NOW THAT HE'S OUT

NOW THAT HE'S OUT

The Challenges and Joys of Having a Gay Son

Martin Kantor, MD

 PRAEGER

AN IMPRINT OF ABC-CLIO, LLC
Santa Barbara, California • Denver, Colorado • Oxford, England

Library of Congress Cataloging-in-Publication Data

Kantor, Martin.
 Now that he's out : the challenges and joys of having a gay son / Martin Kantor, MD.
  pages cm
 Includes bibliographical references and index.
 ISBN 978-1-4408-0261-4 (hbk. : alk. paper) — ISBN 978-1-4408-0262-1 (ebk.)
1. Parents of gays. 2. Child rearing. 3. Child psychology. I. Title.
HQ759.9145K36 2013
306.874086′6—dc23   2012050986

ISBN: 978-1-4408-0261-4
EISBN: 978-1-4408-0262-1

17 16 15 14 13   1 2 3 4 5

This book is also available on the World Wide Web as an eBook.
Visit www.abc-clio.com for details.

Praeger
An Imprint of ABC-CLIO, LLC

ABC-CLIO, LLC
130 Cremona Drive, P.O. Box 1911
Santa Barbara, California 93116-1911

This book is printed on acid-free paper ∞

Manufactured in the United States of America

To my Partner, Michael

Contents

Introduction

In the beginning, few Moms and Dads with a gay son have the special parenting skills they need to cope with and support a son who is gay. Most parents have to acquire these skills as they go along—by trial and error, through education, and, should they have emotional difficulties as a result of having a gay son, via consultation with a professional.

One problem parents with a gay son almost always have to face and overcome is that they believe that to parent a gay son right, they must be entirely selfless people. They ask only, "How do we best handle having a son who is gay?" without also asking, "How do we best handle ourselves in such a situation?" Being paternalistic, they believe, "My child comes first; so our goal is to give him everything we can, and without thinking of ourselves at all." As a consequence, they view parenting a gay son not as a mutual enterprise with shared parent-child responsibilities, but as a one-way endeavor in which their son's requirements alone are of importance, and what is paramount is simply giving him all that he needs, even though that involves neglecting needs of their own and what they want for themselves.

Yet all parents (not only parents with a gay son), being more human than not, must supplement their concern for their child with concern for themselves. They should not blame themselves for everything that goes wrong in their relationship with a gay son as if it's all their fault. They should not too readily buy into others' criticisms of them as being bad parents, to the point that they become sadly self-abnegating and dangerously self-destructive, in the process not only hurting themselves considerably, but also hurting their son. Loving their son, being willing to do anything for him, and gladly advocating for him, and for all gay men, is good; but that doesn't mean that as parents by right they cannot recognize self-concerns that need addressing and neglect being as authentic with themselves as they hope that their son will be both with himself and with them.

One of my patients, a Mom rarely described in the relevant folklore or scientific literature, said to me:

> You know I have a gay son. And he is the one out of five that I am proudest of. And my other four kids have given me grandchildren, so that's no problem. As a mother I am completely satisfied and love him as much as, or more than, my other sons. I only hope that he stays healthy and finds someone to love, and who loves him, forever. His partner is like a son to me too. Only I don't actually remember giving birth to him!

But what she, like many other mothers in this situation, doesn't seem to fully realize, as her (reluctantly made and grudgingly shared) own observations imply, and her even more revealing nonverbals suggest, is that things are not so simple, and that her life as a parent of a gay son is not as carefree as she believes it to be, proclaims it is, and could potentially make it. For while she tells me her story, tears come to her eyes—but she cries silently, so that although she tears, the drops don't roll down her face. Instead they stop short, without ever making it past her eyelids. That alone reveals to me that she is wrestling with, and needs to triumph over, some significant difficulties that she is having with raising a son who is gay. Fortunately, like many other parents of a gay son, she doesn't insulate herself by retreating into a closet of her own making, avoiding facing herself and who she is. Nor does she avoid facing her son as who and what he happens to be. Also, she never faces her son down as some other parents do, hostilely devaluing him, bullying him, putting him under severe mental strain as she silently (but to him obviously) curses the darkness that she feels has overcome her. But her reservations about having a gay son still come through, and they do so enough to walk back on her to hurt her self-image and to walk forward onto her son, lowering his self esteem, shattering his pride, and even silently, but no less tragically, encouraging him to act out against her, against his Dad, and as well against the society they all live in.

And so to meet the often considerable challenges of having a gay son, like many parents in her situation, she needs more help than even she realizes. She, and Dad, as do many other parents in the same position, need to identify, not cover up, the real problems/strong feelings/emotional distortions that they likely experience after discovering "My son is gay." She, and Dad, need more honesty based on the full, authentic recognition that can come only from finally confessing kept secrets—so that once and for all she can stop cursing the lottery that is having children and the unfortunate fate she clandestinely believes has befallen her from above due to "having been stuck with this guy." She needs more honesty so that she can now stop averting her eyes due to unfathomable anxiety and gnawing guilt, and instead hold her head high with self-confidence, free of the erosive feeling that as a parent she is a failure, to instead be suffused with a triumphal sense of her own parental gay pride—knowing that she has a son she unreservedly admires, and a boy she beyond doubt loves, and that he in return is someone who loves her, and his Dad, just as much.

An Overview

In Chapter 1, on responding to disclosure, I discuss how parents of gay sons need to come out too, and in ways that typically parallel how their son needs to do the very same thing. So often both parents and their son, lacking prior experience, are facing disclosure matters for the first time and having to deal with some serious difficulties associated with confessing very personal issues. All concerned are at risk that the outcome of disclosure will be less than favorable, and that they will have difficulty monitoring, coping with, and resolving the problems ahead, including the task of putting disclosure issues into perspective so that they can get on with their lives without becoming so morbidly preoccupied with this one aspect of their existence that they allow it to interfere with their being as joyful and productive as otherwise they might have become.

Unfortunately some parents of gay sons never seem to get beyond the gay issue. Instead they continue to view their son strictly from the vantage point of his being a gay man (and their lives strictly from the perspective of "We have a gay son"). Unable to turn their focus away from "This son of mine is gay," they forget that "This gay man is a son of mine." As a result they become unable to view disclosure as an opportunity to learn—not only about their son's being gay, but also about their son's other, equally human, qualities. They also deal with disclosure issues impressionistically and impulsively instead of scientifically and as a result not in a calm, forthright manner so that what happens next is satisfying and sustaining so that they can make necessary repairs efficiently and do damage control expeditiously. Instead they have harsh words for their son and respond with knee-jerk reactions to his confession. As a result they make mistakes and, overlooking the long-term view, respond strictly as if the here and now will be forever. As a result instead of working problems through, all concerned seriously alienate each other by becoming remote from one another and even prone to angry paranoid outbursts. Thus one couple stopped speaking to each other and to their son because Dad wanted to deny who and what his son had become. He longed to cover it up to avoid facing embarrassment and hurt feelings as others criticized him for having made his son gay then savaged him for handling the outcome badly. Mom in her turn antagonized Dad by being unsupportive due to being unable to decide the question of "Should we try to hide that we have a gay son from our immediate and extended family, or should we openly admit it, even to the point of practicing saying, 'My son is gay' to people we already know or are about to meet?"

In Chapter 2, discarding myths about having a gay son, I identify some of the folklore currently in circulation about having a son who is gay, legends that parents typically buy into then champion, for example:

Myth: Gay pride is always a good thing to have, and most gay men, insufficiently proud of themselves over being gay, need *more* pride to counter that innate excess of shame and guilt that is the burden of every gay man alive.

Fact: There are many gay men, perhaps most, who are not at all ashamed of being gay. Conversely there are occasions where gay pride can be excessive and goeth before a fall—as when too much gay pride is really a manifestation of megalomania (an irrational assurance of one's own extreme importance, righteousness, or authority) so that these gay sons need less pride and more modesty, less narcissism and more realism, to become simply and entirely comfortable with who they are without having to constantly elaborate on their being good not bad, normal not sick, and without continuously having to put their self-esteem to a test their life depends on passing, only one they instead continually fail because, mired in self-criticism, they can't even stand up to and meet their own challenges.

In Chapter 3, about overcoming common emotional problems parents have about having a gay son, I discuss symptomatic responses parents frequently display upon learning that their son is gay, particularly the post-traumatic stress reactions, grief, and depression that flare under this, for some, very trying circumstance. Parents particularly prone to such reactions are generally those already burdened with latent characterological problems such as sadism, masochism, and paranoia. For example, some parents with a *masochistic* bent use their son's being gay to seek sympathy from friends and family for having a difficult son, hoping to wallow in their misery as they surround themselves with the warm cloak of suffering because "We try and try, but with him nothing we ever do seems to succeed." Such parents instead of actively seeking respite, actively seek to collect injuries. Or parents with a *paranoid* bent through projection attribute their own issues to their son and, making these his, demand that he resolve problems they claim belong to him, although they are actually attributes that belong to them, being the product of conflicts that they need to resolve within themselves. Commonly, then, paranoid parents condemn a son for being gay as a diversion from condemning themselves for their own (to them) insufferable (homo)erotic feelings. Just as commonly they project their anger onto their son so that they think not "I dislike him for being gay" but "He became gay as a choice, on purpose, because hating us, he clearly wants to rile us."

In Chapter 4, I discuss family healing. Families rarely get more than one chance to be as one. Just having a family is a gift, but, unfortunately, one that generally is most appreciated by those who are all alone. Losing one's son as a result of one's own voluntary actions, or inaction, is a great tragedy. But too often this actually happens in families who are so negatively focused on their son's being gay that they never come to grips with the really important issues of their lives, or resolve their relevant basic conflicts of living. Instead they continuously switch between hypermorality and civility, putting their son over principle, and their theoretical integrity over compassion and humanity. Failing to soften rigid tradition with flowing kindness, they instead let their angry resentments build up, take over, and make understanding difficult and healing impossible. So often they let homonegative family members take charge and marginalize a gay son just for being gay, creating a monolithic "coalition of rejection" within the family from which their son can't be rescued, at least unless the entire family, including even the grandparents, deal with being caught up in the homonegativity by applying for family therapy and going together, attending faithfully.

It is often helpful for the family to ask its gay son to join in the healing process by saying, "Tell us how to best handle you around the issue of being gay. Give us your honest constructive criticism, and we will return the favor by giving you our full support."

This said, in spite of what many parents think and read, when there is a gay son in the family, *full* family harmony is rarely possible and almost never requires achieving *complete* family closeness—which likely anyway amounts to unhealthy interdependency. Families will actually be closer if they allow/encourage their gay son, as they allow and encourage their other children, to develop a vigorous personal identity through the process of separation and individuation from them, a process that involves breaking too close family ties and one that even *requires* vigorous insubordination and rigorous oppositionalism—through rebelliousness, and that not for itself, but with a specific goal in mind: fostering healthy adult adjustment patterns that require growing up appropriately and moving out expeditiously.

In Chapter 5 I discuss sibling homophobia that makes a gay son's membership in the full family conditional. Not infrequently a gay son's siblings exclude him, and they do so with little to no recognition not only of how they hurt his feelings and destroy his confidence, but also of how they deprive themselves of a potentially wonderful friend and companion—simply for reasons that are illusory, generally theoretical, and often highly rigidly moral.

In Chapter 6 I discuss impression management, which involves parents getting excessively caught up in overconcern about what other people think. So often parents of gay sons worry too much about what people who don't really count say and do, and they do so to the detriment of their son's well-being. Such families need to stop thinking about how others see them and start thinking about how they do, and should, see themselves and their son.

In Chapter 7 I discuss reducing guilt about having a gay son. Many parents of gay sons feel guilty both about having caused their son to become gay and having mishandled him after that fact. They listen to critics who savage them for having a gay son, as if first this is a problem, and second as if the problem rests exclusively on their shoulders. They fail to "give themselves a free pass" by recognizing how hard being the Mom and Dad of a gay son can sometimes be, involving as it does becoming comfortable with a, for them, uncomfortable reality that they cannot change. They fail to develop parental gay pride by reducing parental shame that is fired by rigid beliefs they retain against all rationality; broodings about things they feel they should have done differently; negative thoughts they just can't make go away that lead to negative behaviors they look back upon with regret; and too full recognitions of past misdeeds, such as the awareness that when they should have been practicing restraint, they instead allowed themselves to have only unhelpful responses of an impulsive, entirely emotional nature.

If you are rationally guilty parents, you likely need to take the following steps to feel less shamefaced. If you have been unfriendly to your son, be less antagonistic toward him; if you have been suspicious of your son, become more trusting; and if you have undermined your positive relationship with your son by being significantly unsupportive, critical, and remote, consider apologizing for that and moving on after asking him to make suggestions as to how the next time you can do better.

In Chapter 8 I discuss communing with your son, three aspects of which are communicating with him, getting involved in his life and with his friends, and giving him advice on how he might best live his life on a day-to-day basis. In the realm of communicating with your son, I point out that you don't have to say everything you think, for so often the greater good requires greater restraint. In the realm of getting involved with your son's life, far too many parents believe that a gay son necessarily wants them completely out of his life, and especially away from its most intimate aspects. They believe that all sons are like my young cousin who said to me, "I never tell my parents anything except on an absolute need-to-know basis." They then voluntarily detach themselves from their son's day-to-day personal and professional activities, including—and sometimes especially—his domestic life with his partner. But in truth many gay sons welcome their parents getting involved in their lives, although not of course either in a stereotypical critical "parental" way or in a merger relationship—but rather as friends and colleagues who on occasion gladly join their son (and are welcomed into) his recreational life, and are always there for him as a kind of on-call therapist when, as often is the case for gay adolescents, their son find it absolutely, and so often painfully, necessary to call for help.

In Chapter 9 I discuss handling a difficult/defiant gay son, focusing on emotional problems that afflict many (and possibly most) gay offspring (and straight ones too), making most sons (gay or straight) into somewhat difficult people. This includes the self-preoccupation of the narcissistic son, as well as the suspiciousness and adversarial attitude of the paranoid son. A goal is to help parents understand/not overlook and manage/not flub their handling of a gay son's personality problems. That means viewing personality problems not as gay issues, but as human problems so that parents can come up with remedies that have more to do with psychopathology in general than with being gay in specific.

In Chapter 10 I discuss handling specific problems unique to *adolescents* and thus routinely found in *adolescent* sons who are gay, in particular problems such as attention deficit hyperactivity disorder (ADHD) and conduct disorder. These common adolescent problems are too often missed when the focus is on "My young son is gay" by parents who fail to recognize that "Though my adolescent son is gay, he is simultaneously, just like every other adolescent, subject to the same emotional difficulties to which all adolescents, gay or straight, can be prone."

In Chapter 11 I discuss the controversial issues that arise, and the difficulties that appear, when parents attempt to set limits on and establish boundaries for a gay son. Too many parents seem overly reluctant to set limits on and establish boundaries for a son who is gay because they feel that they have to acquiesce to everything he does lest he, and society, view them, his parents, as homophobic tyrants, martinets, and space invaders. But parents *must* set limits and establish boundaries for their gay sons under at least two circumstances: (1) when their son clearly needs supervision for any reason, and (2) when he is actually in danger and there is no alternative but to try to get him out of it.

Parents can set limits and establish boundaries *directly* by being (somewhat) controlling, saying "no" when "no" is indicated and "yes" is contraindicated lest the "yes" brew trouble that will erupt. At the time, sons hearing "no" will likely complain and resist structure, but in the long run they will as likely, however grudgingly, accept it. I wanted to be a musician and to do what I loved. But being a musician didn't love me. My father saw that more clearly than I did and, as a sensible and practical man, virtually ordered me to become a physician. For years I complained about how his pushing me around kept me from my true calling. But now, many years later, I'm thankful that he didn't give in but continued to urge/press me to go to medical school. Otherwise I might have been free to be free, and free to be me, likely meaning that I was entirely free to be gainfully unemployed.

Or parents can set limits and establish boundaries using an *indirect* approach: by sharing wisdom, avoiding being judgmental by simply presenting viable alternatives and asking their son to choose what feels right for him, not what is right for them.

Setting limits of sorts on a son can also serve you his parents well. For example, a Mom and Dad who want grandchildren, instead of being silently resentful/angry/disappointed/depressed that a son is gay and won't give them grandkids, can urge their son and his partner to use a surrogate, or adopt, and possibly even to accept their parents' emotional support and financial help in this venture. Mom and Dad get what they want and as a bonus help their son live a fulfilling life and please their son's partner who, rather than seeing them as controlling (as they fear), actually welcomes having interested, supportive, concerned, helpful in-laws (as they might wish).

In Chapter 12 I discuss indications for parents seeking treatment. One indication for seeking therapy is to discover if you actually need therapy. More specific indications for seeking treatment generally fall into several categories: lack of intellectual awareness about what you are dealing with, generally because of the obscuring nature of strong emotions; extreme negativity toward, including feeling ashamed of, your son; low self-esteem, especially when that is an aspect of your grieving over or getting depressed about your situation; and a tendency to act out both in a manner that is hurtful to your son and self-destructive. I also present an overview of some of the different therapeutic modalities available, which I go on to elaborate in subsequent chapters.

In Chapter 13 I discuss the psychoanalytic/psychodynamic approach to dealing with parents' troubles with having a gay son. This approach relies predominantly on understanding your inner workings, including the counterproductive defense mechanisms parents likely use in dealing with having a gay son, such as denial (leading parents to become somewhat hypomanic, avoiding painful feelings only to become interventional do-nothings), and projection (leading parents to become somewhat paranoid as they become angrily malcontented over imaginary filial provocations and misdeeds).

In Chapter 14 I discuss correcting cognitive errors about having a gay son. Doing so generally leads to a sense of personal empowerment through acknowledging and correcting anxiety-producing distortions/false notions that arise out of thinking gone wrong that subsequently spins off even greater intellectual biases. For example, as parents you might perceive adolescent anger that isn't there because you see your son's compliments as necessarily being an isomer of criticisms, as when you see his congratulating you for a thing as his condemning you for its opposite. For example, when your son says he is pleased that you accept some of his gay friends, all you hear is his criticizing you for rejecting all the others.

In Chapter 15 I discuss interpersonal therapy, a form of treatment heavily dedicated to helping families avoid destructive negativity by instead employing the healing power of positivity. As for *negativity*, ideally parents should love their gay son fully and unconditionally. But some parents—no matter how hard they try to be completely loving—discover that their background, upbringing, heritage, personality, generation-specific attitudes, and tendency to yield themselves up to homonegative community/social input lead them to feel a degree of disappointment in, and hence anger with, their son for being gay. As a result, they love their gay son but conditionally, and now the best they can do is to keep what negativity is there to a minimum so that it doesn't take over completely. That's okay, for the goal is not to eliminate all negativity, but to integrate what negativity there is and can't be changed into the parent-son relationship so that it doesn't poison the entire affiliation. This done, parents can then accept their son if not fully or unconditionally, then overall and so avoid getting depressed and needing to spin off denial defenses where they unrealistically assess their son based entirely on what they wish him to be, only to miss the reality of who he actually is, and then fail to handle him appropriately based on what he actually says and does.

As for contrasting *positivity*, harnessing its power helps overcome negativity considerably. Parents who are positive encourage, support, facilitate, and teach their son by word, deed, and example. This may involve telling your son what life has taught you, hoping to see him through struggles similar to the ones you had to endure (but got through) when you were his age. Parents who are *empathic* generally automatically become on that account predominantly positive. Empathy allows parents to understand and judge their son fairly by putting themselves in his place. Being empathetic can help you as his parents avoid the necessity of having to issue warnings and threats that impose your own views on your son short of respecting differences and accepting diversity. The empathic parent can see his or her son's true qualities and so avoid divisive moralistic personal pronouncements based on thinking that when it comes to what constitutes right and wrong, because you are his parents you unilaterally, and most certainly, possess the one answer—the only singular truth.

To be effective, positivity must avoid being excessively saccharine as a substitute for being realistic, and be just and fair rather than manipulative. In the realm of the latter, parents are often tempted to use reverse psychology to get their son to do their bidding. But those who do will likely discover that their efforts backfire because their son, failing to appreciate the irony in what his parents say, gets what they mean wrong because, overlooking the irony, he takes what you have said literally.

In Chapter 16 I discuss other forms of therapy such as group therapy and activism as a form of treatment. Many parents seek the companionships and insights associated with attending group therapy. But not all groups are created equal, and there are times when group therapy can prove inadequate and ways that even the best-intentioned groups can do more harm than good.

In Chapter 17 I offer gay sons themselves some thoughts about how they can best integrate themselves into their families. Parents aren't the only ones who bear family responsibilities to "treat their son right." Sons also have a responsibility to treat their parents right. Most relationships, this one included, take two, and there is no better illustration of this than the disasters that occur when a gay son, using being gay as an excuse and any unfortunate response on his parents' part in reply as a catalyst, complains that his parents fail to discharge their parental duties to him, when a good portion of this stoppage is his own failure to discharge his filial duties to his parents.

PART I

Coming Out for Mom and Dad

Chapter 1

Responding to Disclosure

Like their son, Mom and Dad also have to come out. And as with their son, that means being forthright both with others and with themselves. And that involves self-realization leading to self-knowledge. And that can come only when they tell themselves the truth—not by making themselves feel better by erecting barriers to fool themselves, or fomenting denial to hide from themselves, but forging through the blockage that keeps them from really seeing who they are in order to discover what types of problems, if any, they actually have.

Coming out for Mom and Dad is a three-part process, as discussed in this and the following two chapters. Chapter 1, this chapter, describes general problems Mom and Dad might have with their son's disclosure, with remedies implied or stated. Chapter 2 discusses identifying and discarding myths about having a gay son. Chapter 3 discusses overcoming common problematic emotional responses parents have to their son's disclosure, for example, the posttraumatic stress response that many parents develop after learning that their son is gay.

Coming out involves the concerned individuals understanding, accepting, growing, and developing both on their own and in their relationship to each other. That makes coming out a family affair—less the "me" happening that it is often imagined to be/portrayed as, and more the "us" affair involving the immediate and extended family, as well as nonfamily members in the family orbit, that it is rarely thought to be/portrayed as. Also, coming out is not a single, one-time event, but is more realistically a complex, protracted, ongoing, and often difficult process consisting of strong and typically conflicting ongoing primary inner responses guiding behavior, secondary responses to the fallout from that behavior, and tertiary cycling that is generally more vicious than virtuous. Therefore, as I do with gay men themselves, although I still call the phenomenon in question parental "coming out," I really mean parental "becoming out." For that term better connotes important issues and events that occur not only during, but also both before and after, the so-called moment of truth—leading up to it and including what happens next.

We should not assume that all families of gay men have serious difficulties with the coming out process. Many families readily accept that they have a gay son, and, though they would prefer things to be different, don't actually go into crisis mode over the issue—with anxiety spreading and deeply erosive guilt taking over. Such families deal with the inevitable personal and social disapproval related to having a gay son by tolerating it, not much caring about it, or responding not with intense regrets, but by instead facing the criticism down—enhancing their individual pride by ratcheting up their personal defiance.

But many parents do have a degree of difficulty recognizing and understanding what it means to have a gay son, and an equal amount of difficulty making decisions about how to handle/cope with him, themselves, and their situation. Some need a little help recognizing, coping with, and integrating ambivalent to seriously negative feelings about having a gay son. Others, feeling thoroughly ashamed of their son and of themselves, horrified about who and what he is, and guilty about what they have done to "create this monster," need a great deal of assistance. And that includes both those who anticipate, and get, negative backlash from outside, from their immediate or extended family, their friends, and in their houses of worship, and those who have discovered the hard way that the more honest and open their son was in disclosing, and the more he came out to them frankly and honestly, the less accepting they became of him, and so the worse they felt, and the harder they fell. As a result, in both instances, Mom and Dad experience damage to their positive sense of self, lose self-respect, and suffer from inner dissonance proportionate not only to their outer, but also to their inner, discomfort. They get depressed over having to abandon cherished goals for their son, themselves, and their family, and in an attempt to combat their emotional vulnerability, develop counterproductive defenses ranging from projection to denial. Then their son finds *them* progressively more difficult to get along with, and becomes himself hard to tolerate, and thus even more difficult to manage.

Caught up in this bad affair, they seek advice, only—unfortunately—to get some that is unhelpful or potentially harmful. First, they tend to get, and listen to, advice that overemphasizes full positivity as the one and only goal. They are told to love their son unconditionally, as if mixed feelings about him are not inherent either in this special situation or in all parent-child relationships regardless of the child's sexual orientation. (The term "homophobia" falls short because it fails to acknowledge the existence of mixed feelings and so is inappropriately applied in situations where any homonegative trends at all can be discerned. Therefore, I prefer the more accurate term "homoambivalence," however unwieldy it may be and unlikely to ever take hold.)

Second, they tend to get, and listen to, one-size-fits-all suggestions that fail to take into account the considerable differences among gay sons and their families. For their advisors, ranging from laypersons to professionals, lump together everyone gay, as they do everyone in the gay man's orbit, to create a massive collective into which you as his parents, your family, and your special son may very well not fit. This one-size-fits-all advice fails to consider the unique nature both of the individuals involved and of the family as a whole—that is, the special quality of the family "gestalt." This family gestalt, discussed further in Chapter 4 on family dynamics, is a special construct composed of individual contributions that together create the familiar "whole greater than the sum of its parts." This "whole" is unique to each family, lending each family a "fingerprint" of psychodynamics/psychopathology that consists of special needs and passions significantly idiosyncratic to make this one family different from all the others. Thus, not only do Mom and Dad respond as individuals in their own way to disclosure, but the families to which they belong also handle coming out in their own special idiosyncratic way. Therefore, to be properly given, and useful to the person and family receiving it, advice about dealing with disclosure must account both for individual and family variables. As an example, the disclosure process is considerably different if your son voluntarily confesses he is gay or if you, his Mom and Dad, find out about it accidentally; having suspected it all along have cajoled or tricked him into admitting he was gay; or have actively outed him after secretly observing his actions/spying on him. In certain families, for example, those with specific emotional problems, a son's coming out that is a valid affirmation and part of the process of self-fulfillment *for the son* constitutes the reverse *for the family* because it triggers individual/collective familial self-deaffirmation and self-questioning. The impact of disclosure is quite different on more accepting (liberal) families than it is on more traditionally moralistic (conservative) families. Families who are on the whole natively open and communicative often respond to disclosure better than do families who are on the whole fearfully reserved and shy. What can be good for the social can be bad for the *avoidant* family, where emotionality is looked upon as forbidden, or even as sinful. Too often the parents in avoidant families feel that their son's coming out renders the family even more dysfunctional by overwhelming them with revelations, perhaps forcing them to admit things about themselves that they would prefer to hide. Kort says that the "the child's disclosure [gives the family] permission to reveal their [own] secrets."[1] This can be a positive thing—or a negative development when it stirs up family secrets that the family has to date kept hidden out of a need to condemn, and so to suppress, that of which they feel ashamed.

A son's secretiveness is not a burden but a special relief for families with *paranoid* tendencies who thrive on privacy; and for *depressive* families so wracked with guilt about having a gay son that they don't want to be steeped in something they would prefer to ignore. For such families, a son's disclosure, further activating their anger/shame, does not decrease, but rather increases, their burden.

Too, *sadistic* families often perceive their son's disclosure as an exposing of his wounds. Now they smell first blood, then move in for the kill—likely accusing a son who is doing little more than telling the truth of deliberately attacking them by being an unempathic, narcissistic child flaunting his unsatisfactory sexual orientation just to annoy them/make them mad. They may even use disclosure to justify hurtful actions on their parts that would otherwise have made them feel guilty. Typically, such families even welcome hearing they have a gay son, for now they can justify throwing their son out as an unrepentant sinner and telling him to come back only when, after having repented, he can ask for forgiveness—or even ordering him to never come back again at all, no matter what, under any circumstances.

Phases

In many cases, the "parental becoming out" process has some or all of the following phases, one or more of which can be truncated, merged, or skipped entirely.

Phase One: Beginnings

As parents, you suspect that something about your son is special, different, and even unique, but you don't yet know quite what it is, perhaps because you don't yet know what "gay" is exactly, if at all. Or, you appreciate the fact that your son is gay, but you don't want to admit it to yourself, as in, "He may be somewhat sissified, but many straight men act that way." Emotionally in denial, you try to convince yourself that this is just a phase he is going through, and/or act as if he is straight and try to get him to act that way too, and for you. You, your narcissistic concerns ascendant, might try to change his sexual orientation by playing baseball with him or by introducing him to women. Instead of establishing and developing an ambiance of affection, and adopting a tone of overall loving acceptance in a setting of frankness imparting security, you form secret compacts with him, saying to him the likes of, "Tell us you are gay, but don't tell grandma and grandpa, because they are from another generation and won't understand." When I was in my early teens, my parents, already suspecting "something was amiss," took me to a high-level night club burlesque show, presumably to ascertain/stir up my sexual feelings for women. I can't prove that that's what they were attempting to do, but why else would they take me to a strip joint? (Because it was so out of character for them, it was so clearly intended for me.) I went along, knowing full well what they were trying to accomplish, but resenting it as seriously off pitch, intrusive, and controlling—as if they were trying to counter a force of nature, only to ensure that they would be wasting their and my time and energy, and, as a comeuppance for their misplaced effort, lose leverage with me. This attempt, marking an early one of many setbacks in my relationship with them, seriously backfired, for in not asking me if I wanted to go, they were saying to me "We are concerned about ourselves" and "We have expectations for you," not "We care about you" or "We will try to discover and support the expectations you have for yourself."

In this phase, you seek advice from friends, mostly picking those you already know will tell you what you want to hear, like "Don't worry, he will grow out of this" or "Go ahead, make demands that your son change, and do it for your good and for the good of the family as a whole."

Perhaps you call on a therapist to treat your son, likely picking one whose orientation matches your own. (This becomes a futile and dangerous practice should you, disliking your son's being gay, be tempted to send him to a reparative therapist to be cured of his homosexuality.) Too often, if it is you who goes for therapy, you go not for help with your own problems, including problems with managing a gay son, but to see if you can do something through *your* therapeutic efforts to cure *him*.

In your therapy, instead of taking responsibility for your distortive responses, you blame your son for many things to absolve yourself of everything. You rarely get beyond the issues related to his homosexuality to go into personal and relational problems of a more general and even pressing nature. Denial interferes with the progress of your therapy as you can't admit you hate having a gay son; that you harbor thoughts that he is a shameful, weak, defective, bad individual who hurts not only himself but also (mainly) you; that you feel that by being gay he is violating not only your expectations of him, but also society's expectations of what a good son should be; and that you wish you could seriously distance yourself from him to relieve your anxiety and depression about your fate. Instead, you tell your therapist that you totally accept your son as gay and good, and that you therefore have no qualms about raising him in a fully loving way by being the absolutely adoring parent you are. However, your therapist readily observes that you have begun to develop a mild to serious grief reaction. Grieving for your "loss," you bemoan how his life, your life, and (perhaps mainly) your reputation, have been ruined. You remind yourself, "I so hoped he would be a doctor with a standard family, and many grandchildren whose pictures I could put on my cell phone so that I could show them to all the moms and dads at work. But I see that that is not to be, for, alas, I am going to have a son who hangs out in bars, drinks and takes drugs, and doesn't do anything meaningful professionally, but instead aspires to a career in the theatre that he will never have and which isn't real work; or a son who hopes to be an underwear model, or seeks some similarly vacuous job that will last a month and anyway be followed by permanent unemployment (and all my friends knowing that we are supporting him will move in for the kill, further humiliating then abandoning us)." And you worry that he will suffer throughout his entire life alone in some ghetto, and possibly get a serious medical illness and die a horrible death prematurely in the City Hospital, by himself, under a thin cold blanket, and without anyone to hold him close or keep him warm. In other words, you adjudicate your son and foresee his future based entirely on stereotypes you believe to be regularly associated with his sexual orientation, leaving little or no room for consideration of his personal wants, needs, and prospects, and paying no mind to his true capacities, as if because he is gay he gets no credit for the positive attributes that clearly do apply in his case. You forget that he can be personally happy if he is both personable and hardworking; that he can, and likely will, have an extended family of other gay, lesbian, and straight individuals to substitute for a more traditional family; and that he can be professionally successful and thrive if he has the right skills, sufficient education, and relevant experience needed to prosper. You fail to consider that while his being gay changes some things, it has an incomplete influence on what his present and future will be like, and while certainly it doesn't ensure his or your happiness and success, it as certainly doesn't ensure his or your unhappiness and failure either.

Phase Two: Beginning Disruption within and Early Disintegration of the Family

On some level, you accept your son as gay and good, but on another level, thoughts break through that he is a shameful, weak, defective individual, someone who hurts himself and you, his parents, by being gay, and as he violates your expectations for what a good child should be, he violates society's expectations of how a good son should behave. So you less and less come to accept him as he is, and more and more feel that you hate the prospect of having a son like him. At times, you actually even come to hate him personally, so much so that you are tempted to undercut any success you might have had in coming out of your parental closet by going right back in—and trying to draw him back in there with you.

What starts mildly develops into a serious grief reaction due to increasingly pervasive negativity toward your so-called predicament. In your grief, almost certainly you blame your son for being evil himself, and spreading evil throughout your and the whole world, abusing not only himself and you, but also others around him—the adults in his life emotionally by trying to convert them to the gay cause, and the children in his life sexually by seducing and/or raping them—because to you gay = pedophilia. And you start blaming everyone else for causing your distress, scapegoating almost anyone and anything you possibly can. You blame his friends for seducing him into living "a gay lifestyle," which for you is one that is necessarily "from the underground." You blame the media for turning him gay by promoting homosexuality on TV. You condemn any partner your son might go with for having seduced your son and made him gay, or otherwise taken advantage of him—especially if this partner is someone you deem somehow defective, like a man who is older or, if younger, from a "lower-class background." You make his partner take the blame for something personal you choose to dislike and disavow in your son, such as your son's remoteness ("that guy is turning our son against us"). Because you deal with your own feelings about your son's being gay by condemning someone else for causing you to have them—as when you deal with your anger by blaming him or others for making you mad, you are, it would seem likely, becoming somewhat paranoid.

Too, scapegoating *yourself* as well as him, you overemphasize or fully imagine sins you think you have committed to cause your son to turn gay, thus, in true depressive fashion, shifting blame from him and others back to yourself. You blame yourself for having made him gay because of something you clearly did wrong. You blame your bad genes and a handed-down Lamarckian-like inheritance of deviancy you believe you have cursed him with. Or you blame your past and present behavior, as in "If only we hadn't sent him to music classes, he wouldn't have gone gay on us in the first place."

Additionally, you try to relieve your discomfort by distancing yourself from him and his problems. You wish you could, or actually try to, ignore him. When you do interact with him, you become exceedingly judgmental, not only about his being gay, but also about issues you displace from his being gay onto things symbolic—little things he does that you dislike, such as dressing too informally (counterculturally) for family occasions, or staying out too late and hanging around with people who wear skinny jeans and have spider tattoos on their necks.

Sometimes spreading anxiety and anger lead you to consider taking, or to actually take, steps to throw him out of the house, never to let him return again, your way to get back at him for what you imagine he did to you, and to save yourself and your family by reconstituting the family—without him. At the very least, you exile him within the family in small and often symbolic ways, for example, by showing preference for his sisters and brothers. To further what you admittedly hope will amount to a kind of class warfare, you begin to convince yourself that your son is in actuality a "second-class citizen and a third-rate person, no different from a child who is adopted, illegitimate, a love child from another race or ethnic group, or a pathetic kid due to some significant disability that disfigures and cripples him if not physically than at least emotionally." In a vicious cycle that actually causes him to act out, or to act out even more, he becomes promiscuous because you have made him feel unloved and unwanted. You then condemn his acting out promiscuously as "the typical behavior of a typical gay son" and so come to hate his being gay even more, and to love him even less. Though his behavior is likely "a gay-infused primary conduct disorder" resulting not from problems due to sexual orientation, but from problems due to sexual discrimination, you explain his emotional states by citing the homosexual context in which they occur, as if that explains everything. You forget that your son is if not an actual adolescent, then in a prolonged adolescence, in either case possibly suffering from a typical *Diagnostic and Statistical Manual of Mental Disorders-IV (DSM-IV)* "emotional disorder characteristic of adolescence"[2] (as described in Chapter 10). As his acting out worsens and you retaliate, he becomes even sadder, more anxious, and more resentful over being marginalized and sent off to family Siberia. Though this is his response to your mistreating him, instead of your reforming yourself and treating him better, you condemn his behavior even more and treat him even worse—say, by trying to force him to get into therapy, even though he is perfectly happy, and you are the one who needs the treatment.

Instead of becoming overly hostile to their gay son, many parents in this phase cover up their hostility defensively in exaggerated love consisting of a pseudo-understanding that does little to combat ignorance; engineered advocacy that does less than it appears to be doing because it but thinly covers and combats genuine lack of support; and apparently calm but superficial acceptance that but poorly obscures deep, hurtful rejection. But your son isn't fooled, for your hostility still shows and continues to affect him—and does so even more because he perceives that you are clearly being dishonest about how you feel—and to him that means you are being even more hostile toward him than before.

Phase Three: Involvement of the Rest of the Family/the World

So often, members of the immediate family eventually join in to further disrupt what positive family homeostasis remains, threatening the core happy family alliance to the point that a previously at least minimally functional family cohort dissolves into an unhappy coalition where those who feel positively lose their power and influence, and those who feel negatively come to prevail.

You as a family soon allow the focus of your concern to shift from torment within the family to torment about what others think about your family—counting as most important the opinions of your extended family, friends, and professional colleagues along the lines of "What does the rest of the world think about us and our predicament?" Concerns about who and what your son is and what will become of him turn more and more from concerns about "What will happen between us and him?" into concerns about "What will they think, and so what will become of us?"

As the need for impression management swells to prevent you from fully disclosing that you have a gay son, you avoid being as frank and forthcoming to others as you once were, and instead convince yourself that it's better and safer to keep secrets and hide, along the lines of, "If they don't ask, I won't tell" and sometimes "I won't tell even if they do ask." At times you do feel the urge to tell boldly, proudly, and unequivocally—without caring what the family/others might think, or, if they do think ill of you, without worrying about that. So you tell everybody, "My son is gay, and I am proud of him." But most times you feel the urge to stay away from the entire issue, or even to hide that you have, and your shame about having, a gay son. And you comfort yourself over your shamed silence with such rationalizations as, "Why state the obvious?" or "Out or in, there are more important things in this world to worry about than telling, or not telling, people I have a gay son."

You likely consider outing yourself partially/selectively rather than fully—to disclose/hide not all, but certain aspects of, your "problem." Instead of actively spreading all of the word, you merely drop a few hints. You answer only some questions and those only when specifically asked, and share selectively as, for example, when you tell Grandmother but ask her not to tell Grandfather. You also ask your son to be more discrete just to protect your reputation. You say, "I am personally okay with your being gay, but I demand that you be gay out of town, in places where presumably nobody knows you/is aware that you belong to us, so that your being gay doesn't reflect badly on us and threaten the rest of the family." You might even ask, or demand, that your son be celibate, or a hermit, or at least put on a show of sexual reticence along the lines of "I don't need sex," or, lying to the world, say that he is "divorced, and, permanently soured on marriage, never going to get married to another woman again."

As you pull back from others in shame, you come to feel paranoid, for you think everyone, even those who are supportive, is being critical of you. As you think, "They no longer want to have much to do with us," your own social life begins to contract, for you retreat even further into "And I don't want to have anything much to do with them." Your son suspects what is going on and knows it's all about his being gay. He might try to support and reassure you, but mostly he blames you for responding to his being gay negatively the way you do. Whether he is hypersensitive or insensitive, he knows that what you are thinking about him isn't flattering. He hears that your messages to him have become at best mixed, and at worst becomes convinced that you likely would, if you only could, live out the severest most homophobic of morality by issuing forth the most withering of criticisms.

Phase Four: Assimilation (Hope)

You begin to develop useful insight into yourself and your situation. You see that though your negativity toward your son is nominally about his being gay, it in fact mostly originates elsewhere. That is, some of your homohatred is really a displacement from other things, such as worry about the possibility of his growing up and leaving you, so "I hate him for being gay" really means "I want him totally asexual so that he stays with us, safe at home, and there to take care of us in our old age." For many mothers it is easier to accept a son's being gay than it is to accept the possibility that he will find a companion/partner other than you; and for many fathers it is easier to accept the possibility that a son might be a "gay loser" in life than it is to accept the possibility that he might go out and become successful and do better than Dad. In the latter case you, his Oedipal father, actually come to wish that your son will not be a winner—because, as you see it, only a loser won't compete with and diminish your status, or actually overthrow you and take your place.

Phase Five: Evolution (Change)

Much around you has been in flux following initial disclosure. External circumstances change both on their own, as a response to changes in you, and as part of his growing up and maturing. Your ongoing response to having a gay son is influenced by the extent to which he accepts you and forgives your "failings." Your self-expectations change too, hopefully in a healthier direction, allowing you to accept yourself as you are, for example, as being somewhat angry with your son without necessarily feeling that that means you are no longer at all accepting of, and decently affirmative toward, him. You have now started striving as a family to develop a level of adjustment marked by tolerance that works, meaning that as a family you can ultimately become as authentic, generative, and inclusion-oriented as you can possibly be given this unique situation with its not always resolvable challenges, and, as you see it, this difficult situation with its generally "severe disadvantages" predictably leading to seriously mitigated joys.

Recommendations

Try to anticipate your son's coming out by paying attention to the "alerting" signs that tell you that you might have a gay son so that you can prepare your response in advance of, and thus have time to refine your reaction to, his disclosure.

Before he comes out avoid going into denial, as did a relative of mine who "never imagined that my son was gay, although he told me over and over again, starting when he was very young, that he didn't feel like the other boys." Avoiding denial gives you time to actively think through/ rehearse how you are going to respond within yourself and to your son when he discloses himself to you, especially allowing you to anticipate and plan how you are going to handle any negative reaction that his disclosure might produce in you.

During disclosure avoid talking when you should be listening, telling him your problems when you should be encouraging his opening up to you. Listen carefully to what he is saying to, and trying to tell, you so that you can fully use this excellent opportunity to learn about him from a number of perspectives—not only from the perspective of his being gay, but also from the much more meaningful perspective of his being a complex human being. For your son is not only a gay man, but a man with many characteristics, only one of which is that he happens to be gay.

Avoid making his disclosure a hotbed of your own issues. Hear not simply what you want to hear or fear hearing, but also what he actually says. Instead of telling him how you feel, and what you want from him, listen to how he feels and to what he wants from you. This is not the time to state your cherished conservative political views, to affirm your establishment family values, or to bring up your scrupulous religiously based concerns. Hear that what he is revealing is no doubt something important not only about his being gay, but also about his entire self, and in particular about his full relationship with you. Perhaps he is testing your love in a gay context because he feels that if you give him love here, in "this difficult-to-be loving about" issue, you will give love to him anywhere, and about anything. Perhaps he is attempting to gain absolution from you, his parents, people who have until now been critical of him about so many things; masochistically invalidating himself by confessing to some sin (as he sees it); (conversely) narcissistically enhancing himself through showing off by impressing you with his authenticity in order to burnish his personal imago; or telling you what he must have from you in the way of love because that is the only possible source of validation from you of something he has difficulty validating in himself.

After disclosure think about your response and where you can profitably go from there. Quietly make a list of issues that might need addressing over time, such as: What makes you comfortable and what makes you uncomfortable about how things currently stand? How much are you willing to shift and stretch for your son versus how much do you expect/want him to shift and stretch for you? Determine the problems he awakens in you as his disclosure revives special and specific developmental/personality issues of yours that emerge because his coming out relights deep problems sleeping inside of you, problems that you have had for a long time—skeletons in your own closet. In my experience, parents who have had their own parents turn on them and isolate them if they seemed at all individualistic are, when their son discloses to them, the most likely to feel impelled to do exactly the same thing—to their own child.

This is a very bad moment to choose to hurt your son for something else that has distressed you about him/you have resented in him for a long time. It is a bad time to be sadistic and flood him with raw, antagonistic comments to get back at him for hurting you or to devalue him so that you can comfortably exile him in order to get back at him for how he did treat, or you imagined that he treated, you. For example, a father with two children preferred his daughter almost sexually as "the other woman" in his life. His son's very presence interfered with his getting as close as he might like to his daughter, to the extent that he wished he had never had a son in the first place. And he made no attempt to hide that. Always ready to "send this boy packing," he used his son's disclosure as the opportunity he had been seeking for years to tell the son to "get out of my house, and stay away, and be gone forever."

If you don't have it in your heart to fully affirm your son's gay identity at this time, especially if at the same time you can't fully control your temper, at least reserve your negative reactions for later when you have had a chance to first rethink your negativity, second validate or invalidate your negativity, and third calm down enough to respond with a focused narrative that at least starts with the good intention to be reasonable.

Disclosure presents parents of a gay son with once-in-a-lifetime opportunities to become better parents—more flexible, understanding, kind, supportive, and devoted. But they have to allow serious moral qualms about being gay to fade and to embed any mean streaks they have inside of themselves into a kindly matrix that is overall simpatico, empathic, respectful, and sensitive. You have to become less socially autistic with your son by becoming more sensitive to *his* needs, seeing him as a person not just different from you but also as one just as worthy in his own, if to you unique, way. You have to become less theoretically morally sound and more actually humanistic—more concerned with people than with principles; more concerned about what is good and less concerned about what is right. And you must become willing, when indicated, to put being his colleague before being his parent. My parents failed to give me "buddy" advice that I could have used. Instead of giving me constructive criticism both before and after the fact, they waited for me to displease them about something then, pouncing on me, told me what I had done wrong, which they did in a very punitive/castrative way. Also, instead of dissimulating/covering up when that was necessary to protect me from themselves, they were honest with me to a fault and thus hurtful to me to an entirely unacceptable extreme.

Disclosure time is also a good opportunity to model for your son how through common sense and your own beneficent experience you solved, and so how your son might also solve, important life problems of a relational and professional nature. Perhaps you cannot model how to best live a *gay* life, but you can offer relevant solutions for *generalized life problems* he implies or states that he has or might have—problems that transcend those directly related to his being gay. To illustrate, if he feels guilty about being gay, he is likely to feel guilty about other things as well, ranging from sex to success, so be certain to try to help him not only out of his guilty straight closet, but also out of his guilty straightjacket. Divine general anxieties and fears not necessarily primarily related to homosexuality—anxieties and fears that might lead him to become dysfunctional in his relationships—not only with you at home, but also on the outside at school, or at work, and show him how you faced, and hopefully solved, similar or the same problems. Consider acting like a therapist concerned with "transference"—that is, consider using your son's manner toward/actions with you as a measure of how he acts with/toward other people in his life. Let his relationship with you clue you into what is happening in his relationships with others, as you determine how problems you are having with him reveal problems that others might also be having with him. If he is hesitant in coming out to you, he might be hesitant in life, even to the extent that it impairs his general functionality. If he is being nasty to you, he is likely to be mean toward others and so he may be getting along just as poorly with them. If he is tempting you to bully him at home, perhaps that explains why others seem equally tempted to be abusive to, and bully him, on the outside.

Ask him to assist you with any problems you are having due to his disclosing his homosexuality to you. Parents generally fixate on "how I can help my son" but avoid thinking about "And how can my son help me, and help me to help him?" Tell him, if it's true, that his disclosure has been difficult for you. Ask him to assist you to be fairer to, and more supportive of, him by helping you solve any emotional and practical problems that his disclosure has created for, or exacerbated in, you.

Never out your son to anyone else, especially in order to retaliate against him for something he might have done or actually did do to you that you resented. Disclosure is both a sacredly private matter and too complex to be used manipulatively in *any* way, especially in a negative manner. Don't as his parents use disclosure to further long-simmering relational dissention between you and your spouse, or between you and your own parents. If disclosure is to be used manipulatively at all it should be utilized only as part of a plan to salvage relationships; not to drive people apart by getting them fighting, but instead to bring people already warring together once again, by getting them loving.

Parents can facilitate their own coming out by finding out and tailoring their response to what their son expects them to do. For example, without making assumptions, they should ask themselves, "How does my son actually *want* us to respond?"—that is, "What response on our parts does he think will please/help him the most?" and conversely "What response will leave him feeling startled, surprised, and even shocked?" Almost unbelievably, I have treated some sons who reacted negatively to their parents being overly *accepting* of them. If your son seems upset or worried that you are being too accommodating, find out why and what is bothering him about that, and help him handle it. Does he actually welcome/enjoy having homophobic parents because it gives him a reason to defy authority, perhaps as part of his normal/healthy maturational process, for example, so that he can have (parental) rivals he can debate, win over, rise above, then feel proud of/brag about having triumphed over, as in "I beat the establishment?" Sons who are avoidants welcome, and even attempt to induce, parental homophobia as a reason to keep their distance from their parents in order to keep themselves from feeling overwhelmed by in-house anxiety. Sadistic sons actually need resentful bigoted parents to be there to provide them with an outlet/target for their own free-floating sadism. Sons guilty about being gay welcome homophobic parents for masochistic reasons: they don't feel they deserve to have an understanding, supportive Mom and Dad, so they paradoxically judge as disruptive parents who come on to them as too openly loving and accepting. And finally, paranoid sons needing enemies do not unequivocally welcome it when their parents attempt to be their friends. Paranoid sons, needing to be given a difficult time, experience being given an easy one as hard.

This said, most sons being themselves at least somewhat empathic are more compassionate than otherwise. They hope that their parents will, but don't expect them to, accept them fully, and openly. Truly concerned for Mom and Dad, they feel sadness, regret, and even (legitimate) fears for their parents' well-being, which they believe they have compromised by being gay and out. They are concerned, and often with reason, that the rest of the family will shame, exile, and ostracize the parents they love. To be good sons who won't feel painfully responsible for hurting their parents and their siblings, they decide, on their own, to keep quiet about being gay in order to minimize their parents' suffering. "What," a son might ask himself, "will happen when the neighbors spot my parents fawning over me and my partner wheeling a baby carriage?" My parents never acknowledged that I might have any concerns at all for them about what my, their only son's, being gay, meant for them. They saw my coming out as a fully adversarial situation where I, their son, deliberately confessed abrasively to horrified parents in order to have a big hand in creating and welcoming the struggle that ensued. But to an extent I was struggling not with, but for, my parents, and they did not give me sufficient credit for what in my case represented a sanguine attitude—of wanting to spare them as much pain as I possibly could. In fact, I took pains to be gay all the way, but not to let it get in their way. In a similar case, of identical twins, one of whom was gay and the other straight, the gay twin always knew he was "different," but for years he said nothing about it for fear of hurting his brother's and his parents' chances in life

As parents you should remember that sons long to have loving grandparents as much as grandparents long to have loving grandchildren. Therefore, for your son's sake, you should do what you can to keep your relationship with your own parents, his grandparents, positive. That often means finding a way to keep your own parents from acting out by distancing themselves from your "situation" even more—by joining in the general boycott.

A Checklist

Coming out for Mom and Dad involves many of the following items.

Be Patient with Yourself

View the coming out process from a long-term perspective, where the goal is resolving family misunderstandings to achieve a valid adjustment that takes the joys and concerns of all family members into account, and the method necessarily involves therapeutic work that generally requires effort over time. Because coming out is hard work and takes long and hard thought, many parents can come out only gradually, over the days and months following disclosure. Their coming out can occur only in many steps where all concerned seriously rethink and repetitively revise their initial responses—correcting mistakes in order to turn failures into successes until the family somehow manages to cobble a functional, if not a completely happy, family life together.

Communicate with Your Son in a Relevant Way

Freely ask him pertinent questions without unduly fearing that you will necessarily say the wrong thing and provoke a negative response of catastrophic proportions. Ask for any information you need so that you can respond rationally after considering all the facts both from your and his perspective.

Focus Scientifically, That Is, Not on the Emotional but on the Actual Issues Involved

Avoid extremes by steering a course between not overreacting to the situation as if it is catastrophic and not underreacting to the situation by denying or otherwise distancing yourself from its important aspects.

Uncover Unconscious/Suppressed Reasons for Any Homonegative Beliefs You Might Hold

Dad in particular should always ask himself about his own erotophobia and how that might relate to concerns about his masculinity—that is, does his son's being gay enhance not only his fears of his own being gay but also his own personal disgust with all sexuality, and if his son's being gay reflects back on him to cast a shadow on him personally?

Try to Reduce if Not to Eliminate as Much Negativity as Possible

Being at odds with your son enhances the possibility not only that he will be at odds with you, but also that he will be at odds with himself and with his homosexuality. That can lead him to behave in a disordered way because he is feeling ashamed of himself and uncertain about how much he is really loved. In unfavorable cases, it can even be a reason for him to use drugs, engage in unprotected sex, and make one or more suicide attempts. Though you likely blame many things entirely on bullying outside the home, often homegrown bullying is causing many of his problems, one of which is becoming more vulnerable to bullying on the outside.

Temper Being Honest with Being Discreet

Don't lie, but always keep in mind that because less than full honesty can be protective, it is wise to keep some of your thoughts unexpressed and sanitize/neutralize some of your harsher feelings before saying exactly what's on your mind. Always try to avoid becoming openly angry with your son. Dad and Mom should especially watch for making violent statements to their son, as exemplified by the comedian Tracy Morgan, who said, "If I should ever discover that my son was gay I would stab him."[3] Never make openly cruel remarks such as "You are ruining our lives." And never retaliate for his being gay in any way, especially by withholding love for him. Certainly avoid subtle passive-aggressive retaliation, that is, being aggressive by implication as you "merely" suggest that your son should treat himself like a pariah you are ashamed of, banishing and exiling himself from the family and all your friends so that he doesn't ruin you socially should others find out that he is gay. Also avoid becoming judgmentally moralistic and controlling in subtle, indirect ways as by smugly saying, "You can do what you want because we don't care that much about you." Never fall silent to express disapproval and never attack your son in the guise of being overly supportive when that support actually consists of excessive saccharine altruism (as in "We are not thinking of ourselves at all, and we would do anything you want us to do to help you with your problem because we would give our lives for you, and our only wish is to make you happy personally and see to it that you succeed professionally"). At first a friend's mother made it clear by omission (saying nothing negative to or about his partner, yet managing via her silence to clearly show her disapproval) that she wanted his partner to leave her son alone and go away. She later came around, at the last minute, on her death bed, but only after she had done permanent damage to her son's partner, damage that survived her. For years she failed to ask herself, "What is my son trying to do?" and instead only enquired of herself, and of her son, "What are my son, and his partner, trying to do *to me?*"

Learn Exactly How Your Son's Disclosure Affects You

Document how you truly feel about disclosure, and why. In particular ask yourself if you have become so depressed that you no longer view yourself as "good parents" and instead have come to see yourself as failures who missed some opportunities and botched other things. Ask yourself if, and how, disclosure has changed you not only with your son, but also in your relationship with one another, with your own parents, and with the rest of the family, your friends, and your colleagues.

Understand suppressed (psychodynamic) reasons for any discomfort you may be experiencing around disclosure. Look at the historical origin of your present feelings, trying to see if any or all of your current attitudes about your son's coming out basically represent not a purely current rational position, but a flowering of previously held, often latent, attitudes newly stimulated/revived by your son's disclosure.

Specifically focusing on the discomfort that you believe to be about sexual matters, see if your displeasure is actually over, or at least fueled by, such nonsexual matters as:

- *Dependency* issues involving who is going to be succored by whom, where you have difficulty differentiating your reacting to your son's revelation of *homosexuality* from your own response to your adolescent son's developing *sexuality*—leading to his becoming less sexually innocent and growing up and developing interests and companions outside of the home, meaning that he is pulling away from your world, effectively rejecting and even disowning you.
- *Control* issues involving who in the family is going to tell whom what to think and do, starting but not ending with sexuality.
- *Competition* issues (struggling among family members) involving who is going to be the one to decide and determine the overarching nature and course of the family attitude/response/approach to a gay son, even involving struggles to determine whose ideas are going to attain ascendancy.
- *Avoidant* issues where anxiety that at first seems to be about sexual issues more specifically is about closeness.

Try to determine if you are reacting not only to your son's disclosure, but also to how other parents and family members are responding to your "predicament," that is, are you responding primarily to your son's disclosure, or is your response to its wider fallout?

Examine the Interface between Your Core Personality Problems and the New Reality of Knowing You Have a Gay Son

Especially look for your own (paranoid) responses where as you project yourself onto your son you turn your worries about and suspicions of him into what you perceive to be realistic observations/interpretations of how he is behaving toward you. Minimize (hypomanic) denial defenses where you trivialize his disclosure by feigning disinterest and a lack of surprise, saying, "That's okay," and/or flippantly treating your son's being gay as "just a phase he is going through" so that you can now safely preoccupy yourself with other matters you (defensively) deem to be "more important."

Recognize the Possibility That Adjusting Can Be as Difficult for Him as It Can Be for You

Don't think only, "He is giving us a hard time," think also "He is having a hard time of it himself." Not once did my parents even acknowledge the possibility that my being gay presented certain problems for me. Their entire orientation was how my being gay was a problem for them. So regularly ask your son, "Is there anything that I can do for you, any help you might need that I can give you to make your life, and your life as a gay man, easier?"

Avoid Scapegoating Others

Especially avoid criticizing/blaming your son's friends/boyfriends for making your son gay/ruining his and/or your life.

Strike a Balance between Affirming and Enabling

When disciplining your son, do so in a way that represents a compromise between being arbitrary and controlling/routinely challenging/hovering, and abdicating to all your son's needs and wishes, even encouraging him to act out for you by saying nothing about what should stop.

Practice Modeling for Your Son What a Good Relationship Consists Of

Show your son the way by example, using your own (hopefully healthy) marital relationship as illustrative. At the same time avoid modeling what a bad relationship entails by encouraging him to do the questionable things you do and/or have done.

A gay son will be more likely to be happy and joyful if he grows up in a home where all concerned have a good life and *want* his life to be as good as theirs. Because here, perhaps as nowhere else, good wishes toward him can really make good things happen for him.

Learn to Recognize Your Limitations

Always tell yourself, "I don't know it all," and ask yourself, "How can I supplement what I know by learning from him about what being gay means, and how it affects us and him?"

Become Willing to Apologize when You Are Wrong

If you say or do something that in hindsight you wish you hadn't, invalidate it by taking it back, and as soon as possible.

Recognize the Bad News

Appreciate the downsides of your coming out (your as well as his). As parents of a gay son, you should expect fewer benefits from your coming/being out than you might at first have anticipated. Being out, even as a family, can do a lot but not everything. On the positive side healthy coming out helps you feel freer, and be more honest, so that you no longer have to waste time alternating between depressive self-hatred/abandonment of your authentic self and blaming others to proclaim your innocence. Likely it will help you cope/survive by showing you the folly of believing your circumstances to be hopeless. It can foster a cohesive conflict-free family atmosphere by sealing over family conflicts/divisions—by instead of fracturing the family in dissention, uniting the family around supporting a gay son and his cause. It can activate a positive family identity.

But it won't fully counter a persona/group identity seriously compromised by damaging guilt-driven punitive self-devaluation, and it won't definitively solve serious emotional problems that plague family members as individuals or the family as a unit. And lack of any family strife may not be an entirely good thing in the first place. It can have a negative homogenizing effect, obscuring individuality and thus hampering true personal authenticity and growth.

Also on the negative side is that coming out too assertively can expose you to prejudice and discrimination from homohating others. For in the real world it's best, or at least safest, to achieve a balance between inner peace and reduction of stress through openness, and outer security through reticence that involves being closeted in some, even crucial, respects with difficult, and possibly even dangerous, people.

Recognize the Good News

The good news is that your son's being gay doesn't mean that he or you will have a problematic life. As with any other life, gay or straight, it's not the life itself but how life's problems are handled that determines what is to be, and whether it is to be joyful or challenging.

Chapter 2

Debunking Myths about Having a Gay Son

Parents have difficulty coming and staying out in part because they buy into myths about being gay/having a gay son and then, thinking accordingly, and often emotionally, fail to face the contrasting facts and consider the absolute realities.

Myths consist of distorted viewpoints/beliefs that belong both to laypersons, who spread them by word of mouth and on the Internet, and experts, who advance them in the media and in the scientific literature. In fact, laypersons often distort the facts less than do the experts because while the former tend to be, and keep, current, the latter tend to fall behind as they, their often complex theories, and their publication schedules fail to keep up with the rapidly changing gay world and its subculture. Thus much of the literature from the 1990s dramatizes the problems with being gay in a way that is more suitable for yesterday than today. As further discussed later in this chapter, while the layperson, knowing better, realizes that most gays of today have learned to take good care of and protect themselves, the experts continue to portray too many gays as excessively sensitive men likely to be bullied and to respond by becoming shattered by all the bullying—to the extent of becoming dysfunctional, often to the point of becoming suicidal.

Instead of buying into myths about having a gay son, parents need to think for themselves about what being gay, and what having a gay son, actually means. An important assignment takes you as a gay son's parents beyond simply reality testing myths about having a gay son to learning why you buy into and respond so unrealistically to what you hear. Many parents respond as they do because they are told that that's the way they should react—because that's how others respond. So they fail to react, and act, authentically, that is, in their own way—the way that feels, and is, right for them, and that is appropriate to their special makeup and circumstances. Commonly, for example, parents feel traumatized by having a gay son because they hear that their friends were never the same after disclosure. And they feel ashamed about having a gay son because they hear that when other families found out their son was gay, the whole family both fell into a depression and suffered severe social disgrace. So they emerge even from disclosure that goes smoothly feeling not only as if things have completely changed in their lives, but as if the changes have done them considerable damage. They overreact by feeling and acting more traumatized than they actually are in order to empathize with others, by meeting others' expectations of how to respond, and in order to be able to react in a way that is both politically correct and au courant. Too often this involves responding catastrophically, for example, with a pervasive sense of guilt coming into play about having done something wrong to "cause this terrible thing to happen" and having done nothing right to correct it.

Here are some specific distortive myths currently in circulation in parental circles. All in some way deform the true nature and meaning of disclosure (and afterward) and being gay, as a result disrupting, often seriously, how parents think about and behave toward their gay son.

Myth: Gay sons must be parented differently from straight sons.

Fact: There is no reason to parent a gay son much differently from a straight son. In fact, doing so involves reverse discrimination based on sexual orientation. All children, straight or gay, girls or boys, should be treated as equals and with equal care and concern. That starts with assessing their individual needs using objective criteria and continues with never depriving one child of what he or she requires for the express purpose of gratifying another. The goal is to integrate your son into the family, not to seal him off by making him special in any way. Both the following positions are unacceptable: "My straight children are the most valuable to us; so let's deaffirm/ignore our gay son not only for their sakes but also to punish him for being gay" and "He needs us more now, so we will give him all of our love, even if it means depriving our other children of some of our affection."

Myth: The main job of parents is to be martyrs, to self-sacrifice 100 percent so that they can give their absolute all to their children, including, or especially, their gay son.

Fact: *All* concerned—Mom, Dad, and son—have to work together to help each other feel comfortable and do their best. Although their needs may differ, parents are as needy as their children. Parents, like their sons and daughters, need handholding and support. So as parents you have to get beyond totally focusing on, pleasing, appeasing, and entirely avoiding being hurtful to your gay son, to also focus on pleasing, appeasing, and entirely avoiding being extremely hurtful to yourself. For here too, or especially, what is good for the gosling is good for the goose.

Yet many parents of gay sons are tempted to treat their sons far better than they treat themselves. Devaluing their all-too-human need to be self-protective and failing to recognize that whatever they might be they too "were born that way," they self-sacrificially fail to establish an even playing field with their sons. They think, "I mishandled him" when in fact he mishandled them; and they accept anything that comes their way "given the sensitivity of the situation" when in fact they are actually being bullied by their own insensitive son. I have treated a number of families where the parents were depressed because their son, and their society, were in actuality unfair to them. For example, their son unjustly demanded that they advocate for him although at best he, being personally difficult, required more deaffirmation than affirmation. They heard and read that if they didn't love him unconditionally and issue infinite permission slips, they didn't love him at all, and that they were being homophobic if they controlled and suppressed him in any way. They tried to meet their son all the way and always give him a free pass, when they should have met him only part of the way and awarded him free passes not based on perceived, generally theoretical, need, but on actual, real accomplishment.

As Kort says, "[F]amilies have a right to their reaction, *negative* or positive [emphasis added], and need the time and space to experience it."[1] Kort implies that parents of a gay son have the right to feel any way they choose about the situation, without necessarily condemning themselves, or being condemned, for the way they respond. They may feel, "It's not easy for parents to have a gay son" and as a consequence feel disappointed and get angry. But what they must not do is to suppress, without integrating, such negative feelings to the point that they dismiss these feelings as not being an integral part of their authentic overall response, one that is inherently part of their makeup. Conversely, parents who roughly follow the rule of "self-acceptance too, although not regardless" can generally get along better with their son—if not perfectly, then at least well enough—by being able to retain an enhanced relationship with him—because they have retained an enhanced relationship with themselves.

Too often, unfortunately, having a gay son tempts parents to masochistically self-abnegate, going beyond the self-sacrifice inherent in properly raising a child to hoping to attain a kind of sainthood that ultimately has the reverse effect of the one intended, and is in fact unconstructive and damaging overall to their ability to parent their son. For one thing, personal masochism enhances a son's sadism, for parental begging to be loved, a form of self-bullying, generally attracts bullying from others—including, or especially, their son. Parents who beg to be loved come across as weak, and weakness tends to encourage adolescent sons, most of whom have a sadistic streak in them in the first place, to disdain their parents even more fully and feel freer to bully Mom and Dad to an even greater extent. At the same time, begging lowers parents' own self-esteem and self-confidence, making them even more of an object of their son's scorn and derision, further undermining their authority and subjecting them to the greater attack that could have been averted if they instead had approached their son from a position of strength.

Also, masochistically abdicating parents predictably come to feel resentful over having to play a role that unavoidably sooner or later makes them feel uncomfortably like patsies. They resent abdicating. But instead of honestly saying so, they deny it. And instead of doing something about it, they continue as before. Next, feeling devious and dishonest, they lose self-respect and with little to no self-respect set a bad example for a son himself struggling to be proudly self-respectful. Besides, rewarding by ignoring their son's bad behavior generally has the opposite, unintended, effect of enabling it.

Therefore, it is important for you as parents to remember that being a good parent does not necessarily mean that you have to fully like who and what your gay son is or completely agree with everything he stands for, says, and does. Just because you do not feel entirely positively toward your son doesn't mean you feel highly negatively toward him and are therefore despicably homophobic. True love neither requires complete idealistic acceptance of another, nor involves taking sides against oneself.

Worse, being too concerned, overly caring, excessively supportive of, and extremely affirmative toward a son (when there is little reason or need to be) often comes across as condescending—and therefore paradoxically as itself homonegative. Many sons interpret the parental view of them as "not bad but needy" as their parents seeing their being gay as the same thing as their being weak and defective, thus implicitly devaluing gays as beggars along the lines of "He must be a beggar if he needs our handout." Some sons so devalued turn on their parents. They hate their parents for infantilizing them by viewing them as helpless, and for demeaning them by seeing them as hapless. Others, going to extremes to prove their parents wrong, become not healthily independent but overly free in a way that looks less like freedom and more like rebellion.

In conclusion, while you might have to change for him, he might also have to change for you. Both you and he should be flexible and willing to consider alternative views and positions. As he needs to develop personal pride independent of what others, including you, say and do, you need to develop personal pride relative to who you are, independent of what anyone, your son included, says about and does to you. It is an exaggeration that the first and only job of parents hoping to bring their children up right is to lose themselves and disappear into them. As parents you count too, and for as much as your child; your feelings and well-being are just as important as those of your children. Besides, you can't ensure your children's well-being unless you first ensure your own, for valued blessings cannot come from devalued saints. Never believe that you have so few significant needs of your own that you must focus exclusively on your gay son's needs and sensitivities, even when they seriously conflict with your own. As you take the same measure of yourself as you take of him, refuse to entirely suppress your self-interest to the point of marginalizing yourself, thus making your son a first-class, and you a second-class, citizen. For sooner or later, all people who view themselves as second-class become resentful of their self-imposed purportedly inferior status. And resentful parents, without exception, can't help but become less supportive than they should be of their son, and will possibly even become unsupportive to the extent that they ultimately withdraw their support from their son entirely.

Finally, parents who fail to support themselves out of excessively altruistic feelings for a child make bad role models for their son. The son hears "self-interest equals selfishness." And he learns that lesson all too well.

Myth: All coming out is exactly the same.

Fact: Gay sons and their families are not all alike and do not represent a collective; rather, they possess different personal, pathological, and sociocultural characteristics, which means that different disclosure scenarios will apply. Commonly parents who hold a one-size-fits-all philosophy respond with one-size-fits-all reactions and so tend to intervene simplistically with one-size-fits-all responses that though meant to be therapeutic are actually antitherapeutic. And in dealing with a theoretical, they fail to deal with an actual person. They forsake their son's total personal psychological profile and sociocultural specificity to deal only with his confessional as they fail to individualize their response to who their son is, as they knew him once, and as he has newly become after his personal revelation. If your input is not precisely applicable to his output, you are stereotyping not only your son as a gay man, but also your family as an average family. And you are likely doing so not only without special consideration for the different needs and philosophies of different gay men and diverse families, but along pre-determined, more politically than scientifically correct, lines. For example, as you assess your son's prospects in life, remember: It's not only a cultural but also a personal thing that while some gay men are hedonists, others, natively of a more conservative bent, tend to disavow polygamy and trend toward monogamy. Also, as you assess yourself, remember that some families are by nature overall more liberal while others are overall more conservative. And different families have different group emotional make-ups. *Passive-aggressive* families traditionally respond to disclosure with anger, which they first suppress then express indirectly by seething instead of blowing up. *Paranoid* families traditionally have an immediate "you-against-us" response with a condemnatory and adversarial flavor, for example, "You chose to be gay to get back at us." *Obsessively* rigid families tend to take up entrenched positions characterized by active stubborn resistance that likely supersedes even their own desire to be nonthreatening and passively accepting.

In addition to different personal and family types, different real-life family constellations tend to, or should, determine different family responses to disclosure. Families in which the gay son is an only child are likely to view disclosure with more alarm than families in which straight siblings can provide Mom and Dad with a buffer. Suburban and rural families often respond more negatively than do urban ones, as do families from certain socioeconomic backgrounds. Two-parent families differ in their response to disclosure from single-parent families in which the father or mother is absent. Families with happily married parents respond differently from families in which Mom and Dad are on the verge of a divorce. And close-knit families differ from families hanging/living apart. Families in which other children are gay differ from families with only one son, perhaps one who is older, who is gay, if only because in the first instance the family has by now had a chance to practice its response. Religiously conservative families differ in their responses from reformed or atheistic ones. Religiously conservative families often use dissociation to cope with the contradictions involved between what the Bible says and how they themselves actually want to and do feel about their son, as if they are trying hard (and often successfully) to keep their right brain, where they feel, from knowing what their left brain, where they comprehend and think, is all about. Conversely, more liberal families less conflicted about having a gay son may have problems not with reconciling conflicting moralities within themselves and with their Bible, but with defining (and defending) their views (and themselves) to less liberal or openly homophobic outsiders. Finally, families lucky enough to be able to effectively manipulate their environment respond to disclosure more flexibly than families unluckily unable to physically protect themselves, say by moving to another neighborhood, by sending their son away to school, or (in unfavorable cases) sending their son to rehab, thus getting out of the difficult, unalterable, and perhaps realistically unbearable reality in which they might otherwise find themselves.

Myth: Problems surrounding disclosure always have to be met and solved immediately.

Fact: Parents who find out they have a gay son and have problems with that should consider challenging the belief that lest opportunity be lost the immediate issues that come up should be their full focus. For so often if parents wait out the problems, if any, that are associated with disclosure, they will find that the problems resolve themselves spontaneously through the healing tincture of time. Time alone is on your side and is often powerful enough a remedy to itself seal difficulties over, especially when fortuitous external events occur to help the process along.

Myth: Disclosure is a limited, one-time, event.

Fact: There is a lifetime of work to be done after disclosure, and the whole family should be part of that (ongoing) process. Therefore, it is important for parents to recognize that disclosure is a process, not a one-time event. That is why I prefer the term "being out" to the term "coming out." For the actual disclosure process occupies just a few days, weeks, or at most months out of the long lives of all concerned, and what happens next and in addition to the issues immediately unleashed by disclosure is generally just as, or more, important. After disclosure, factors directly or more distantly related, or unrelated, to a son's being gay—especially educational, professional, and relational matters—do, or should, become important/proper targets of parental interest and legitimate concern.

Myth: Gay issues are the most (only) important issues for a family with a gay son.

Fact: As parents you must, at least some of the time, change the gay subject and instead focus more directly on the life subject. Once you get over the initial shock of learning that your son is gay, if indeed you do experience shock in the first place, you should focus on/worry about the kind of life your son will live overall. Focus not, as my parents did, on being gay and its negatives, but on the problems associated with growing up immature (gay or straight). Then intervene in a way that helps your son, gay or straight, develop into a mature person. Address all realistic concerns, not just those that are gay related, and suggest appropriate helpful corrective action your son can take—not to go straight, but to be gay in a sanguine way. Devote your attention to the difficult aspects of *his* life that no doubt exist. Especially check to determine if there are any problems he might be having that you might have been the cause of.

My parents rarely if ever mentioned problems I was having in my life. They rarely if ever offered me their wisdom about how I could live my life better. Instead they, or at least my father, only—and incessantly—complained about my being gay, and how it embarrassed him and my mother. I could have used a little direction presented in a helpful therapeutic parental advisory way. But they never got beyond the negative feedback consisting of criticisms for being and warnings about remaining homosexual. It seemed that what was furthest from their thoughts was helping me in areas where I was obviously unhappy and having problems. Perhaps I could have used the therapy they insisted I enter, but not to turn straight. If it were not my sexual orientation but my unhappiness that mattered most/most alarmed them, I would have gladly acceded to their wishes and sought the treatment they said I must have. And I would have done so without resisting, as I most certainly otherwise did.

Parents generally need to intervene when their son's life is lurid: overly steeped in the search for excitement and immediate gratification, particularly that of a sexual nature; and trivial to the core, as when one gay patient of mine celebrated too long and hard the joy of spying an attractive younger man wearing fabulous yellow sunglasses. Parents should help such a son become more concerned with things likely to be more important/central to his ultimate happiness and well-being than, however flashy, a pair of alluring sunshades. If your son is acting out self-destructively in his relationships, help him stop by asking him "Why?" in preparation for looking into what, if anything, you can do about it. Is he the way he is because you don't accept and love him enough at home, and so is seeking substitutes for love outside the house to make up for what he feels he isn't getting from you (only to go on to pick bad substitute parental figures as he neurotically, and self-destructively, repeats his traumatic relationship with you on the outside to once and for all try to come to terms with, and resolve, problems he is having with you at home?).

Yours is a dilemma: If you ignore his acting out, he might feel rejected, as if you don't care, and so become more defiant (through acting out more, and more outlandishly) to call your attention to him so that you now at least notice him and, even better, do something about what you see just to prove your concern. Yet if you crack down too harshly on him, you will likely cause him to act out even more by rebelling against you. A possible solution involves avoiding lecturing him in the recognition that doing so is being controlling and can worsen the problem. Instead (perhaps even without mentioning the problem that needs to be solved) simply give him a stable loving home environment, anticipating that he will use that as a base upon which to build a new, more upbeat, more joyful, more creative, and likely all-around more rewarding personal life.

Myth: All gay men are okay just the way they are.

Fact: The literature generally implies/states that gay = okay and thus implies/states that few if any gay men have emotional problems worth considering. Thus McDougall quotes a parent from Perth, Australia, as saying that "all gay men are gentle, kind and gifted souls with a warm sense of humour. They bear no malice to their fellow man."[2] By extension parents can supposedly readily forgo an in-depth personal psychological assessment of their gay son even, or especially when, they suspect that it might turn up flaws mixed in with his virtues.

While there is nothing bad about being gay, neither does being gay automatically make a person good, sweet, and loveable when a relevant problematic constitutional or emotional problem exists. Some gay men, less rascals than otherwise, are and stay family men. But others, responding negatively to parental love, though the love is strong and sincerely offered, reactively remove themselves entirely from their families because their family's *loving* paradoxically arouses deep ongoing inner conflicts, leading them to retreat into their very own, very gay world, closing off their family and sometimes also distancing themselves from everyone else around them. Some gay men consciously or unconsciously deliberately provoke others, their parents especially, pushing their buttons and arranging to be a "poor fit" out of a need to be a misfit so that they will be different as outsiders who as such can view themselves as unparalleled and unique, thus enhancing their self-esteem through differentiating themselves from the establishment by copping an angry antiestablishment attitude—one that in some cases comes dangerously close to paranoia. They present their stance as a legitimate sociocultural/philosophical outsider position when it is in fact more like adversarial injustice collecting. They feel that they can prop themselves up only by successfully fighting some imagined enemy who is supposedly scornfully and contemptuously putting them down. Homophobia is common, but these sons assume it is there when it isn't, often just so that they can fight the worthy cause against bigotry and by doing successful battle with demons come to count for something—sturdy warriors, guardians of what is right, and keepers of that which is just.

Myth: for gay men, advocacy/affirmation/positivity = a panacea

Fact: Often positivity is (as described in Chapter 15) an extremely helpful interpersonal therapeutic approach to take with gay sons, and especially with those who have low self-esteem. It can heal entire families, even those who can't get along at all. But as also mentioned in that chapter, positivity has its limitations and must be presented judiciously to avoid crossing the thin line between affirmation and enabling. Excessive positivity can make some sons too smug and overwhelm others by causing them to feel devoured to the point that they literally need to get away from home or if they stay at home, to withdraw in place just to maintain their comfortable distance and safe space. Therefore, parents must be selective in being supportive of and advocating for a gay son. No parent must feel he or she needs to see everything exactly the same way their gay son does and come to a full meeting of the minds with him every time, in every instance, even if that means disavowing their own philosophy in order to completely shadow that of their son. Often the best course, the one that in the long run is actually most supportive, involves sometimes agreeing with your son and sometimes disagreeing with him, and sometimes agreeing to disagree, always depending exactly on the specific issue at hand. And when a gay son's life is dangerous and self-destructive, your job as his parents is not to affirm him, but to set standards, establish boundaries, and enforce limits—then, if he complains, to remain steadfast even when, as is likely, he says something along the lines of "You are telling me that it's not alright to be gay." At this point you should probably iterate, or reiterate, that while you continue to offer him your unwavering basic support, you nevertheless feel that he needs your actual guidance, and that requires your taking a stance, one that consists of a happy medium between being blindly permissive and being overly forbidding.

Myth: All gay men are sensitive and especially so to being bullied, and so all have to be treated more gently than straight men.

Fact: Too much folklore, the media, and the scientific literature portrays all gay men as being ashamed of being gay and consequently as being fearful of being criticized/rejected by friends, family, and society at large. Thus Jennings states that gay men "having absorbed society's rejection of them reject . . . themselves."[3] Supposedly thus having become all too aware of their shortcomings, and overly alert to their failings, they presumably all require being treated as sensitive people who quake because they are too easily hurt and so respond to any degree of bullying, including parental negativity/abuse, by withdrawing, becoming depressed, and even attempting, or actually committing, suicide. Hence, it is often said, parents especially must always be fully positive to their gay son. And necessarily that requires that parents hide all their negative feelings—although negative feelings are always mixed in with the positive and thus always present in all parent-son relationships, even with good sons and the best of parental intentions.

It is true that there are some gay sons who are truly hypersensitive, brittle individuals with whom parents have to be very careful, watching every move, censoring every statement, always alert to avoiding the many pitfalls that potentially exist from not being tamed and polite enough to avoid unwittingly hurting their son's feelings. But so often gay sons are hypersensitive not because they are gay but because they are troubled—generally paranoid, and depressed, and it is that issue that puts them at special risk for having a catastrophic response to parental abuse. Paranoid gay sons not only can't easily ignore any parental bullying at all, they rather always have one eye open to and so are prone to exaggerate the devaluation from the bullying they often assume is there even in its absence. Depressed gay sons who are also unable to ignore any bullying instead overrespond to being bullied by becoming dejected simply because one or both parents even hint that, as Jennings says, "you just don't fit in,"[4] leading them, as Jennings continues, to feel "devastated, vulnerable, and alone"[5] and to a far greater extent than warranted. These are the gay men who already suffer from low self-esteem that leads them to become self-unaffirmative—again, not because they are gay, but because they are more tender and brittle, and less resilient (on average) than other gay men due to their depressed emotional state. And it is that emotional state, not merely the parental bullying, that constitutes the biggest danger of all and thus the most important measure of what their parents need to address.

Two gay siblings existed in one family. The view of all gay sons/gay men as tender, brittle people likely to wither and die, and even to attempt suicide if Mom and Dad merely mistreated them in any way, even if they just looked at them angrily or used a term that was, or that they could perceive to be, bigoted and critical, like "lifestyle" instead of "life," was applicable to one of the gay brothers but not to his sibling, who instead of responding in a catastrophic fashion to negativity/being devalued remained unconcerned with what his parents thought and had to say (as he did with everyone else other than his intimates). Instead he knew what his life should be about and didn't actually want or need to factor in other people's opinions about how he should live it. The sensitive brother told his parents everything and hoped they would nod in approval. It seemed that inherent in the other brother's being gay, in being gay's very DNA, was his love of freedom, which included freedom from caring about the impression other people, including his parents, had of him. If he cared about what his parents thought, it was only to discern what he shouldn't tell them. To illustrate, when they dropped him off at Grand Central Station to take the train back to college, he stealthily went down one staircase and up the other for the little R and R he believed absolutely necessary after a weekend at home with the family. His favorite expression, at the time all too familiar in the gay world—"You do that, and I'll scratch your eyes out"—revealed an ageless truth: The view of all gay men as shrinking sissies is a stereotype because many gay men—like him, a force to be reckoned with—are not (and resent being viewed and treated as if they are) weak, helpless souls in need of hothouse maintenance—lest they wither from lack of nourishment and die from the cold.

Though neurotic in many ways, one gay patient, relatively invulnerable to insult, was hardly subject to swooning at the first sign of being bullied in or outside the home. Once he even humorously threatened to "destroy" a friend for "criticizing me for not wanting to hear Gloria Gaynor's Disco anthem I Will Survive one more time." He was rambunctiously and even defiantly proud of who and what he was, far less fragile than tough and durable, and as likely to bully as to be bullied by others, including his parents, of whom he said, "Being a problem for my parents is my job." I myself regularly fear emerging from a certain train station in Greenwich Village early on a weekday morning when the previous night's crowd is still there, acting more like predators than victims. They are gay men who are not as ashamed of themselves as the experts and the literature frequently suggest all gay men are. Rather they are ashamed of, likely to protest against, and themselves apt to bully others who don't speak and act in a way that *they* approve of.

It follows that all gay sons are not only not sensitive persons who need continuing hothouse care, but boys and men who can well handle the abuse they routinely get from insensitive, unthinking bullies—including parents who don't know how to, or won't, properly manage them. So it follows that if you as parents dish out abuse to the wrong son, you should be prepared to take abuse back from him. And the remedy in such situations involves not sending your son off to therapy, but making an appointment with that therapist for yourself.

There is an important upside to recognizing your gay son's lack of exquisite sensitivity. That upside is that freed from your worry about your son's brittleness, you can just be yourself without being unduly concerned about hurting your son seriously and permanently. As parents you can, thankfully, expect your son to survive even your bad mistakes and to do quite well in the process. Reassure yourself that your fears that anything you might say or do wrong will necessarily hurt him badly are generally unwarranted. Recognize that these fears partly derive from a *culture* of parental overprotectiveness of children, straight and gay, and partly from emotionally based *cognitive distortions* such as the one that minor negativity on your part indicates a totally homonegative attitude toward your son, with highly negative results consequently clearly predictable and devastating. So reassure yourself that you can't hurt your son as easily as you fear, and that even if he feels hurt, it will generally be temporary and in the long run count for little. Also consider the possibility that his hurt feelings can even be a good thing—a necessary healthy step in growing up and out of your family, a first move away from your house, one that will likely lead to his ultimately becoming a mature functioning adult through having triumphed over imperfect you, if only in self-defense. Besides, in a general way, working with what you have is usually adequate because when *your* being perfect is impossible, being simply good enough will likely suffice.

In conclusion, while most if not all gay sons are subject to a degree of emotional and physical bullying in and outside the home, the legendary shy, scared, and extremely vulnerable gay son as portrayed in much of the literature—that sensitive soul who cringes in fear when he senses negativity around him on his parents' part and negative feedback from his peers—is in fact a stereotype, and an insulting one at that, for it brands all gay men as "sissies" if only because they supposedly cannot survive being assaulted in any way. So while you as parents do have to be somewhat cautious in how you handle your gay son, you don't routinely need to be as careful as you at first might think and certainly not cautious to the point that you fully abdicate to him just to spare what you believe to be his undoubtedly fragile ego. So many gay men well survive being seriously stigmatized and ostracized, emerging relatively unscathed. They handle this well, generally on their own, and instead of killing them, it goes on to make them even stronger.

Myth: All gay men are sufficiently resilient to be able to handle themselves adequately under all circumstances.

Fact: This said, a number of gay sons are vulnerable when others victimize them for who and what they are, and for things for which they bear absolutely no responsibility. These are the sons who most need help with bullies and best get it from nonbullying parents. First, as parents you have to stop bullying your son yourself. Second, you have to categorically support and take his side when others are bullying him. As parents you can help a sensitive son who is being victimized by bullies in several ways. You can help him *directly*—by giving him advice such as, "Walk away after considering the dangers involved." And you can intervene *indirectly* by providing him with an affirmative home environment that gives him the strength he needs overall to handle bullying on his own and on his own terms. You can do this by being empathic and understanding—accepting him as much as possible, taking his side whenever appropriate, and cheering him on when it makes sense to do so—by recognizing his achievements over his failures and in other ways conveying to him the message that he is if not special then at least as good as anyone else, reaffirming that he is not being bad by being gay, while still letting him know that if he is "bad" it is because, as is true of most adolescents, he still has some growing up to do.

Conversely, if you do the opposite and quash your son's self-esteem at home, you reduce the self-affirmation he needs to draw the line against permitting outside others to quash him just as you did. Parents who impart a sense of worth to their son help him feel good about himself no matter what. And this holds true even when others are taunting him and won't stop. For a good sense of self allows him to—depending on the circumstances—either not care or effectively fight back against others who are treating him badly.

Myth: All gay sons are ashamed of being gay.

Fact: Gay shame does exist, but it doesn't always constitute a serious problem for the sufferer. Some gay shame is due to internalization of the homophobia that exists in the outside world, and some is due to innate self-homophobia, that is, to that homophobia that originates not from without but from within, often in that personal erotophobia that seems universal in the human condition and exists in straight as well as in gay men. Under the circumstances, gay pride cannot come fully from without but has to somehow be acquired from within. Also, even when a gay son is self-critical and highly ashamed of himself, it is not necessarily because he is at odds with being gay. Many such sons are mainly at odds with unrelated aspects of themselves, perhaps, like anyone else, over having forbidden thoughts of a nonsexual nature, for example, irrational hostilities. As a rule, that which occurs in a gay setting is not necessarily homosexually generated.

In fact, relatively few gay men unduly concern themselves, if they concern themselves at all, with what other people think. Because they are well-defended against criticism, they really just don't care what other people, besides their chosen gurus and intimates, have in mind. Alternatively, they have *high* self-esteem—innate pride that while traditionally deemed absent or inadequate in the gay man can in fact be reasonably high or higher than on average. Indeed many gay men truly see society's victimization of them as seriously misguided, and believe that if anything and anyone needs to be victimized, it is the society that they live in, both for its negative ideas and for its victimizing behaviors.

Sons who feel very guilty about being gay may need professional assistance. But advising your son to get that help can be counterproductive should you as his parents fail to exercise care in suggesting that a son already ashamed of himself needs help. For most sons will find the suggestion that they get therapy demeaning and itself a source of further shame. They will think that they are being told they need help because they are gay and so will respond antagonistically. Similarly counterproductive is going to the opposite extreme and attempting to be too reassuring by belaboring how your son is okay as he is and so doesn't need to feel any shame at all. For likely he already thinks he is fine, and if he even cares what you, or anyone else, thinks about him in the first place, he is apt to wonder if, and be correct in assuming that, you are protesting too much.

Myth: The ideal parent loves a gay son unconditionally and never falls short in this regard.

Fact: Parents should not convince themselves that to be ideal parents they must not make even one mistake with a gay son, and if they do then all is lost. For it is only the mythic parent who meets the ideal of being a selfless, self-sacrificing, always giving, always altruistic, never ambivalent, routinely entirely positive, constantly realistic Mom or Dad completely free of base emotions like anger, disappointment, and even disgust—in all ways, and especially where gay issues are at stake, in all spheres. All parents have negative thoughts and feelings about a gay son and at times even show and act upon them. And parents who try to completely suppress their negativity are generally disappointed to discover that it ultimately bursts forth unexpectedly and inappropriately. Trying to feel like "good people," they proclaim that "this is the most wonderful thing that could have happened to my son, and he is particularly special to me because he is gay." Only they discover that their wounds are still there and festering, for the bad feelings go not away but underground. Therefore, parents have to not deny but candidly work with their negativity to integrate it in order to make it an acceptable, authentic part of themselves and their relationship with their son. For that's the best if not the only way they can create harmony out of the interpersonal dissonance that so often comes not from inner ambivalence per se, but from its outer misrepresentation to others.

Myth: All families have to be loving family units who stay, and cry, together.

Fact: Your goal doesn't have to be to keep your family happily together. Rather it can, and perhaps should, be to form a functional family unit that is close without being repressively so. That is, it does not have to be so close that your son cannot grow up, apart, and out to the extent that he needs to so that he may develop fully as an individual. Families don't have to go through, and perhaps shouldn't live, life together in a kind of pathological merger where, dissolving the normal boundaries that do and should exist between family members, they do everything with one another, crying together in sadness and celebrating together in mutual joy, full understanding, and unmitigated shared love. Some of the most functional families stay together by hanging separately. Individual family members should consider pulling back just enough to keep a loving home going while not maintaining family ties too strictly, and too closely, to the point of flirting with mental illness. A truly loving family allows a son freedom to find love outside of the home. That generally involves letting him break too close family ties that bind. Some parents I have treated even found it wise to *encourage* their son to break away from them, at least to some extent—while still carefully leaving the door open for him to come back as a stronger, more independent person than he was before he left.

Myth: Always communicate with your son in a fully open and completely honest way.

Fact: You will hear people say, "Always say how you feel and, should you have negative feelings, always bring them out into the open." It is true, as Jennings says, that "if your child feels your displeasure it will only compound the dissatisfaction [he] may already feel about [him]self."[6] Yet it is also true that he will feel dissatisfied with you if he detects you are hiding your negative feelings from him and don't trust him enough to tell him about them. Therefore, sharing your thoughts with your son should be a selective—considered, nuanced, goal-directed—process, with honesty not always the best policy, and discretion almost always the better part of valor.

Of course, secretiveness is never supportive if you are covering up how you really feel in a passive-aggressive way through disingenuousness only to have how you really feel nevertheless come through clearly, if only by implication, with withheld disapproval seeping out and thus seriously disturbing basic trust. So if you have negative feelings about your son, first admit how you feel *to yourself*, then admit how you feel (*selectively* at least) to your son. While doing this, disavow, when true, the feelings as "not me," making it clear to him that you selectively deaffirm *yourself* as you make your negativity into something belonging to a part of you that you isolate from the mainstream of "me as a person" as you *struggle* with being negative so that it doesn't take over to the point that it comes between you and your son. Admitting this internal struggle with yourself and telling your son about it exactly avoids being inauthentic with yourself and appearing so to him. As well, it avoids setting a bad example for your son by showing him exactly how to be inauthentic, that is, how to be a phony.

Myth: Stay out of advising a gay son about his personal life.

Fact: Too many parents buy into the concept that parental involvement in their gay son's personal life is necessarily intrusive, for "It's his life, and he should lead it the way he wants to." And the literature generally agrees, for example, when it tells you to stay out of your son's intimate affairs, with only a few exceptions (e.g., when there is a medical issue you need to address). It is true that when parents make suggestions or give advice, they often find that they agree with Dumas, who says in *The Three Musketeers* that "People in general only ask advice not to follow it; or if they do follow it, it is for the sake of having someone to blame for having given it."[7] Typically they also find that their son in response to their considered advice distances himself from them, complaining that "You are meddling." Under such circumstances many parents forfeiting their parental responsibilities (if not their parental rights), abandoning common sense, say and do nothing directive, then feed themselves reassurances that their son is happier without their input because their guidance would clearly be more constricting than it could ever be broadening. These parents pull back because they worry that involvement = overinvolvement, which to them means being invasive/controlling/overly disciplinarian, which risks offending or even alienating their son. This fear may even lead them to stop setting any standards and limits, and defining any boundaries at all to instead rubber-stamp all things in their gay son's life just so that they will not see themselves as having meddled in it. But this fear of somehow challenging their son's inherent wisdom leads them to miss the opportunity to share their considerable knowledge—both native and acquired—with him. Parents who fear being invasive will not be instructive and so for that reason are unlikely to be nearly as helpful as they could otherwise be.

As parents you can, and should, retain your personal profile throughout the parenting process. Be judicious about what you say, but never be afraid of speaking up/speaking your mind simply because you feel that you, as somehow an inferior member in the partnership with your son, don't count for much, or at all, and as such what you think as a person older and so no longer wise therefore is presumably noncontributory. You will, of course, be overly critical, deaffirmative, and rejecting should you make suggestions abrasively, issue commands with finality, and failing to bargain, instead conclude what is right unilaterally and threaten reprisal if your son doesn't go along. But there *are* ways to register your vote without cornering who your son is and taking away the space he needs—encouraging rather than discouraging him not to simply do your bidding, but to at least consider your input as possibly being helpful. Want grandchildren? Don't bemoan the fact that since your son is gay you can't have them, or order him to get married to a woman and reproduce. Instead consider encouraging him to find a wonderful partner and adopt, or have children with a surrogate—for you as well as for himself. Tell him what you want and ask him to give it to you. But do so in a compassionate way, for that increases the chances that you will get something for yourself and at the same time prove to your son that his well-being is of interest and concern to you. As you guide him on the path that is right for him, help him walk the parallel path of what is also right for you.

In fact, many gay sons I have treated, though they refuse to admit it (at least at the time), were actually eager, or starving, for direction and discipline. Yet they held their parents off because they didn't want to think of themselves, or be thought of by their peers, as being too dependent on their elders, that is, under the thumb of Mom and Dad and as a result losing their true identity completely and giving up their freedom entirely.

Myth: Typical parent-gay son interactions need to be understood strictly from a middle-class perspective.

Fact: There is a tendency in the literature/the media to focus on problems of intact middle-class families, as if their concerns about having a gay son are not only typical, but also the only ones worthy of exploration, the proper focus, and the sensible objective for taking remedial action. Yet where I live in New York City, many gay sons come from families who are not middle class, are far from intact, and are overall quite different from the portrayals generally found in the standard scientific and lay literature about families of gay sons, and in essays in the lay press about ways to most effectively parent sons who are gay. Many of these families, struggling for survival, don't have the time/energy/money to resolve merely philosophical conflicts, either on their own or in therapy. Some abuse their gay and straight children equally. They are often concerned less with sensitivity, serenity, authenticity, and self-fulfillment, and more with actually making it. They care if their son is gay less than they care if he performs what they consider to be his crucial filial duties, like fixing things around the house and making money so that the rest of the family can eat and otherwise survive.

Myth: Your gay son is necessarily in for a troubled life.

Fact: Parents generally hear and believe that being gay supposedly means having a lonely life, and dying alone and full of regrets about what might have been. They don't hear that, as Bernstein rightly says, "the much maligned lifestyle of the average gay person is about as lurid as [one's] own, centered on such mundane matters as job, family, friends, home, hobbies and church,"[8] for gay men on the whole live stable, happy lives. Clearly being gay doesn't necessarily imply a specific type and quality of life that depends entirely on and strictly "goes with a homosexual orientation." The individual gay man's quality of life depends on many factors, including his individual personality, the luck of the draw, and the solidity and effectiveness of the input that you as his parents, and others in his world, have into his existence—input that can either help him do better, or inhibit his overall growth and development. As for individual personality, what kind of life your son will lead depends less on his sexual orientation than on his interpersonal savvy, and this in turn depends a great deal on whether he is accepting of, or unaccommodating to, others, as well as on whether he is a pessimist who, figuratively speaking, doesn't drink because he feels all drinks are poisoned, or an optimist who quenches his thirst even from a glass that is half empty. For some men it's harder being gay than straight; for others it's harder being straight than gay. There are many straight men who no matter what will remain unhappy, even depressed, throughout life, constantly fretting about who they are, never achieving full inner peace on their own terms, and instead going through life full of fear and disappointment, regretting much but changing little. And there are many gay men who wouldn't change a thing about their existence, having achieved full inner peace, fearing little, not at all disappointed about their lives, regretting nothing, and doing what they can to make any and all ongoing changes that they believe to be necessary to achieve full joy and fulfillment. So your job as parents is not to bemoan the fact that your son is gay, but to assess your son's strengths/liabilities/particular circumstances and then to act constructively by making any proper and necessary provisions you can and should make for him, seeing to it that a son who, as most sons, needs you both personally and financially gets what he needs, even when that involves saying "no" to him when a "yes" is not indicated and saying "yes" to him when a "no" (though the wrong thing to say) would just be your easy way out.

Myth: Nothing has changed just because your son is gay.

Fact: According to Jennings, when you have a gay son, "nothing has changed."[9] That is, he's the same person as he was before you found out he is gay. But *life* with a gay son while neither necessarily better nor worse can be somewhat different from life with a straight son. Therefore, disclosure, while it doesn't change *everything*, is likely to change *some things*, and for some families even a great deal.

True, the changes often occur less in reality than in its perception. But perception is what puts parents through changes, and it is these that are the ones parents have to deal with.

Myth: Your son should be judged strictly according to standards you as straight people apply to yourself.

Fact: Your son should be judged according to standards applicable to him as a gay man and in the context of the specific circumstances in which as a result he finds himself. Saying, "He will not be just as happy being gay" involves making invidious standardized comparisons based on stereotypes. He may or may not (but likely will be) just as happy, but he will likely be happy in a *different* way. You must not judge his happiness according to your standards of what should and does make people who are not gay happy. You must judge his happiness according to what makes a *gay* man happy. Being gay is not better or worse than, but simply a variety of, being straight, like left-handedness is a variety of right-handedness, or the express train is a variety of the local. Gay happiness comes about in alternate ways, neither better nor worse than straight happiness.

Myth: It is your fault for making your son gay.

Fact: Some of the literature suggests that certain family constellations "make" a son gay. For example, one favored formulation suggests that a son will become gay if he has a weak father (preventing a masculine identification) and an aggressive/seductive mother (scaring him off women). Others suggest another formulation: He will become gay if he has a strong (castrative) father and a weak mother (who doesn't intervene and protect him from Dad).

While being gay is itself almost always inborn (genetic in origin), a gay man's personality/personality problems likely will be, like any other person's personality/personality problems, at least in part the product of specific family interactions. For that reason, what a detached mother married to a too-strong/intrusive/demanding father (or some other version of a "pathognomonic parental constellation") may (or may not) promote is not a son's being gay, but personality problems in a gay son. For example, it is not uncommon for a son to identify with troubled parents, leading him to become troubled on his own, along similar lines. But even here it is difficult to relate process to outcome, for multiple factors, none of which are by themselves either necessary or sufficient, generally determine results. Therefore, while your son was born gay, and his being gay itself is not your doing, secondary aspects of his being a gay man *are* likely to be a response to how you brought him up. So Kort's statement that parents of gay sons "need to be reassured that they did nothing to cause it, shape it, or develop it"[10] is correct only if by "it" he means actually being homosexual. That is because parents can and often do shape their son's being gay in a certain way. (Parents can sometimes help tip innate bisexuality to homosexuality or discourage that shift. They can help promote opportunistic homosexuality or discourage it.) Therefore, as parents you should take some responsibility not for your son's being gay, but for how he turned out over-all. If there are ways you went wrong, admit it to yourself and him, and put things behind you by making amends specifically geared toward undoing any mistakes you may have made, and harm you may have caused, and go on from there to help your son make any necessary adjustments he should be putting into place to improve his life as a gay man.

Myth: Diversity always beats homogeneity (traditionalism).

Fact: Diversity is both a virtue and a fault. There is nothing inherently bad about decrying diversity and wanting sameness, such as the sameness associated with maintaining family tradition. So don't condemn yourself if you believe that your son's being gay involves his being more disloyal to you and your family than you might like. That the world would be a dull place if everyone were the same is true, but it is also true that the world might be (is?), though a brighter place, more problematic if everyone were too idiosyncratically individualistic.

Myth: Learning about being gay diminishes homophobia.

Fact: According to Bernstein, learning about what being gay consists of will predictably trump antigay prejudice. As he says, "[O]nce Americans learn the truth about homosexuality, their sense of fairness will not allow them to continue to discriminate against our gay kids."[11] This implies that the genesis of social distress with homosexuality is *strictly* due to society's *conscious* reluctance to renounce archaic myths, superstitions, and hatreds that tacitly encourage homonegativity, with the remedy clearly implied. But a main source of bigotry is *unconscious* and as such comes from a dark place within ourselves that is not readily subject to airing and influence. Put another way, prejudice, including homophobia, will always be with us because it serves a psychological function, and so changing one's conscious mind doesn't always fully change one's unconscious attitude. For that rea-son, activism won't always effectively change society (and a changed society will not always walk back to change all those who live in it). While educa-tion can make inroads into prejudice, education—because it doesn't touch the unconscious roots of bigotry—won't expunge it entirely. Therefore, as parents you should continue to learn about the reality of your son's being gay but expect that other interventions/actions will be required to turn what you have learned into a fully nondistortive, and hence more positive, view of what your son's being gay actually entails.

Myth: All parents of gay sons can benefit from group therapy, especially if the group consists of other parents of gay sons.

Fact: A search of the literature reveals many authors who suggest that the best thing parents can do for themselves and their gay sons is to enter group therapy, such as a group run by PFLAG (Parents, Families, and Friends of Lesbians and Gays). The literature cites as being among the benefits of group therapy opportunities to get one's feelings out and obtain consensual validation, and the encouraging of activism to help both the individual and his or her society.

But in reality, only some parents can benefit from some group therapy. First, many parents don't need therapy of any sort. They may think they do, or be encouraged to go when in fact their pain and distress are too superficial (or nonexistent) to actually represent a strict indication for obtaining help. Sometimes group therapy makes things worse, as can happen when leaderless nonprofessionally run groups lack, as they often do, the ability or willingness to handle parents who are deeply disturbed. Worsening can also happen if the group is biased against those with unique but rational philosophical persuasions that don't fit the group mentality to the individual in attendance, for example, making groups that embrace activism wrong for parents who are "passivists." And those who are truly in pain may desire, or do better in, individual therapy, especially if they are private people who actively prefer to air their problems behind closed doors in individual treatment. Those who must be the primary focus of the therapeutic process may feel excluded by the large numbers of individuals attending group sessions. Some parents complain that from past experience they know that members of a group who are excessively needy, or angry and vengeful, can do more harm than good to the group's individual members and the functionality of the group as a whole. And some parents of gay sons complain about lesbian, transsexual, bisexual and questioning issues being mixed in with gay men's issues, as they often are in groups that deal with parents of anyone who is not heterosexual for any reason.

In short, it is always necessary to fit the treatment to the patient, and the reverse. The same principles apply when entering/recommending any form of therapy, group or otherwise, and to anyone—parents of gays, parents of straights, parents without children, unmarried people, and gays themselves. Whether or not a son is gay, as emotional problems don't discriminate according to sexual orientation, so should solutions to these problems be considered to be equally blind.

Chapter 3

Overcoming Common Emotional Problems Parents Have Due to Having a Gay Son

Parents commonly develop emotional problems as the result of difficulties they themselves associate with having a gay son. These problems typically make it hard for parents to be as knowledgeable as possible, as accepting as desirable, and as effective as they could conceivably be.

Most observers minimize how hard it can be for Mom and Dad to handle learning they have a gay son. And many parents themselves, feeling overconfident, believe that they are able to deal with the situation easily—more easily than they actually can. For example, a patient denied that her son's being gay presented a problem for her. Only on further discussion did she reveal that it was more difficult for her than she at first realized. She admitted that she wasn't able to fully cope with all the problems involved, at least not as quickly and effortlessly as in the beginning she believed she could. First, as she discovered, she wasn't clear about what the problems actually were and to whom they belonged. Was she being a difficult parent who couldn't properly handle her son, or was her son and "his situation" a proper source of a reasonable amount of concern, and so of her personal angst? Did she need to learn more about how to handle herself, or did she need to learn more about how to go about encouraging her son to treat her better? Second, she began to identify previously overlooked negative feelings about her son's being gay. At first she tried to cover them up, only to discover that they were so strong, persistent, and unyielding that she could not meld them into an overarching positive whole—one that acknowledged, but did not emphasize or fully encompass, her negativity. So when she felt highly antagonistic to her son, she developed a fully negative self-concept based on her belief that she was a bad person mistreating her child. Third, while she acknowledged that she had made some mistakes, and perhaps continued to make them, she fretted that she couldn't repair the wrongs she believed she had already done. Fourth, she was confused as to whether the usual principles of good parenting applied in this case, or if her son's being gay meant that her interaction with him was unique, as if matters of proper parenting somehow discriminated according to sexual orientation. In short, as she in essence herself summed things up, "I do realize that I am getting too emotional about having a gay son and that that is causing me, I would imagine like most parents in the same situation, to think unrealistically and to act impulsively. So what I need to know is how I can fully identify and face all my irrational responses so that I can develop a realistic overall strategy for coping with and normalizing these—my clearly excessive, much too passionate replies to a situation that for me is more highly charged than it should [be] and than I at first ever realized it could be?"

Here are some recommendations based on classical time-tested methods for identifying/coping with/healing from/treating the main emotional reactions so many parents, without necessarily realizing it, have in response to finding out that their son is gay. In many cases making the right diagnostic observations and instituting the remedies I go on to imply or suggest can result in a healthier adjustment not only for Mom and Dad, but also for the entire family, including, or especially, their son.

The Posttraumatic Response

The posttraumatic response to having a gay son, which may or may not progress to full posttraumatic stress disorder (PTSD), consists of the *biphasic* reaction characteristic of most posttraumatic responses to events perceived to be traumatic—which, for some parents, having a gay son clearly seems to be. This biphasic response contains both an *initial* acute and a *later* more chronic response to the trauma, the second either running in with or separated from the first by a shorter or longer period of time many observers call the latency period.

The *initial* response typically consists of repetition of the traumatic event in the form of insistent, recurrent, partial, or close-to-exact conceptual and visual memories of, or flashbacks to—if not to all, then to a significant aspect of—the original traumatic experience. Traumatized parents have preoccupying horrific visualizations of what a gay son is supposedly doing both in the bedroom and in his life, and these can amount to a partial or full-time preoccupation, one that can be likened to obsessive brooding shading over into depression. (According to Pinsker in a personal communication of August 12,

2012, the posttraumatic response needs to be distinguished from "a phobia, with spreading sensitivity [requiring] desensitization therapy. And it needs to be distinguished from obsessions where there are intrusive thoughts which may be of a nontraumatic nature.")

There are associated ongoing feelings of anxiety, agitation, and anger, the latter consisting of raging at one's fate and the person(s)/situation supposedly responsible for it, as in, "That son of mine is ruining my life" and "That boyfriend of his is making him gay." Anxious/agitated/angry parents typically brood about the past, the present, and the future—theirs and their son's, as they worry "What did I do wrong? Did I do anything to make him gay?" They feel that for them life as they know it is over both now and in the years to come. And they convince themselves that their son will also fail in life. Depressive preoccupations like this are generally embedded in engulfing sensations of spaciness (feeling detached from reality), which can amount to an "altered state" (called depersonalization), for example, "I can't believe that this terrible thing is happening to me," but "I *am* actively freaking out over the fact that my son is gay."

Most parents try to relegate the trauma, and their traumatic response to the past, that is, to "just get over it," to "forget all about the fact that my beloved son is queer." But commonly the harder they try, the less they succeed, and instead what often happens is that self-abuse begins, prevails, and strengthens as they can't stop blaming themselves first for having brought the traumatic situation down upon their own heads and second for not being able to put it aside. And at the same time they blame others for their state: their son, his partner, and each other. In a typical case, parents both blame their son's being gay and all that that supposedly entails on themselves, for example, "If we had raised him up differently, we might not have caused this to happen." Paradoxically they also might think, "I don't believe we did this to him because his being gay is his choice, and that's the choice he made, so don't blame us, blame him."

Totally shamed, guilty, yet outraged, they attempt to right all wrongs and make changes they feel to be necessary and for the better—only they mostly try to do these things not for their son, but for themselves. Thus "I want him to change for his own good" is often a self-statement, not so much a wish that *he*, but a wish that *they*, would have a better life. They say, "We don't want him to feel so bad about his situation." But they really mean, "For our sake, we want him to marry a nice girl, and have a big family to give us grandchildren." Frantic but generally ineffectual attempts to change their son, to make him straight, may begin. These generally range from subtle, indirect persuasion to giving him orders accompanied by forceful actions hoped to have a direct, immediate, effect upon him, as when parents attempt to push their son into reparative therapy while claiming altruistic motives (so that he can have a better life—because the gay life is so hard), when in fact the "repair" of "reparative therapy" is more for them than it is for him.

In the delayed leg of the response, flashbacks resume and continue in the form of tortured, increasingly lurid images of their son having gay sex. Parents typically describe these images as "dancing through my head," and the process consists of the inability to stop thinking of their son in various sexual poses. This leads to a degree of phobic avoidance of gay things (not wanting to know) taking over as they defensively avoid their son, his friends, and many or most aspects of his gay life, none of which they now want to hear about or get involved in. This becomes their way of actively dealing with passively feeling helpless over having been thrust into a situation that they believe they can neither handle nor extricate themselves from, however much it puts their lives and reputation in danger, and keeps them from achieving their personal goals. For example, they balk when their son insists on bringing his new buddy over for dinner, and even go so far as to threaten to throw this buddy out of the house and disown their son in the process. A partner's parents at the beginning of their relationship tried to fix their son's homosexuality by getting rid of his partner—by offering to pay for their son to go to their favorite medical school—one that just happened to be on the other coast from New York, in California.

Commonly since you cannot avoid the traumatic situation in its entirety, you try to avoid it partially by avoiding it symbolically—by avoiding only one of its more minor but still salient facets. Thus using the defense of displacement, you try to get more comfortable by putting all of your fearful eggs in one sacrificial basket and then making it all okay by breaking that basket's contents—dealing with the problem as a whole by emblematically dealing with/avoiding/destroying one of its significant aspects. For example, you concentrate the blame on your son's partner. You accuse him having seduced your son. Then you avoid him so that you do not have to avoid your son.

You as his traumatized parents simultaneously and frantically try to avoid thinking "scary thoughts" such as about how longstanding/cumulative family traditions will crumble, and you won't be able to function as usual, for example, "With him around we can't have our friends over, everybody will shun our whole family, and we will no longer be able to attend church/synagogue as a family without the congregation staring at us and pointing so many fingers that we might as well stay home."

Unfortunately truly traumatized parents can no longer think of much else than having a gay son. So preoccupied, they are no longer beneficially occupied with what is important—with the entire process of parenting. They become unable to deal with their son's being an adolescent/being in a prolonged adolescence, and with all the life problems attendant upon that, to the point that they can no longer function effectively enough to adequately discharge many of their other pressing parental responsibilities, none of which they can effectively handle because of their concerns about this one—their son being gay.

Once parents determine that they have such a serious emotional problem of their own, they should seek treatment to avoid coming to the point where they respond to disclosure with paralytic worries without foundation, continually imagine the worst, act hurtfully toward their son, and make little progress toward understanding who their son is and why he does what he does so that they can come to reassuringly see their son has as much chance of having a good future as does any other son, gay or straight.

Therapy may, however, not be indicated when the symptoms are mild to moderate. As Pinsker continues, "I suspect that [some people today] have learned that PTSD is a lifelong, disabling condition. It always has been for some, but for most it fades away unless there is a specific trigger. [Some people, having] watched a fireworks display, ... can't sleep that night. [Some] can't watch movies that have German soldiers. But [these people] don't necessarily need a pension or lifelong care for this. I think [that even some] men and women [who] have been forced into unpleasant sexual experiences had problems [that were not as great as they themselves/others initially felt/claimed]. Patterns of mental and emotional disturbance are learned. Columbine was the first school shooting ... there have been 80 since some of which have been 'copycat.' Some experiences are so traumatic that they cannot be overcome. [But many people can unlearn being traumatized]—or at least [to just avoid] events [that] trigger the painful reaction. If a movie introduces a Gestapo officer, people can get up and leave the theater. Avoid the triggers and there are [fewer] problems. My speculation is that some combat veterans, sexual abuse victims [, and mothers and fathers of gay sons] are being taught that they have a grave disability rather than a condition that can be dealt with by avoiding certain trigger stimuli that revive their trauma" and render them too weak to fight and stave off an eventual catastrophic response to the posttraumatic event.

For parents of a gay son these (generally daily) triggers that induce posttraumatic responses consist not only of the fact of his being gay, but also of specific interactions with others that devastate them, especially those that do so by inducing shame, particularly the shame that is a response to being humiliated, as when others savage them for their inability to be good parents, for example, when others demean, devalue, and deprecate them by accusing them of being responsible for making their son gay and for being lazy/incompetent in raising him up as a gay man. Such parents can help themselves by staying away from difficult personal encounters with hostile and intimidating people—people who say things such as, "You are a disgrace to your heritage. I told you that you brought him up wrong. People with bad genes and a history of homosexuality in the family shouldn't have children. You aren't doing enough to discourage him from being gay/to turn him straight." When staying away from people who act as triggers isn't possible, parents of gay sons should try to prepare themselves in advance to be better able to deal with hearing such things. They should try to remember that most critics are highly insensitive people and less knowledgeable than they believe themselves to be (and claim that they are), having had little firsthand experience with the issues and little or no relevant professional training—because they themselves have never been parents or have never actually worked as therapists treating patients in a similar situation.

Self-analysis can help by guiding parents to determine if they feel excessively traumatized because they attach a specific (negative) value to a son's being gay, one not inherent in his being gay, but rather arising from their own background—out of their past and present emotional experiences and as a continuation of problems with their past and present intellectual and emotional makeup. Determine what your son being gay means to you exactly—why it upsets you so, to the point that you allow this *relatively* neutral matter to decisively undermine your comfort. Recognizing that the significance of your (so-called) trauma is as symbolic as it is real, and as personal as it is absolute, can go a long way toward helping you dispel the pessimistic feeling that your son being gay is a reality that is virtually guaranteed to ruin not only his personal and professional life, but yours as well.

However, do not try to avoid actively participating in your son's life in all ways because you believe that participating in it will of necessity be so traumatic that it will predictably revive your serious posttraumatic symptoms. For completely avoiding getting involved in your son's life can have a paradoxical effect. It can cause you further grief due to inflicting even more trauma upon you—as the product of your having become distant and remote from your basically beloved son.

So often traumatized parents can feel/get better by improving how they deal with one another. Instead of taking their disappointments and anger out on each other, they can resolve their differences to the point of being able to work as a team.

Parents should avoid seeking and gratifying "insatiable traumatophilia" where they actually *want* to feel traumatized out of a sense of guilt that makes them compulsively seek self-abuse. To this end, they go about looking for punishment from others to the point that they become injustice collectors who almost in spite of themselves learn, and even feel compelled, to assume an ultimately unrewarding and unpleasurable victim role—one characterized by being overwhelmed by constant painful intrusive thoughts and disturbing flashbacks that won't leave them at peace or let them rest.

Parents should certainly avoid therapeutic approaches that go nowhere or make matters worse, ranging from magical approaches like the application of crystals to the body by a shaman who calls himself Big Bear, to attending too many group sessions too frequently (compulsively) in a desperate attempt to resolve continuously feeling traumatized. Constantly therapeutizing "your trauma" and yourself can become less a therapeutic solution than part of the original (posttraumatic) problem. For this can lead to dwelling on the trauma and its repetition that subverts the need to cope with/master its effects once and for all. I have treated parents who attended too many therapeutic groups only to discover that the sessions stirred so many traumatic things up that the therapy defeated their attempts to put the trauma behind them. This led not to trauma resolution, but to trauma repetition. Their attempts to make a new life out of therapy instead turned into making therapy into their new life.

Grief

Mom and Dad often respond to the revelation that their son is gay by experiencing symptoms of grief (short of full depression).

According to many observers, grief consists of a mixture of emotional reactions, among which are posttraumatic and separation anxiety features. Many parents grieve over having a gay son because they anticipate that they will of necessity have to separate from him. Preoccupied with his bad points while overlooking those that are good, they brood about troublesome aspects of his life today and to come, to the point that they begin to believe that the only way they can deal with something so discouraging as having a gay son is to remove themselves from him entirely, thus creating a sense of loss that leads to despair. They also convince themselves that even if they respect their son, he will disrespect them by removing himself from them to live his gay life, one that doesn't include them, to the point that they will lose him completely to some figurative or literal gay ghetto. Anticipating years of loneliness, they become convinced that their nest will always be empty and certain that their life will sooner or later be entirely devoid of meaning.

Self-blaming responses also predominate, particularly self-blame for having produced a gay child. Self-abuse then begins and escalates through a process of vicious cycling to ultimately become demoralizing self-hatred. Thus the thought "I am not now and never will be a good parent if this is the best I can produce" and the feeling "I am too ineffectual to influence the situation no matter what I do and how hard I try" take over and spread. That seriously compromises Mom and Dad's self-image to the extent that they believe themselves to be unworthy persons and as such not entitled to have a worthy, ideal family.

The opposite of self-blame—resentment for what their son is putting them through—further severely deepens their grief. They blame their son for making them feel bad; then he acts out in a way that leads to even more self-blame for being bad parents.

Grief is often associated with feeling blank accompanied by feelings of disbelief along the lines of, "We can't fathom that this is happening to us." Grieving parents want to weep, but they find themselves unable to shed tears partly because they feel too stunned and dazed to do so. Many have difficulty functioning not only at home, but also at work. A great number experience bodily symptoms such as mysterious functional (i.e., emotionally induced) aches frequently misdiagnosed as physical, for example, fibromyalgia. Also present are resentful feelings of unfairness, bitterness, and envy of other parents who don't have such a problem. These feelings, part of a more generalized anger, lead parents to feel increasingly negatively about, if not to actually become abusive toward, their son. Thus one Thanksgiving my father severely chastised me for being 10 minutes late to pick him up and for the way I was dressed. I thought my dress was appropriate for the occasion, but he nevertheless deemed it inappropriate because what he believed to be my too informal appearance made him uncomfortable and embarrassed because he thought it would not sit well at the suburban straight restaurant we were planning to go to. As was the case with my father, typically anger is released by trivialities like this, that is, set in motion by "trivial prompts," with the result that parents become labile as almost anything "gay" causes them to feel enraged. Many next defensively displace their anger about their son's being gay to homo- from nonsexual issues, and from anger to fear, so that while they think, "I feel revolted by gay sex," in fact what revolts them in their son is the concern that he will grow up and out, leave home, and—seeking gratification elsewhere—permanently abandon them.

Often going beyond being bothered by the prospect of losing their son to getting upset about almost everything about him, they develop a generalized neuroticism that affects both them and those around them, potentially isolating them from others who, finding them off-putting, become impatient with them for being "such difficult people, so unpleasant to be with."

Some parents, having long suspected that their son was gay, have already experienced anticipatory grief, that is, grief in preparation for disclosure—grief over the inevitable admission. When disclosure finally occurs, they feel that they were right all along and now not only blame themselves for creating a gay son, but also for not having been sufficiently aware of what was happening soon enough to have done something to prevent it.

Grieving families almost always become ineffectual in working out significant parent-son problems both of a general and of a specific nature. For they find themselves sidetracked from being good parents as they cope with, master, and alter "the (grief-inducing) gay situation"—an unnecessary task because no change is in fact called for, and being gay in any event is unalterable. By being preoccupying, their grief renders them unable to view their son dispassionately enough to deal with him effectively overall. Rage and self-blame make it hard for them to think clearly, at least clearly enough to sort things out and understand what is going on. They so condemn themselves and their son for being gay that they become entirely unsympathetic and unempathic, rendering them unable to give their son, however needy he may be, their full support. And often they also become so self-pitying that they fail to take into account the negative effect that their self-pity is having on their son.

However much they may compassionately try to bury these (unwanted) feelings in altruism, they find themselves nevertheless still selfishly more concerned with their own than with their son's needs. Though they feel that they have failed as fully responsible parents and say, "We worry that you, our son, will be unhappy and lead a tragic life," what they really mean is, "We are unhappy about you making us unhappy by causing us so much grief." This self-preoccupation makes them reluctant to even consult with their son to find out who he actually is and what he requires. That makes it difficult or impossible for them to help him make any needed course corrections and to do so in *his* preferred, self-fulfilling, entirely personal direction.

When grief is so severe that catastrophic feelings take over, parents tend to panic and act impulsively, and often inappropriately, based on the whim of the moment, not on the plan of a lifetime. Having become desperate, they become more loss- than restoration-focused, too emotional and hence too uninsightful to be properly task oriented. Unable to recognize that they as parents are grieving unnecessarily over having a gay son, they turn into desperate mourners—without an actual sorrowful cause.

Depression

Grief and depression overlap in the sense that both share many clinical characteristics, making severity, a subjective quality, as much a differential criterion as any pathognomonic (specific) signs and symptoms.

Parents who are depressed are routinely excessively and unfairly critical not only of themselves, but also of others, in this case of their gay son. As a result they seriously abuse him by invalidating him much as they invalidate themselves and by being as judgmental of him as they are of themselves, and for many of the same reasons. Such parents magnify their son's human flaws and ineptitudes much as they do their own. They become as unforgiving of their son as they are of themselves, misunderstand him as they misunderstand themselves, and devalue him emotionally or hurt him physically as they do themselves. Sometimes, parents even ultimately throw their son out of the house just because "out of sight is out of mind." They do so in much the same way that they completely abandon themselves over being "worthless and defective" both as parents and, more generally, as human beings. Yet rather than viewing their attitude as symptomatic of their depression, they see it as a reasonable response to their circumstances—that is, as a proper and correct assessment of, and reply to, what they consider to be their truly tragic reality. Then, failing to appreciate the irrational emotional nature of their response, they attempt to alter not themselves, but their supposed reality, typically by insisting their son enter reparative therapy to go straight.

What they as parents fail to recognize is that in most cases to feel and do better, they need to:

- Become less pessimistic about their son, just as they ought to become less pessimistic about themselves

- Become less condemnatory of their son, just as they ought to condemn themselves less
- Stop taking their negative feelings about themselves (and life in general) out on their son, just as they take them out on themselves
- Abort the self-defeating behavior that in many such cases shows up as a suicidal action once removed (killing not themselves, but their relationship with their son, even doing so beyond repair)

A depressed Mom and Dad suffered from low self-esteem that manifested as their tendency to be as unfairly critical of their son as they were of themselves. They felt worthless in comparison to parents whose sons were straight. They also blamed themselves for making their son gay. Though in fact they both had been fairly good parents, and all the evidence pointed to how their son's homosexuality—being inborn—had nothing at all to do with any relevant actions on their part (their son even told them on a number of occasions that he had always felt different from his brothers and sisters, starting when he was just a few years old), the father nevertheless blamed his son's homosexuality on himself because "I am a classical case of a passive father," and the mother nevertheless blamed her son's homosexuality on herself because "I too am a classic case—of an enveloping mother." Also they severely condemned themselves for all their negative feelings, even those that were perfectly natural under the circumstances, and for having taken actions that though regrettable were equally understandable and so minor as to be within the bounds of normal. After the fact they seriously condemned themselves for not properly handling the situation, although many parents would have found it difficult to handle this particular set of circumstances, especially when their given situation was uniquely hard to manage because their son, himself a problematic person, would have tried, as one of his parents put it, "the patience of a saint."

While they thought that all their anger toward themselves was justified (for they *had* made and continued to make mistakes), in fact much of that (self-directed) anger was not the result of what they did, but a product of having bought into others' unjustified criticisms of them to the point that their (negative) evaluation of themselves came to exactly mirror others' negative opinion of them, according to the formulae of "I don't love myself because you don't love me" and "We are unworthy just because you think we are." Particularly galling was that grandma, the mother's mother, criticized them for being "too good, too loving to your gay son, too tolerant of him, coddling him too much (although he doesn't deserve it) just to get him to like you" and for "giving him more than you give your other children just to appease him, and to avoid his calling you a bigot, then turning you out onto the street when you get older in retaliation for perceived wrongs on your part—I bet even forcing you to sign your home over to him and agree that when the time came you would enter the nursing home of his choice, and do so entirely without a fight."

When parents get *seriously* depressed, it is often due to preexisting depressive tendencies on their parts *combined* with having actual reasons to be realistically concerned about their son—less because he is gay than because he uses drugs, seems likely to acquire or has acquired a Sexually Transmitted Disease (STD), or his life and cultural style take him away from home (not always to the best places) and sometimes without his giving his parents hope that he would ever even consider coming back.

In a typical core vicious cycle that depressed parents have to identify, intercept, and interrupt, disclosure creates parental depression that snowballs. It starts with self-criticism for not being able to handle the situation better. This spills over to become a tendency to be overly critical of others—and specifically of their son for being gay. That further separates them from their son by driving him away. After he pulls back they become even more self-critical should others, including their son, lock into their self-criticism by actually criticizing them along relevant lines, for example, "If that's how you feel about yourself, why should I feel any differently?" Feeling unacceptable and unaccepted, they isolate themselves from their son and the world. They become lonely, which enhances their depression and leads to future shock that causes them to feel helpless to ever face what is to be and to cope with oncoming difficulties. Unable to see their true value, and concerned only that others might, or do, think ill of them, they find it difficult to give themselves the vote of confidence they need to counter others' disdainful attitude toward them. That makes them less able to see what really matters—not what others think they are doing to their son, but how loving they are actually being to him. This renders them unable to turn their focus away from the names the sadists in their lives (both outside as well as in the family) call them and to remain aware of their actual merit as parents. So they become vulnerable inspiring sadistic others to harm them even further.

Depressed parents should seek treatment when they find that they cannot disrupt these vicious cycles enough to allow them to get over their depression. In choosing a therapist, they should be alert to the possibility that they are making a masochistic choice of helper—a therapist who for theoretical reasons shames them (as they believe they deserve to be shamed) instead of offering them needed support and positivity to break the cycle of escalating self-abuse that can but lead to further isolation and hence abject despair.

Therapy may need to focus on how one depressed parent hurts the other, as when the wife blames the husband for being a too-weak identification figure, thus creating a sissy of a son, and the husband blames the wife for being either overly seductive or overly aggressive toward her son (or even both), in either event thus scaring their son off women. So often one such parent starts drinking heavily or cheating on his or her spouse. Or, going to the opposite extreme, one or both parents deny that a problem exists, as when a defensive hypomania takes over, and one or both proclaim that having a gay son "doesn't bother us at all." This was the case for one mother who said, after finding out her son was gay, "It's perfectly all right with me." What she really meant, though, was "Now change." She then became an advocate for gays less because she wanted to and more because she was becoming euphoric, using her euphoria to cover her depression with a defensive "You are wonderful just as you are, so stay as you are, because I wouldn't have it any other way" attitude—thus wallpapering over feelings that she instead should be facing, and protectively shunning problems that she instead should have been resolving lest they break through later and with ever greater impact than before.

Depressed parents depress their son, and that poses a serious risk for causing him to become seriously dysfunctional. So many depressed parents destroy their son's spirit by sending him, a valiant son and person, unintended (or even intended) messages that defeat and even cripple him, ultimately enhancing his loneliness and isolation and thus potentially causing him to act out self-destructively, not only with them, but also in other areas of his life. Then the parents blame the gay life, and such of its potential complications as being bullied, for being entirely the cause of their son's misery and/or unacceptable behavior. But the thing at fault may not be the gay life, but their own depressive stifling of their son's admirable attempts to live as a happy gay man—a wonderful life he could much more easily create if he didn't react to his parents' bullying of him by developing an affective disorder of his own.

PART II

Family Processes

Chapter 4

Family Healing

Families of gay sons respond to disclosure both as individuals and, as Beels says, as a "natural group" that demonstrates behaviors whose laws and principles are somewhat "independent of its individual constituents' [thoughts, feelings, and motivations—group relationships that have a] natural history which can be studied."[1] Therefore, each family needs to be aware of its unique reactions occurring before, during, and after disclosure, focusing not only on the responses of the individuals within the family, but also on the interconnective issues/adjustment problems of the family as a whole. Families thus alerted will likely discover problematic idiosyncratic patterns of response that while influenced by and reflective of the individual personalities/personal difficulties of the involved family members collectively form a well-defined, often pathological coalition whose (likely problematic) profile is also distinguished, as Beels notes, by "superordinate dynamics and laws of behavior"[2] applicable to the family as a whole. This group response in turn suggests points of therapeutic intervention that can be employed to help the family contain/overcome family crises that typically occur when a son discloses that he is gay. As Beels says, the family that manages the temporary and permanent changes in "the homeostasis of the family system"[3] that occur postdisclosure can now redesign/redeploy old family coalitions to foster the healthiest recovery agendas possible, helping ensure the most favorable development of the family by avoiding family dissonance and, in a virtuous cycle, creating reduced interfamily group tension that walks back to reduce personal conflict and the anxiety attendant upon that.

Of course, unhealthy family coalitions form not only around the son's disclosing that he is gay, but also around issues other than those immediately related to this particular disclosure. Many of these issues existed in latent form up to disclosure time. But now, newly revived, they once again come to have influence on and threaten the family's integrity as much as, or even more than, issues directly related to a son's telling the family that he is gay. What has happened is that disclosure, a current event, has revived old but still active complexes, having triggered and energized old formerly latent, but to date still active, anxieties and the unresolved conflicts that once caused and still accompany them.

Negative families need to seriously and rapidly assess the damage they are doing to their son and stop it before that damage causes the whole family to become dysfunctional and their son turns to promiscuous sex, drugs, and suicide; leaves; or gets himself kicked out of the house because Mom and Dad come to feel that they *must* send him away—for as they now see it, that is the only means they can use to maintain individual comfort and family solidarity. Therefore, families potentially in this harm's way should not wait too long before getting help lest unhealthy negative coalitions becoming permanent lead to disturbed alignments that create fixed misunderstandings that in turn become lasting vendettas as family members become irreparably alienated first from their gay son then, likely as not, from one another.

Different Developing Coalitions

The following are some different coalitions that commonly develop postdisclosure.

The Siege Mentality

In one typical postdisclosure coalition, family members develop a siege mentality, thus creating a monolithic homonegative family structure aligned to exclude the common enemy, their gay son. In this siege mentality coalition, the gay son becomes *the* and sometimes the *only* actively manifest family problem. Indeed, as Beels notes, "the focus on [a gay son] as a problem [becomes] part of the [family's] stability, and with that [it seems as if few] other things [have] to be faced."[4] This is a family that in its entirety turns on and possibly threatens to exile their son unless he renounces his homosexuality and goes straight. Predictably, such a coalition ultimately becomes more like a cartel as the individual members progressively mutually reinforce each other, tightening homophobic family bonds through consensual validation and communal stimulation (kindling) to create a final, devastating, averse pathological antigay voting bloc characterized by a fully homonegative front where the family (united, as if with one voice) condemns the gay son for who and what he is, and en masse demands that he change over to become exactly what they want him to be.

In one family, in the beginning each of the family members who were later to comprise a coalition of the besieged had a different reason for being antagonistic to a gay son. In this family the different issues were originally:

- The brother's religious convictions
- The sister's erotophobia that led to her general disgust with all sexuality
- The mother's disappointment over not having grandchildren
- The father's wish to have a masculine son with whom he could play sports

Soon enough, however, the different individual motivations (as well as differing personalities and personality problems) ultimately melded and became transformed into unity as the family united in negativity toward their gay son with one mind (it seemed) and for the same reason. A new family gestalt had formed where the whole family made the son into a pariah, thus ensuring that his rejection would be full and complete. Each family member had become a team player and, now on the same team, was acting with one goal and motive—under one banner—making division of labor subsidiary to unity of purpose. As a result, the son faced a negative family attitude so seamless that he was unable to exploit breaks in the family's (homonegative) façade. Helpless to breach its solidarity to his benefit, and unable to remake the coalition along more favorable lines, he stood no reasonable chance of ever protecting himself from this, his own family. As he said, "The only possibility for my salvation lay in my leaving home." And so one day he packed his things and walked out of "this unbearably hateful place." Each family member (at least initially) secretly had his or her own response to the loss. But ultimately the family as a whole became united in their negativity.

In another family, the son also became the common enemy. Convinced that they had lost or would soon lose their son to the gay jungle, this family soon came to feel that they needed each other even more than before. Eventually the entire family came to pride themselves on how their son's being gay brought them together. As they became closer, they further consensually validated each other to the point that the whole family became convinced that the gay son was the source of all their family problems and so the person who made the proper, best possible, and most available enemy to unite against. The family members actually bragged about how having a gay son was a good thing for it *reduced* family tension by enhancing the family bond, thus making it firmer. They said that they didn't care about the great sacrifice involved in exiling their son from the family—and his exiling himself from them. Unfortunately as they progressively distanced themselves from their son, he paid them back in kind. Predictably their relationship with him deteriorated even further as he—coming to feel totally unwanted and thoroughly unloved, isolated, emotionally bereft, and depressed—formed an "adversarial coalition of one" at home then left permanently, saying that he refused to ever return.

Sometimes a gay son finds a simpatico sister or brother to lean and rely on. But most often a gay son's siblings also align with and become part of the family siege coalition. For unfortunately too often siblings feel that they benefit from their family's antigay negativity because it means they have both of their parents all to themselves and although they lose a brother, they gain practical advantages.

Mom and Dad Divided (Often, but Not Always, Mom and Son against Dad)

Another characteristic pattern involves not one but two warring coalitions, as when one coalition forms between the positive parent, often the mother, and the son, and another forms aligned against them, typically the father joined by the rest of the family. In this formation the parents—at first allies—break their prior federation and become rivals. The mother uniting with her son after learning that he is gay feels, "Poor thing, he needs me now more than ever." But the father after learning that his son is gay and becoming rivalrous feels, "I've got a gay son. That's a disgrace. I don't anymore want to have much, if anything, to do with him or my wife, his mother." Typically while the mother says, "I think he needs our understanding and love," the father says either, "Maybe if we ignore this it will go away," or "We can't ignore this—I think we better order him to go straight." Ultimately the father mourns for the son (and sometimes for the wife) he feels that he has lost. He deals with the resultant grief by attempting to get the son to change, claiming it is solely for the son's benefit (although it is really for his own) so that "Do it for yourself because I want you to have a better life" actually means "Do it for me because if you stay gay, you will ruin my (and the rest of the family's) entire existence."

Often at this point the mother begins to fight with the father. She accuses him of being harsh and cruel, and suggests that if he continues in this mode, he will do irreparable harm to her son and to her relationship with him, his father. The father fights back, with the mother. He complains that she is being too accepting of something unacceptable, forbidden, and even disgusting, and accuses her of being overly permissive and thereby removing all hope that their son could ever be rescued and that his straight sexuality could ever be restored.

The father's negativity toward the son tends to enhance the mother-son bond. As the mother protects her son, she enlists him in old and new battles with her husband. Now the excluded father comes to believe that he has lost both mother and son, and he may be right. As a result he gives up and becomes no longer available to deal with the problems all Moms and Dads have to face together when they have a growing son, gay or straight. Unfortunately the son, faced with one parent fighting the other (over him), begins to guiltily think, "My being gay made a lot of trouble for my parents." Both parents recognize that he feels this way and how that makes things worse all around—for the mother blames the father for upsetting the son, while the father attributes the son's being upset to the mother, accusing her of creating problems by not siding with Dad and thereby causing a family rift that is, according to the father, the thing that is actually most negatively affecting the son.

Mom and Dad Joined Together in Denial

In another characteristic coalition, the parents (and often the rest of the family) go en masse into denial. Instead of saying, "I don't like it, but you are still my son, and let's come together over this," they instead say, "We don't worry about what you do. It's your life, live it as you choose (for all we care)." This manifest lack of concern about matters as they stand spares the son the burdens associated with parental disapproval and parental control. But it deprives the son of having parents who lovingly fully participate in his life, giving him needed guidance and offering him sustaining love. For that reason, not caring can become just as destructive to the son as negative involvement. For while negative involvement at least leaves the son feeling that someone is noticing and paying attention to him, lack of concern likely leaves him feeling that by ignoring him, his Mom and Dad are abandoning him.

Mom, Dad, and Son Together versus the Rest of the Family

In this coalition, both parents feel positively toward their son, but the extended family and friends feel negatively toward him. This negativity forms an anticoalition with the goal of breaking down the positive parent-son coalition The parents resist, only to find themselves isolated from the rest of the family—"them versus us." This alignment has its advantages for the son, for since he is important to (and loved by) his parents, he can retain a positive sense of self. But there are disadvantages to this arrangement as well. In the main these are obvious—those that predictably follow upon destructive divisions of any sort appearing within the family.

Psychopathologically Determined Coalitions

Shared psychopathology (which causatively can be genetic, learned, or the product of a folie a deux or plusieurs [the madness of many], or all three) drives the formation of coalitions so that there is an alignment against the son that is characterized by avoidant, paranoid, histrionic, posttraumatic, obsessive, depressive, and passive-aggressive jointly manifest homonegative attitudes on the part of the family as a whole. Thus families with collective *avoidant* traits tend as a unit to pull back from a gay son as if they are en masse afraid of him. Because they respond to disclosure by feeling trapped in a narrative they don't want to hear/be involved in, they view disclosure not positively, as their son might hope, but negatively, as their son often fears. Thus they long for and demand not more (but less) openness, more (rather than less) dishonesty, and a son's not coming out of the closet (but staying in). Or if he is out, they expect him to hide in the rest of the house.

Families with collective *paranoid* traits as a unit angrily view their son as their adversary, along the lines of, "You did this terrible thing to us," and "You chose to be gay because personally you are against/hate us." Also as a unit they project their own feelings of inadequacy onto their son, creating the belief that "He is a disgrace" as a reflection of their personal belief that "We are a disgrace because as a family we feel inadequate because having a gay son makes us an embarrassment to the neighbors."

Families with collective *histrionic* traits as a unit become alarmist due to an all-is-lost mentality that leads to excessive end-of-the-world anxiety/guilt about "this catastrophe" that is accompanied by passionate condemnation of a son they accuse of destroying the whole family by being gay. In one family the uncle and aunt were the tolerant ones, but their children, the gay son's cousins (reversing normal generational progress from older conservative to younger more liberal thinkers) were the ones who chose to avoid the son as being a "complete disgrace to the clan."

Families with collective *PTSD* traits as a unit relive their problems with learning they have a gay son over and over again. For them triggers are everywhere and create flashbacks to "this family tragedy," undermining closure by constantly reviving original despair. Almost masochistically, these families figuratively beat themselves up. Consequently, they enhance rather than cope with the pain, open rather than heal wounds, and so in the very process of attempting to cleanse themselves of the infection actually spread it. Many things about their son "traumatize them," and they vocally blame their son for "everything" until he begins to feel, to quote one patient, "Mom and Dad, pardon me for living."

Families with collective *obsessive-compulsive* traits as a unit become overscrupulous about issues involving morality. For them homosexuality is not different from, but immoral compared to, heterosexuality. They also typically emphasize issues of control, for example, "No matter what any of us say and do, he still likes boys better than girls." As a result all come to view their son being gay not as self-realizing for him, and deserving of their support if not admiration, but as antagonistic toward them and so deserving of their animosity.

Families with collective *depressive* traits as a unit blame themselves for having a gay son to the point that they become preoccupied with "What did we do to cause this?" They also become a worrisome group en masse focused on how their son being gay will of necessity cause him to abandon them if not actually, than at least symbolically. They also fear that to save themselves, they of necessity must abandon him. Additionally they preoccupy themselves with how their son being gay lowers them, in the competition of life, in the eyes of their extended family and friends ("Now our family looks bad compared to families with straight kids where the children make their parents happy instead of sad, and proud instead of full of shame").

Families with collective *passive-aggressive* traits as a unit feel anger toward their gay son. But instead of expressing it directly, they express it in roundabout ways—not as rage but as annoyance, worry, sadness, and self-blaming with hostile implications for others—(for them) safe alternatives to attacking their son openly and for who and what he is. This is not an entirely unfortunate development, in part because mixed feelings lead to reticence that softens fully negative responses and thus protects the son from having to bear the full brunt of his parents' negativity. However, underneath it all these families are sparing their son less than they are sparing themselves. One family typically conveyed how it feels to have a gay son both by pejorative implication and through too-readily interpretable symbolic negative actions such as giving different, preferential treatment to the family's straight children. The parents not only gave their daughter and her husband one gift for Christmas and their son and his partner two separate ones, they also always "forgot" to invite their son and his partner to family functions. Then they apologized afterward, only to repeat their actions the next time. At Christmas dinner the father, a Christian, gave everyone a Christmas card except for his son's Jewish partner. The father, after announcing he had a hard time finding a card for him that was appropriate for this solemn occasion, handed the son's partner a card with flowers and a blank message and said, in essence, "Given the circumstances this was the best I could do." For party gifts all the rest of the family got expensive trinkets with a religiously neutral theme—all, that is, except for the son's partner, who opened his gift to find a dreidel (a toy top with Hebrew lettering on it).

Remedy

Sager, a family therapist with whom I trained, focused on identifying the family coalitions in which some or all family members responded to, coped with, and attempted to solve "the problem of having a gay son" in idiosyncratically psychopathological ways. As Sager noted, to a great extent these different family coalitions require different recovery agendas. That means that the specific interventions chosen in any given case depend not only on the temperament of the individuals in the family and the nature of their personal problems, but also on each family's behavioral patterns/psychopathology considered as an intrinsic interactive whole.

Thus Sager's remedy might involve firstly treating pathological family coalitions/adjustments by attempting to influence the negative monolith directly to reverse its fundamental antagonistic composition so as to allow the son to be readmitted into to the fold as an active, equally contributing family member. Then secondarily Sager, like many family therapists, might supplement family therapy by evaluating and treating the family members individually. As Beels says, "[M]eeting with more people than the presenting patient helps . . . make a thorough evaluation as well as lay the groundwork for consultation to the family as to what form of treatment should be undertaken: couple, family, or individual. From this starting point one can always go to individual therapy"[5] where the therapist seeks to learn more about the parents' individual contribution to the monolith, the therapeutic goal being to help individual family members become themselves less adversarial and so overall form more inclusive coalitions.

Thus in one family the therapist ultimately dealt with a mother-father versus son coalition by uncovering the father's problems, in this case his difficulties with dependency/rejection, control, and competition. In the realm of the father's issues around *dependency/rejection*, he felt his son was rejecting him by being unlike him, that is, by being less of a real man, clearly not someone he spawned and so not someone he could comfortably embrace or who could comfortably embrace him. Also the father worried, "I am losing my gay son, for sooner or later gay sons all become closer to their mothers than to their fathers. Having more in common with Mom, he will pull away from me and run to her, not to me, every time he needs something."

In the realm of the father's issues around *control*, the same father, upon hearing that his being emotionally absent was what caused his son to grow up gay, tried to make up for "what he had done wrong" by getting more and more involved with his son, only to overshoot and become *overly* involved—but not necessarily in a helpful way. For he began to push his son too hard to go straight and additionally tried to get his wife to take his side in defense of his actions.

In the realm of the same father's issues around *competition*, though he was manifestly displeased that his son was gay, he secretly welcomed it because to him it meant that if his son was "less of a real man" he, the son, had by definition become less the competition. Secretly desiring a weak son, he took steps to ensure that he had one. For example, he unconsciously tried to cause his son to get depressed, actually hoping he would develop work inhibitions and possibly even become suicidal. Himself a successful surgeon, he rarely complimented his gay son because he feared that this son might thereby "get a swell head and measure up to me." The son feeling "Why bother trying" remained unemployed throughout life except for picking up junked furniture on the streets and rehabilitating it so that he could sell it in the local consignment shop.

The mother, herself a successful computer programmer, helped the father crush the son by encouraging the son in a futile quest: his desire to make a career out of writing a particular kind of music—music that combined popular and classical styles. She told him, "Great idea, you'll make a mint," while admitting to Dad, "Instead of encouraging him I should have told him that that had been done before, numerous times, and by some very talented people, like George Gershwin." While she consciously felt frustrated by and angry with her son for being a failure, unconsciously she was helping her husband get her son out of the way so that he, the father, would have one less contender to the crown to face and could now get the grand prize he (the father) had always wanted for, and only for, himself. For now Dad could be the one at center stage, soloing in the spotlight. The mother further supported the father's need to keep his son down because she believed that she would feel less guilty over getting too close to her son if she were able to devalue him. (She had sexualized the relationship between Mom and Son to the point that everyone noticed that they were getting "just too close"—and so she felt she needed to "put some space between me and him.")

I first saw both parents in therapy. Then I continued with the father alone. Before I terminated with the mother, I encouraged her to help Dad tone down/eliminate as many of his negative feelings as possible. In therapy I worked with Dad to try to get him to stop seeing his son as a dangerous adversary and start seeing him as his friend, ally, and hope for the future.

One remedy that tends to work very well in most if not in all troubled families with a gay son involves undercutting negative coalitions and thereby enhancing family stability through inducing positive growth via the power of positivity, thus, as Beels says, "revitalizing the family by maintaining or reconstituting the homeostasis of the family system."[6] Invoking the "power of positivity" is a technique I go on to describe throughout. In brief, this process starts with asking the question, "What can we as parents in this situation do that can make our child and ourselves happier, our relationship with him more fruitful and creative, and our whole family into one that resolves instead of perpetuates disruptive interpersonal conflicts?" It then focuses the parents on understanding in order to diminish/silence angry feelings that lead them to traumatize their son in the first place—passively through neglect or actively through overt displays of vengeance.

However, like many techniques, becoming highly positive can have its downsides. It can mean covering up differences and disagreements just to get along, thus creating a blanket conforming that can bleach out the richness and complexity of family diversity. Like any other technique, when too globally applied it can become a one-size-fits-all approach that additionally self-defeats through being based on false assumptions, such as the assumption that, as Beels says, the "individuals who make up the family have equal constitutional endowments"[7] involving equal intelligence and the same psychopathology. Parents who assume thusly give positive feedback indiscriminately overlooking constitutional differences between them and their son, as well as age-related differences associated with being on opposite sides of the generation gap. I have had parents think they were doing the right thing by giving their blessings to their son having multiple partners even when their son viewed his own promiscuity as inherently problematical; telling him that it was a good idea for him to maintain the old gay way of sexual freedom—for himself lest it disappear from his life, and for his society lest it disappear as a trend that should last because it well characterizes the gay subculture and differentiates it from being straight.

Positivity does not necessarily involve universal agreement that is the product of unmitigated love. Rather it involves mutual respect and flexibility where there is a willingness and ability to accept idiosyncratic differences after hearing what these are from individual family members—members progressively able to speak freely without shame and without feeling that they have to apologize for how they think or to go back abjectly on everything that they sincerely believe.

Chapter 5

Sibling Homophobia

A gay son's brothers and sisters, although likely involved in the disclosure process, do not always handle it in an uplifting way. Since a negative response on their parts necessarily affects the entire family, the whole family must be prepared to deal directly and definitively with sibling homophobia before it takes over and simply destroys all involved. In particular, the parents of a son who is the victim of sibling homophobia have to become doubly protective of him, offering him special sanctuary even if that means for the time being creating an uneven playing field in which they give to this one child more than they give to the others—if only just to keep his straight siblings in line and from acting out against their gay brother. Parents in this situation need to make it clear that they strongly advocate for their gay son on two grounds: because he is gay and being deaffirmed, and because he is their son and being marginalized. While ideally both Mom and Dad should offer their son their protection, generally that job falls to one or the other parent, often the mother. She at least must take a strong stand insisting that her son's full membership in the family is not conditional so that the entire family's need to accept him totally is in no way optional. The following is a typical case example illustrating the mother's but not the father's being forthcoming with support.

On one occasion this mother told her gay son's sister that she, the sister, couldn't boycott a major birthday party the mother was giving for her son, and proved that she meant it by threatening meaningful financial consequences if her daughter didn't comply and instead continued to distance herself from her brother on this, or on any other, occasion. Unfortunately the father looked the other way and condoned the distancing, using as his excuse, "I only have one daughter, and I don't want to insult her because *her* daughter is my only grandchild." Ultimately the father actually encouraged his own daughter to act out—not only *against* her brother, to displease him, but *for* her father, to please Dad. This father was effectively sacrificing his son for his own emotional benefit. Though the son complained that Dad was being obvious in displaying his preference for his straight daughter over him and asked him to stop giving his sister preferential treatment because he, the father, was making him, his son, feel seriously devalued, the father nevertheless still refused to comply. He denied that he was doing anything wrong, and instead insisted that he was being fair to both his daughter and his son by treating them not preferentially, or exactly as equals, but "only as the situation warranted."

The son decided to enter therapy to get help dealing with his difficult father. As his therapist I helped him understand that while his father was clearly displaying homonegativity, his homonegativity was in some respects impersonal because it reflected less his true stance than his neurotic conflicts, with the root of the father's neurosis the father's relationship with his daughter, a person who, going beyond being a daughter to him, had for her father become the "other woman." And as people do when they are "in love," the father was ignoring his daughter's flaws while paying full attention to her attributes, thus offering her admiration she didn't fully deserve because of the abominable way that she was behaving toward her brother. Also, I said I believed that the father's Oedipus complex was creating some of the havoc. For the father saw his son as his rival for his own wife's, his son's mother's, affection, making it unlikely that Dad would protect his son because Dad, if only unconsciously, wished to see his son if not completely destroyed than at the very least effectively out of the way. Feeling that what the son got he, the father, lost, the father actually wanted to make his son feel bad—to feel ignored and thus so weakened that he, the father, would, remaining superior to his son, be the one who garnered all the attention and the person who got all the stuff.

On her part, the sister's active, complementary Electra complex led her to join the father in acting out not only against her brother, but also against her mother, *her* rival. For being homonegative to her brother was her way to spite her mother, who loved her brother. Also playing an active role here was the sister's generally competitive nature: she was also fighting for primacy with everybody not just at home, but also on the outside—especially in her professional life, where feeling as if her status as a licensed practical nurse was somehow inferior to the status of being "a real nurse," she constantly fought for medical primacy by putting the "real nurses" and the (mainly male) doctors down. So like her father, she secretly enjoyed her brother's being gay because that became an important reason for seeing and keeping him one-down and, as the devalued one, less of a threat—not only to her exclusive relationship with her father, but also, as she put it, in essence, to her "identity as a vital woman in no way second to any man." All told she could now affirm her status to herself as the most important and significant member of the family and so rest easy that now she had become a very big fish, however much she swam in an extremely small pond.

The following case history illustrates other stresses that can occur between siblings in the family of a gay son. A sister, one of two children in the family, had always been a sickly child whose vision problems required extensive, expensive, and time-consuming medical treatments. As a consequence she (not unexpectedly) became the favored one in the family in the sense of being the one who the parents attended to the most. Partly as a result, later in life she became testy whenever she sensed someone who ought to fulfill her needs was not meeting them and not doing so on schedule, and whenever someone, in this case mainly her gay brother, was getting anything at all from her parents, something, as she complained, that was rightfully hers. Even to the most casual observer she had become so overly sensitive to the possibility of deprivation that when anyone in the family didn't coddle her enough, in the sense of being less positive and attentive to her than she might have liked and expected, and more attentive to her brother than she might have desired, she interpreted that as an attack upon/criticism of her and, becoming restless and temperamental, began counterattacking, with the counterattacks especially directed toward her gay brother. She put her attacks on him in terms of "he is gay." But in fact the attacks on him went far beyond that to also encompass even his good points, for the better he was, the more problematical for her he became.

In contrast her brother, always healthy and independent, never particularly needy, and with a personality that was more altruistically than selfishly inclined, skated through life mindful that in his relationship with his parents he was getting less than his sister got, but having long ago gotten used to it, didn't particularly mind. In fact from the early years of his life on, he actually preferred to function as an autonomous individual, happy in his own way, not needing to compare what he had to what others, including his sister had. Unfortunately after he disclosed he was gay he was not able to continue in his preferred "anonymous" way. For the moment it was *he* who had newly become the (to the sister unwelcome) center of the family's attention, their immediate and central (to the sister, excessive) object of interest and concern.

Predictably his sister now raged over feeling sidelined, as if the family were once and for all abandoning her for him, leaving her to fend for herself. She hated that, despised her brother for having brought it on her, rebelled, then did what she could to undermine his ascendancy. Hoping to eventually and permanently recapture her own favored position, she did everything possible to turn the family against her brother—including eloping with an intensely homophobic man who brought considerable homohatred directly to bear on his brother-in-law, his wife's gay brother, further inflaming the whole family's negativity toward the gay son. For example, each time the family met, and only then, would the sister's husband make a big show of reminding the family that he was a religious man. He did this by handing out Bibles and suggesting, with clear implication, that the entire family bone up on what the Good Book said—mainly what it prohibited and how that was entirely "applicable to the current situation."

Since the family had previously ignored their son for years with impunity, they now confidently and comfortably believed that he would never turn against them no matter how harshly they treated him over being gay. So after a short while they confidently once again turned away from him and back to his sister, as she had hoped. But the sister felt the damage to her had by now already been done. And she believed that the turnaround was jerry-built, inadequate, and likely to be impermanent. Now she protested even more vehemently each time her parents paid attention to the brother/intervened positively for him in any way. And she did this in two ways. The first was by getting sick. For example, she assiduously refused to eat anything at one summer barbecue after another because, as she said (providing little real evidence to back her claim up) she suffered from food poisoning. And the second involved issuing warnings that she would retaliate against her parents for paying so much attention to her brother by keeping them from visiting her children, their grandchildren. These threats were so effective that ultimately the family newly closed this circle, completely reconstituting their formerly close relationship with her just to keep her well, and calm, and excluding their son just to retain their relationship with their grandchildren. They had decided that clearly it took sacrificing the brother to prove to his sister that with them she was still number one. They then rationalized their behavior as "because he is gay" and made it very clear to the brother that that was why they were excluding him. In turn he increasingly had no choice but to distance himself from his family. Yet the family, denying that this was as bad as it seemed to be, and never considering that his removal would be permanent, continued to increasingly distance themselves from him—without ever worrying that unless they stopped what they were doing immediately, they would cause a permanent rift.

Fortunately the parents, at last suddenly aware of how dysfunctional the family had become, just in time applied for family therapy asking for help in getting their son back. I responded by encouraging the mother, who loved her son if not more than, then differently from, the father, to intervene with the father on her son's behalf. To do this the mother had to first detach herself somewhat from her daughter, however difficult this was for her, and however much it threatened the daughter directly. The mother was better able to do that after coming to understand an important aspect of her own psychology—that she lived out her own excessive dependency needs through too much caring for her "sick" daughter hoping, even though that meant losing her son, to keep the daughter dependent on her so that she wouldn't lose either her daughter or her grandchildren. In turn, I helped the father see that he mistreated his son because he, the father, suffered from an unwholesome relationship with his daughter, one that involved an Electra complex vis a vis his daughter, the "other woman," and a supplemental Oedipal complex vis a vis his son, where the son had become his rival and the father needed to treat him as such because the son's good looks, intelligence, and youth threatened the father's primacy with his own wife—as well as the father's status with himself.

Yet in spite of developing insight, the father continued to devalue the son, rationalizing his need to mistreat and ignore him by citing one negative (his homosexuality) and one positive (his daughter's neediness). The father, it soon became clear, had made his choice: his daughter over his son.

Not only was the father unable to stop coddling his daughter at his son's expense, when his son met a man the son loved, a man who was to become his partner, the father actually intensified his negativity, now to both his son and his partner. Even though he liked and respected his son's new partner, he deliberately distanced himself from the couple just to form an even stronger prodaughter/antison coalition, now excusing that by claiming that the son was flaunting his homosexuality by bringing this man home, something his daughter wouldn't like, and, according to the father, rightly so, because it would clearly set a bad example for his daughter's children.

Ultimately the whole family became splintered. At first they got together only at Christmastime. Then they didn't see each other even then. Also, because the sister's husband had poisoned his child's mind, the child became remote from her gay uncle. She showed her disdain by removing herself almost entirely from him during what few family gatherings still occurred. At first when the family visited she retreated into her playroom with her video games. Later she would sit in the middle of the crowd texting her one and only friend, paying scant attention to her family and none at all to her gay uncle—to whom, as the months went by, she spoke very little (and she spoke even less to his partner).

She not only became isolated from her uncle, she ultimately became a totally bitter and lonely isolated woman herself, full of shame about her "dysfunctional" family, and so about herself, a shame that extended even to her own (hetero)sexuality. Shame about her own family became shame about wanting a family of her own "because my heritage would affect my kids." Partly as a result she never married and ultimately became a lonely woman stuck her whole life in a city studio apartment in a large anonymous white building, in love with her few and paltry possessions and (with the encouragement of her father) not seeing her family much, and her uncle and his partner not at all. She never even went on to develop a fictive (substitute) family of her own to substitute for the family of origin she had ultimately completely dismissed.

I finally interrupted treatment with this family because I had become convinced that desirable realignment was not possible and that even partial healing could never occur. I accidentally discovered I was right to stop because the situation had in fact worsened as the son grew older and it became clear to all concerned that he had no intention of changing and going straight. Still the family never gave up trying to get him to stop/reverse his homosexuality. And Mom and Dad continued to fully embrace the sister, which essentially meant banishing both their son and his partner from all their houses and then, in entirety, from all their lives.

Sisters and brothers of a gay sibling have to deal with their own strong emotions about their brother being gay. Sometime they "merely" feel disdain and disgust, often to the extent that they pull back from their brother to live their own lives and, if married with children, hide their brother from their children's eyes. Not a few go to extremes, as did one patient of mine who refused to ever take her daughter to visit her gay brother because he lived with his partner in a town with a large gay population and she, in essence, didn't want her child contaminated by the surroundings. In a common pattern, such brothers and sisters feel perfectly justified in showing remarkable insensitivity to their gay brother's feelings—and how what they are doing to him hurts. Yet at the same time they are remarkably sensitive to what their gay brother is doing to them. So often they form a coalition whose members generally fail to recognize that they need any help at all in dealing with their negative feelings and altering their negative attitudes about having a gay brother, thus making it difficult for concerned others to offer helpful and doable suggestions/constructive criticism to them. Instead so often they respond to therapeutic intervention not as if they have some explanations to give, apologies to make, and changes to implement, but by intensifying their antigay cabals even to the point of completely exiling their brother. Characteristically rationalizing personal spite as culturally induced, they propagate the fiction that forming their negative coalition is in fact an appropriate response to their difficult situation. The coalition supposedly is reactive to their gay brother; not a reflection of who they are and what they bring to the situation, but a response entirely appropriate to the stimulus, incentivized by the society in which they live. As they see it, they, not the gay brother, are the victims; he, not they, is their victimizer.

Whenever possible, such negativistic siblings should be encouraged to enter treatment to discover exactly what they so resent about having a gay brother. In particular they should be encouraged to ask themselves why exactly they are so homophobic. They will likely respond to the questioning with something like, "It is because we are living in a homonegative town, and our local society dictates that we look unfavorably on gay men." Or they will say that they are "homophobic" less because their brother is gay than because their brother is a difficult person. But so often the real reason is that *they* are the ones being difficult because *they* have emotional problems of their own, and it is these problems that need attention. Chief among these are:

- *Paranoia*, where they see a brother being gay as an attack upon them. Resentful toward their parents and the rest of the family, they themselves want to leave home only to find that in order to do so without guilt they have to blame someone for driving them away, conveniently their gay brother.
- *Narcissism* that makes them envious people who attack their own brother for being, at least for the time being, the center of attention in a family concerned (and likely overly concerned) with him, focusing on him alone, thus displacing them (his sisters and brothers) from their central position.
- *Histrionic personality disorder*, marked by jealousy, not only about all the attention the gay son is getting, but also about his having a life characterized by enviable sexual freedom—especially grating to those who feel constrained by their own erotophobic guilt. As histrionics they are also enmeshed in competition issues, where their negative feelings toward a brother for being gay are less over his being a homosexual than because his being gay has possibly led, or might in the future lead, to his becoming professionally successful/making an outstanding partnership/marriage. So when such a sibling says, "You are

a disgrace to the rest of the family," he or she might very well actually mean, "What is a disgrace is that your life, and your partner, is too good, and I envy you, because in comparison to yours, my own life is so pedestrian."

Of course, in fairness siblings of a gay brother can have problems that are less emotional than they are real. For a son who outs himself also outs his siblings, not as being gay but—almost as shameful (as they see it)—as being in a family where there is a gay brother in the first place. When my cousin's wife outed me, the entire family (with only a few exceptions) responded by thinking not only "He is a disgrace to the family," but also "Our whole family now is a disgrace to the world." Clearly such a family has to overcome its (less than empathic) preoccupying concern for themselves and start thinking about what their brother being gay means not for them but for him.

Generally multiple issues exist, and they can require prolonged intense therapeutic discussion/intervention. In one case a sister claimed she pulled back from her brother because being involved with her own children, she hung around only with families who were compatible because they were like-minded due to also having children. And so she felt she had more in common with them than she had with her gay brother. Additionally she was a notoriously difficult person who went on to make excuses for her own inhumanity by citing her community's antigay sociocultural leanings and homonegative religious teachings. Another factor was her envy of her brother's exciting life, something she dealt with by defensively elevating in her mind her own pedestrian existence by seeing her life as "morally far superior to his." Also extant were her selfish wish to have not one but both parents all to herself, both for their love and for their money, and an innate avoidant and paranoid personality structure that led her to be natively remote both as a sibling and as a person. Another factor involved her competitiveness whereby she compared herself unfavorably to her brother's partner (he was a doctor and she was "only a social worker"), and still another was her having a husband who discouraged her from seeing her brother because of his own fears of homosexuality and how they came welling up in her brother's presence.

In therapy we were able to resolve these issues to the point that she ignored her brother less and less over the ensuing days. Ultimately she at least saw him and his partner on some holidays. As time went by the two became closer, for their mutual hostility diminished as at first she, and then he, worked through the many fears that had once kept them apart.

Chapter 6

Impression Management: Dealing with Overconcern about What Others Think

Parental overconcern about what other people think about them for having a gay son increases emotional tension and realistically interferes with supporting/loving/promoting a son who is gay. My parents constantly worried about what their friends and family thought about my being gay. In their defense they were somewhat at the mercy of the opinion of a homophobic family cartel who, as I just recently learned, saw me as a "disgrace to the family." Unfortunately my parents didn't much rely on their own opinions or worry about my response to their reactive concerns. Apparently it wasn't meaningful to them that I, their only son, a person who should have been more important to them than any of the members of their extended family/their friends, might feel like a second-class citizen due to their giving first priority to their own self-esteem and reputation. It didn't seem to bother them that thus preoccupied with their own self- and outer image they failed to be sufficiently concerned with mine, and instead of helping me solve some personal problems that I did have condemned me for having them, and overall for who and what I was. So even though they were wise, they failed to use their wisdom to make my life easier. Concerned for their needs compared to mine, they failed to tell themselves "This is my son, my only child," and ask themselves "Who is my son, and shouldn't we respect him, then do what we think is best for him, and what he might think is best for himself?" Instead they mainly, or only, asked themselves, "What do my peers and my community think or say about us?" Then they forced me to see a psychiatrist to go straight, at least partly so that they could tell the family, "He's getting over this, so just be patient and forbearing." Then when they saw that my psychotherapy wasn't turning me heterosexual, they started pressuring me to at least act straight in front of the family, or when anyone else they cared about was around. Particularly shattering to me was that they would invite me but not my partner Michael to family events. And when I insisted on bringing Michael, they would have the event cancelled—just so that I wouldn't show up as one half of a gay couple.

To a great measure their overconcern with impression management had serious consequences for all concerned because it led to vicious cycling along the following lines. Underconcerned about my well-being and functionality, they allowed their loyalty to their own relatives, friends, neighbors, and even strangers to fully co-opt and trump their loyalty to me, their son. This both created and reinforced my shame and disillusionment with myself. As a result I had no choice but to attempt to repair my self-view by becoming defensive—and I did that increasingly by viewing my parents in a negative light—valuing myself by devaluing them by refusing to listen to anything they said and deliberately subtly undercutting their authority however much I could have used some advice, and even control, from them, undermining them by counteridentifying with them just so that they would have less of a negative impact on me, mainly, on my self-image. Then I moved on to actually acting out against them by being openly oppositional. That locked into their already negative mindset involving me: "My son is a difficult boy, and the real reason for that is not that we aren't very nice to him and he feels our disapproval and responds accordingly, but that he is gay." Now they, and the whole family, became even more ashamed of me, which they did on two accounts: I was gay, and (they were not entirely incorrect about this) I was behaving badly. That led me to become even more oppositional toward as well as remote from them, and ultimately to become depressed because I had so distanced myself from my family. Depressed, I tried even harder to get them to validate me by accepting me for who and what I was. But I had a difficult time accomplishing that. Instead, failing at it over and over again, I became progressively desperate to have them authenticate me, and angrier and angrier that they did not. As an outcome, I began to act in a way that led me to more fully deserve the approbation that I already was getting from them—and ultimately getting as well from my extended family, and (because I began acting out with a vengeance) from society at large. I then started alternately retreating into myself and lashing out at my parents. They now completely stopped making excuses for me and instead simply hid me from the rest of the family, and as much as they could from the rest of their world.

Many experts state that these days parents are less ashamed of having a gay son than they were at an earlier time, when the term "homophobia" didn't even exist, when they were still raiding gay bars and arresting their occupants for being unlawfully gay, and when there was no PFLAG to help anxious guilty parents recalibrate. This is only partly true, for while shame has a large (changing, and thus temporal) social aspect, it also has a large personal component to it. Therefore, regardless of all the social advances that have occurred in the last decade, many contemporary parents still remain somewhat ashamed of having a gay son much as their counterparts from years ago. And those who do still feel shame have a special need to ask themselves, "Why?" then answer that question exactly, "Because. . . . "

Here are some possible answers. They assess their situation illogically. They pay *selective attention* in assessing their reality. Selective attention is a cognitive error that occurs when parents attend to only the negative, not the positive, things others say about their son and then—listening only to what they dread hearing, they create a distorted picture of what others are actually thinking about them, which is, predictably, the worst. To illustrate, many parents' families consist both of members who are conservative thinkers and members who are more liberal. Yet so often parents of gay sons focus on the negative feedback they get from the former and disregard any positive feedback they get from the latter. To the negative people they reply, "You are right, our son is as much a burden to us as he is to society." But to the positive people they reply, "You aren't telling us the truth, you are just putting an optimistic spin on a negative situation when you say, 'Take him for who he is and appreciate that overall he is worthy,' and you are doing that because you simply don't know the whole story, or what you are talking about, or because you want to make us feel good, even though that involves not telling us the truth." They also somewhat (but not entirely) erroneously conclude that other people properly can, should, and do evaluate the producers, them, the parents, according to the nature and quality of their production, their son. And so they come to see themselves as flawed—simply on the basis of "having created that monster son of ours."

They have specific personality problems. A chief one is passive dependent personality disorder, which makes parents overly compliant, self-doubting people who instead of thinking for themselves assign their critics the power of expertise. Now they take everything their critics say seriously, believe it to be true, and convince themselves that "They wouldn't say it if it weren't correct." (Criticism from others, and dealing with it, is discussed further in Chapter 7.)

They believe that by the very act of going along with others they can enhance their own (already compromised) self-esteem. They feel good about themselves only when they are being "cooperative," as they see it. They need to have others approve of them for not being "argumentative types," so instead of fighting others' opinions off they instead fully parrot them. So they go along with others' disapproval of their son and willingly themselves disapprove of him in turn, and in a parallel way—simply to get along, and so just to be loved.

They have their own depressive need to seek outside approval to countermand their own inner, guilty self-disapproval. Failing to get it, they become unable to give themselves a vote of confidence.

Critical others hit home when they touch upon parental self-criticisms. This is because others' critical evaluations seem to make sense and stick because they, the parents, already criticize themselves, and their son, for the very same things. Thus as parents they buy into criticism of their son's identities because they already criticize their son's identities along similar lines: his sexual identity (gay not straight), his gender identity (feminine not masculine), the gender role he plays (being more female than male), and his nonsexual identity. ("He is just going to be a ordinary plumber, not somebody special like a doctor or a lawyer.") They criticize their son's identities for at least two reasons. First, they themselves have (excessively) rigid expectations of their son and he isn't meeting them because he is going his own way. Second, they are secretly struggling with their own identity issues and projecting these struggles onto their son to create a simplified narrative consisting of "My son is bad because he embodies what I most dislike in myself—my latent homosexuality, my shaky gender identity (father is not as male as he would like to be, mother is not as female as she believes she should be), my gender role (father doesn't act as manly/mother as womanly as he/she should), and my nonsexual identity (as they think of themselves as being bad, ineffective parents and evil people for who and what they are and so have done to produce this boy)." In turn, making their issues into their son's issues, they come to feel not only disappointed that their son is not a heterosexual, but also despair that he falls short of being an *ideal* male due to acting unmanly and is professionally inept, for he is not the good, solid, strong, admirable citizen and successful worker that they so want their child to be.

Reducing the need for impression management starts with you as his parents becoming more accepting of your son as he is in order to be better able to overlook others' criticisms and condemnations of you for making him what he has become. Now rather than being ashamed of your son you will instead be proud of him, and sufficiently proud of him to defend him against mortified others.

It also requires becoming comfortable with who you are and what you stand for so that you challenge the views, statements, and actions of people who don't like you that way—telling them that they are not getting it, and not getting it right, after challenging yourself for in the first place thinking that what how others evaluate you actually matters one way or the other.

Now your son will feel you are backing him up. When he feels this he will likely feel less ashamed of himself. Then he will act in a way that leads all concerned—you, your extended family, and your friends—to become prouder of him. Mom and Dad will now feel as if they are the worthiest possible persons. Also, feeling less deserving of criticism, they become less likely to provoke others to criticize them and, more self-satisfied and for a good reason, less prone to buying into the negative things others think and say about them. Others' impression of them will now likely improve, at the very least because others will, sensing their new positive spirit and hence their newly enhanced invulnerability, be less prone to want to, or feel that they can safely, express their negative feelings so freely.

A son whose parents made it clear that they were ashamed of him vowed out of spite to give them a real reason to feel that shame. He deliberately walked and dressed in a way that would embarrass them to punish them (and not so incidentally to manipulate them into giving him as a "disabled person" money they didn't have so that he didn't need to go to work so that now, unemployed, he could stay home all day long, doing essentially nothing).

I advised the family to try telling him that, no matter what, they basically loved him. I also asked the relatives to tell him if not the same thing then at least that they wholeheartedly supported and embraced him, and wanted to welcome him back into the family fold just as he was, no further questions asked, no matter what kind of life he chose to live. They did this, where-upon he felt that he had a family and "Since I have one, I must be worthy of it." As a result he no longer felt forced to seduce a parade of different men to buy him drinks and otherwise "demonstrate their love for me, only to leave me and never to be heard from again." And he no longer felt that he had to rely on pickups in bars for social contacts just to fill the void that was life without a supportive family. So he was able to rally emotionally, settle down into a committed relationship, then become less antagonistic to his parents. They, their fondness for him increasing, felt less and less concerned about what other people thought of someone they now basically admired/loved, and simultaneously came to worry less and less about what others thought of them. As they began to put loyalty to their son first, they became his advocate, defending him when others devalued him, touting his worth because they knew that he "was a good kid, and we don't need outside validation to determine that that is the case."

Guarded against negative fallout from the outside, they were now better able to go on to correct negative information circulating within the family, thus denying their son's and their own critics the opportunity to criticize him and them. Refusing to cower in the face of persistent criticism from their own parents, siblings, cousins, and some friends—not buying into it and so feeling as if they needed to change accordingly—they no longer felt helpless due to feeling/being overwhelmingly devalued by their and their son's critics. Next they began openly to challenge others and, when indicated, to devalue those who sought to devalue them and their son. This allowed inflicted wounds to heal so that as a family they were able to go on to develop a healthy fundamental sense of adequacy and solidarity entirely independent of the evaluative input from the curious, prying, negative people who still swarmed around them. For now sadistic others, no longer able to affect their target, turned elsewhere to obtain the cruel satisfaction they so readily sought—from people more vulnerable to their abusive ministrations.

Chapter 7

Reducing Guilt/Dealing with Criticism

In my experience most parents of gay sons feel somewhat guilty about "their situation." They feel most guilty about being hypocritical because they have one set of rules for themselves and another for their gay son. For example, when it comes to sexuality they expect their son to do as they say not as they do, an expectation that diminishes their sense of personal rectitude if they sense they are not being fair.

They feel guilty about being selfish. They know that they should be concerned about their son's, not about their own, aspirations, but regardless they feel impelled to impose their values on him to get him to do as they see fit. Then when they can't stop nagging him to do their bidding on command and, as predictable, he fails to yield, they feel that they have imposed upon, and so as his parents have totally failed, him.

They feel guilty about having gotten angry with their son—even over having allowed themselves to feel a small amount of rage toward him, for he is "someone we love."

They feel guilty because they can't follow others' well-meaning advice, of which they get plenty. Everyone offers them suggestions as to how they can do better, but they feel sheepish because they can't or won't buy the suggestions. Everyone gives them advice on what not to do, but they can't or won't follow it. As a result they feel as if they are being uncooperative and incompetent. Others tell them:

- To rejoice in what they have, but they can't because it is not what they want
- To view their son's being gay as a force of life, but they can't suppress the feeling that this particular force goes against the force of nature
- To appreciate the beauty of diversity, but they want conformity/uniformity
- To offer their gay son unconditional support, but they feel that he does some things that are unsupportable and other things that they can't help but see as "contemptible"

- To tell their son every day that they love him unconditionally, but they believe not in unconditional but in tough love
- To respect their son even when he disrespects them, but his disrespect causes them to disrespect him in return
- To feel and act proud of their son being gay, but they feel ashamed of him for being homosexual

Parents who feel guilty about having a gay son generally find that the harder they try to feel less so, the guiltier they become. In a typical sequence parents who try to love their son more completely find that overwhelmingly their natural leanings and inescapable tradition make that hard to do. So they feel guilty about their failure, and to feel less so they shift over into blaming their son for causing them to fail. Their son then retaliates by blaming Mom and Dad for being unsupportive and critical. Then Mom and Dad blame their son for having a "generally hostile attitude" toward them, which they attribute to his being gay. Now they come to feel even angrier with him than before. Then they fall short in their own eyes for having such negative feelings about their son. And that makes them feel even guiltier than formerly.

Dealing with Guilt

Dealing effectively with parental guilt over having a gay son requires identifying its source, which ultimately involves criticism—both self-criticism and criticism from others.

In the realm of *self-criticism*, guilty parents become self-critical largely due to making cognitive errors about themselves. Therefore they can reduce their self-criticism by assessing and correcting the cognitive errors that lead them to misguided self-assessments that in turn create the assumptions of fault and failing on their part—particularly the belief that they are responsible for having caused their son to become gay. Many parents indulging in black-or-white, part = whole thinking cannot treat themselves as good because they cannot put their bad points into perspective as being "not all of who I am." As a result, they view themselves as all bad because they view themselves as, and quite possibly are in some respects, imperfect. They have made their entire self-view out of one or a few of their "flaws." Because they disapprove of certain aspects of themselves, they disapprove of themselves on the whole. They deem themselves wholly undesirable because of a few traits they dislike in themselves and because they, like everyone else, have actually done, and are still doing, some things that they rightfully regret. Hierarchical thinking on a scale of 1 to 10 leads them to believe that since a tree doesn't grow far from its fallen apples, parents who have a gay son are not as good as parents whose sons are straight. Therefore, they see parents with sons who are straight as winning in the competition over those people, themselves, burdened by sons who are gay—making them as parents with a gay son second-best individuals in a second-best family: their own value diminished, and their personal status in life reduced.

In the realm of *criticism from others*, parents of gay sons generally have plenty of critical people in their lives whom they must identify, understand, and cope with. These are the people focused on parental wrongdoing as if that completely accounts first, for their having produced a son who is gay and second, for their having afterward badly mishandled the situation.

These negative people criticize these parents for wanting their son to go straight (even though they do or should know that that can't be); for determining their son's true value based on what *they* think it ought to be (not on what *he* thinks it should be) and is; and for setting professional goals for their son that are inappropriate for this particular given child.

Such parents feel particularly guilty (and get especially depressed) when others criticize them *passive aggressively*. Others generally aren't so bold as to tell parents of a gay son, "That son of yours is a disgrace, and so are you, his family, for having, and putting up with, him." But others frequently do criticize them in more subtle ways that though more superficially politically correct are not for that reason ultimately any less personally devastating.

Passive-aggressive criticism directed toward parents of gay sons tends to have the following characteristics:

Though initially it appears to be of modest proportions, it can in the long run be even more devastating than overt criticism—by virtue of its being constant and so highly motivated to be hurtful that it makes up with devotion to purpose and commitment what it lacks in immediacy, strength, and focus.

It tends to be displaced onto other, often distantly (but sometimes closely) related matters, for example, from having a *gay* child onto having a *difficult* one.

It masquerades as impersonal, which though supposedly less hurtful can be just as, or more hurtful than, attacks that are overtly personal. Passive-aggressive critics of parents of gay sons often convince themselves that because they speak but theoretically, they have avoided doing harm simply because they have avoided getting personal. For example, they say and believe that they aren't criticizing Dad personally when they speak of how sons become gay due to "Your difficult father-son-relationship"; "You his dad

rejected your gay son during the critical gender identity phase of development, thereby inflicting narcissistic injury on him, causing him to detach
himself from yourself, leading your son to relinquish his masculinity due to
having been dealt a fatal blow to his male confidence because he no longer
has a suitable identification figure to emulate"; "Your lack of closeness to your
son led you to withhold affirmation, creating a weakness of confidence in
him"; or because "You withheld strokes, which led your son to question if
he is loved, leading to him becoming personally impotent and so less masculine both in a general way and more specifically in the sexual realm."

I treated a patient, the father of a gay son, whose prior passive-aggressive
therapist made him feel guilty by implying that he made his son gay by not
giving him what he needed in the way of happy, warm, and intimate closeness, causing the son to self-protectively/defensively detach himself from
Dad and thus forever carry silently within himself a longing for warmth
and love in the encircling arms of a father figure, one he could, however,
feel, but never get close to. This supposedly led the son to lock into an
intense need for "any substitute for masculine intimacy, warmth, and love
I can find," something he sought from other males, generally strangers.
I also treated a mother whose prior equally passive-aggressive *therapist*
made her feel guilty by implying that she had been engulfing/smothering
to the point of causing her son to "regress to infantilism" so much so that
he, the son, was, in essence, no longer able to "function as an independent,
successful, real man, but instead could only regress to being a gay person,"
which she interpreted as her son becoming "a shrinking violet."

Guilty parents can reduce the impact of others' criticisms by *analyzing
themselves* along the lines of, "*Why exactly* do you let your critics bother
you?" and "*Why* exactly do you care what people who buy ink by the barrel
think?" Is this because developmentally speaking you currently accept
others' negative, but you can't accept their positive, view of you because
having long ago incorporated your parents' negative view of you to become
your own negative view of yourself, you continue to devalue yourself even
though you know that your own parents had problems of their own that
rendered their judgment of you as deficient?

Parents can also help themselves feel less guilty by avoiding blindly
buying into what their guilt-inducing critics say about them via identifying
the cognitive errors embedded in the criticism *of others*—errors that make
these criticisms as irrational as they are undeserved. They can help themselves deal with being critically abused by being alert to others' *part-to-
whole* thinking along the lines of, "If you are not all good, then you are all

bad"; others' *selective abstraction* where critics recognize, and emphasize, only parents' weak points and flaws while overlooking, and deemphasizing, their strong points and virtues; and others' *arbitrary inference* where parents' critics "know it is so because they know it is so." Parents can also be alert to others' playing guilt cards such as the "I am entitled to criticize you because I am your mother" card; the "It's a free country where I have free speech and so am entitled to say whatever bad things about you that I want to say, even though they crush you" card; the pseudo-altruistic "I am just trying to help you and to protect society by ensuring personal and social order to avoid the slippery slope into chaos" card; and the "You are wrong and stupid simply because I, the expert, disagree with you" card.

In actuality parenting is a complex process where so many controversial elements come into play that there is no one right way to parent applicable to all situations. Still, as Pinsker says in a personal communication on June 26, 2012 in another context, "[W]hile people don't expect all the answers when orthopedists disagree about the consequences of an accident; while no one says that economics is a fraud because economists not only can't agree about what to do now, but don't agree about what caused or cured the Great Depression, the recent Japanese deflation, or whether it is better to save or spend; and while no one says that traffic engineering is a fraud just because there are divergent views about how much parking should be required/allowed for a new mall," many people aver, and mean it when they say, "It's perfectly clear: you as parents say and do what you know to be absolutely wrong, thus contributing to your son's being gay, or having caused, have subsequently mishandled the results of your actions with subsequent actions that made things even worse."

Importantly, parents should distinguish constructive from destructive criticism. Constructive criticism's goal is to create not guilt, but improvement through change. It is in the main justified, involving as it does not an attack, but an assessment while softening any tendency it has to wound by pointing to the potential for positive results, for example, "Do better and you will thereby enhance your already low self-approval quotient by not giving others any excuse they might be seeking to put you down." It is directed to problems that can be solved because the remedy is not merely needed but also accomplishable. When directed to problems parents have created through their own actions, or fault, while affixing appropriate blame, it simultaneously gives absolution and suggests specific changes that parents can make in the future to avoid repeating any unfortunate past.

As parents of a gay son you should accept constructive criticism—from your son, his friends, his partner (your son-in-law), your extended family, and even from strangers, and use it to make indicated and needed course corrections. You should not respond resentfully with defensive excuses and rebuttals meant to avoid seeing and accepting your so-called imperfections. Learn from the criticism, then rise above it by putting the reasons for it behind you once and for all and setting off in a new direction. For all parents make mistakes in child rearing, and that is okay—if they subsequently apologize then make timely adjustments. And when you make corrections, you will likely discover that your son, like most sons (gay or straight), is eager to forgive and willing to forget.

In contrast, destructive criticism is unjustified and consciously or unconsciously is meant to be harmful. It is often unsolicited, that is, forced upon an unwilling victim. Though it is seemingly object-directed, it is in fact mainly self-directed—in the sense that it expresses a mindset of the critic as much as it represents a considered evaluation of his or her subject. It is typically intended to make the critic feel less devalued through the devaluing of someone else, the critic's victim, a person brought in to serve as a foil, that is, as "the comparatively more disreputable one." Therefore, critics who defile you for having a gay son are generally less concerned with your lack of decency than with elevating themselves in their own minds by comparing themselves to you favorably, along such lines as "I am more decent than you because all my children are straight." That is, they are improving their self-image by diminishing your self-esteem, diverting themselves from feeling inadequate by telling you how far more inadequate you actually are; propping themselves up by tearing you down; and expressing how they are better and brighter than you as a self-soothing on their part that says, "I deserve admiration and love for being right and good (and you, just the opposite, for being wrong, and bad). Critics of parents of gay sons are often attempting to diminish their personal guilt feelings about having mishandled their own child by shifting the blame onto you for doing something similar, or much worse, in order to convince themselves that "I myself never did such a thing" or "such a bad thing." It is said that behind much criticism of another lies a self-criticism. As such, many critics are in fact expressing anger/disdain toward themselves by shaming, criticizing, and humiliating others along similar (projective) lines. Thus those who criticize fathers for being distant and mothers for being engulfing generally do so because they see themselves as, and condemn themselves for being, just that, making their criticisms self-reflections, however much they frame them as perceptive, justified attacks upon others. It follows that parents of a gay son can feel better about themselves if they hear (and disregard) the critical things people are saying about them as self-statements—on the part of those making the negative comments.

Parents can often help themselves feel less guilty by assessing their critics' mental health/identifying their psychopathology in preparation for evaluating whether to accept their critics' so-called expertise or to discount it as the product of their critics' troubled minds. Parents can help themselves by specifically identifying the following emotional disorders that are so often at the core of a critic's need to be critical, as well as his or her actual critical formulations.

The *megalomanic* component of criticism involves critics *narcissistically* overestimating their knowledge of the subject at hand.

Often critics are also excessively *paranoid* individuals. As such, hearing differing points of view as constituting an adversarial challenge to their expertise, and so to their identity, they intensify their attacks retaliatively and so defensively that they come across as believing that others have no rights at all, and are not entitled to any of their opinions

Often they are also *depressives* denying their own "personal badness" by affirming their "unalloyed goodness," telling the world, and God, that as people they, not like you, uphold family values—doing what is moral, and doing so out of respect and love for their own Mom and Dad.

As overly competitive *histrionics* they need to best all rivals, which for them is everyone. They are exceptionally envious, jealous people who are able to feel less personally deficient if after identifying you as the competition they do you one better in order to piggyback on you to their personal glory.

As excessively perfectionistic *obsessive* people they pride themselves on scrupulously and consistently following social rules (not as you purportedly do, being inconsistent, breaking the rules when, and just because, it suits your particular personal bent or real purpose). They are overly controlling individuals who feel justified in ordering you about "for your own good" because, clearly knowing more than you do, they have the right to demand that you go along with them because clearly they are more powerful than thou and clearly they feel that they are the ones entitled to be in control.

As excessively *masochistic* people they are effectively "cruising for a bruising" so that when you get mad at them, they get exactly what they want.

As excessively *sadistic* people they are fundamentally hurtful individuals who like to make others feel bad, so they comfortably abuse you by challenging you, often by denigrating you personally by calling you names (such as "stupid") or by hurling pejoratives masquerading as scientific formulations that rely heavily on the use of sophistry as they, for example, cite the primacy of the negative downsides that in this imperfect world do regularly exist for every positive action (for something "shameful" can, by those who want it to be so, always be found to be inherent in, and so go along with, something admirable).

Guilty parents should inure themselves to criticism remedially by elevating their personal self-esteem. The most resilient self-esteem does not rise and fall dependent on winning or losing battles with others over how good and moral one is. It comes from two main sources: within and interpersonally from responding to criticism by subjecting it to a reality check. The latter in part involves demanding critics offer specifics. Parents who do this do not accept name-calling without demanding to know what the names refer to precisely, and what is the evidence exactly for the put down. "What," they might ask, "is the confirmation of critical theoretical assumptions leading to accusations that as parents we have been ineffective? How exactly did you arrive at the conclusion that because I as a mother was remote I turned my son against women and to men, or because I as a mother was engulfing I turned my son off women and to men? Let me counter with research findings that clearly show that gay sons exist in so many different family contexts that no theory as to what causes a son to be gay is valid, if ever, in more than a few, highly select, cases." Sadistically calling your critics names and otherwise confronting them aggressively by challenging them as troublemaking homophobes, misanthropes, or vengeful sadists is not likely to be helpful. Replying scientifically to their distortions with a reality-based fact check about yourself that originates in well-reasoned arguments about who you actually are, advanced without becoming counterproductively overly defensive, is more likely to have the desired effect. Most likely to hit home is a scientifically researched rebuttal dispassionately offered "to set the record straight," as in "My research proves that having a son who is gay is a biological development that generally no one can influence and so for which no human being, least of all us, his parents, should be held accountable."

Parents should scrupulously avoid masochistic involvements with their critics. Such involvements focus them away from doing the best possible job they can do as parents and onto feeling hurt by the disharmony caused by self-appointed authority full of smug unilateral self-justification of its negativity. Masochistic parents become so preoccupied with their critics that instead of ignoring them, they try to change their minds or, developing Stockholm syndrome, even want and beg their critics to love them. They become so submissive that they passively assign status and influence to their critics (which their critics don't merit) just because their criticism is so vocal; and they accept criticism even from those who have had no relevant proper training and are possessed of less than impeccable credentials. As a result they fall under the spell of false gurus prone to steer them wrong about parenting a gay son based on conclusions arising out of the guru's personal distortions/prejudices that have been carefully honed to effectively bully parents so that the guru can gain emotional (self-esteem enhancing) and even practical advantage. Now parents self-destructively condemn themselves in lockstep with their critics. In particular they blame themselves for overreacting to criticism when their response is in fact understandable and unsurprising given how sadistic critics desire to be and how persuasive certain critics can come across as being. And finally, they actually can, and often do, bring criticism, or further criticism, down upon themselves, and they do so unnecessarily not for what they have said and done via actual poor parenting on their parts, but by first parenting well only to then seek out others who are by nature abrasive, deprecating, and never satisfied no matter what, and inviting them in and practically begging them to stay to savage them (the parents)—to back up their own misguided need to savage themselves. So they change for their critics when their critics in fact need to change for them. They imagine that they benefit from being overly remorseful and apologetic only to likely instead find that being that way only causes their critics to savage them further—because the critic, sensing high vulnerability, feels ever more emboldened to continue and escalate his or her assault.

This said, always recognize that overt intimidating confrontation of critics can be unsafe. So instead consider a *healthy* passive-aggressive counterresponse that while making your point avoids being overtly combative. For example, you might induce guilt in your critics not by attacking them, but by simply acknowledging what is right about what they say and thanking them for their perceptive analysis, while "gently" pointing out its flaws.

Seek consensual validation from simpatico friends, family, therapists, or self-help books judiciously selected for being rational and having a proven track record. This, an especially good way to enhance self-acceptance, involves keeping supportive company, that is, surrounding yourself with other parents who basically like and accept you and yours (and staying away from those who don't). You can do that on your own by relating mainly to parents and friends selected for being supportively homopositive, or you can do it by attending group therapy sessions with other parents who have similar problems and personalities, and are motivated to come together to pool what rudimentary high self-esteem each has in order to, in effect, pull one another up by each other's bootstraps.

Seek out/read about people who model for you how in situations that parallel yours of today they were in the past able to continue to be self-accepting without succumbing to others' lack of acceptance of them. Also seek out people who can show you where you may be going wrong—doing so without carping on your deficiencies, but rather emphasizing your strengths and indicating how you can use them to your advantage by their telling you exactly how you can do better.

Parents can help themselves feel less guilty by looking for the positive sides of their critics' negative assessments. Sometimes the "bad" things critics accuse you of can actually (if only unwittingly on their parts) on further examination turn out to be compliments in disguise. For example, a positive take on the engulfing mother stereotype is the caring, sharing, and loving mother. A positive take on the passive father stereotype is the man who allows his son to be himself without unduly interfering in what his son himself wants to be. Thus your response instead of being "I'm sorry," can be "And what's wrong with that?"

Unfortunately, so often coping with criticism involves coping with the depression that results from having been criticized. One of the many reasons parents of gay sons get depressed is that, already somewhat depressed, they see the criticism that comes their way as just and as just punishment for having been unworthy—for having been people who destroyed their son's life, their own, and that of the rest of the family. Matters can become particularly desperate when vicious cycling starts, beginning with depressive self-blame that leads to fault-finding directed toward your son—for his being difficult/doing you wrong. This seriously harms the parent-son relationship, ultimately isolating you from your son and so making you even more self-critical (for what you have done) and depressed (over what you believe to have been the result of your actions).

Some families most effectively handle their criticism-induced depression not by meeting it head-on, but by waiting it out. They just accept being depressed for now, hoping the depression will resolve itself in time as intimidations that once seemed insurmountable come, as if on their own, to matter less or actually get resolved. Meanwhile they continue to function in spite of being depressed. That way they avoid a double depression—getting depressed over being depressed—and additionally they avoid decimating relationships because others, falling victim to their moodiness, leave them behind, giving them a real reason to feel even more down.

You might choose to seek out helpful supportive treatments involving taking care of yourself physically to help you feel better about yourself. Improved diet and adequate exercise can help in a general way. So can individual or family meditation, which can lead to improved self-esteem as you find comfort through temporarily removing yourself from others who think ill of you, thus allowing you to think about yourself in a new more sanguine light. Bibliotherapy (reading literature about having a gay son and the problems that most families experience in this situation) can also help, but you must avoid writings with a one-size-fits-all approach with a narrow agenda that is subtly or grossly inapplicable to you personally.

Never attempt to cure a guilty depression by abusing/bullying your gay son, thus enhancing *his* shame in order to reduce *yours*. You might get temporary relief that way, but unless your son basically needs/loves you too much to even contemplate making a break with you, you will likely miscalculate and overdo, and later regret it as you discover all too clearly that having misfired, you have caused him to pull back from, or actually leave, you.

Fortunately most parenting mistakes guiltily depressed parents make are reversible—as long as parents admit/confess them after the fact and backtrack in a timely fashion. However, in situations where there might be a point of no return, seeking therapy if needed, and doing so as soon as possible, can prevent a serious and possibly permanent rift with your son from developing.

It is particularly important for depressed parents not to expect themselves to be perfect. In fact most benefit from admitting and counting their imperfections, identifying, accepting and understanding them in anticipation of trying to determine what they are—but only in preparation for making constructive changes. All parents, and especially those prone to depression, need to recognize that they can get things right only some of the time, and that they, like most parents of most sons, can never do right by a gay son all the time. Feeling less guilty doesn't mean never questioning and blaming yourself when self-blame is warranted, and never criticizing yourself when you deserve to be brought up short. It does not simply involve becoming more self-accepting even though you are still thinking and doing some unacceptable things. It does mean losing the focus of "Who is responsible and at fault?" and instead realizing "We simply accept who and what we are, and enjoy what we have, yet look forward to altering that which, if anything, needs to be corrected."

If you feel you need therapy, consider seeking insight-oriented therapy aimed at providing you with a full awareness about and understanding of the personal difficulties that spin off guilt and the family tension, unhappiness, disarray, dismay, confusion, and anxiety and depression that come in its wake—all virtually guaranteed to spread to involve the whole family. Consider seeking a therapist who additionally incorporates a cognitive approach into his or her insight-oriented therapy, helping you not only to understand yourself, but also to correct such erroneous thinking as the belief that thinking = doing, a belief that leads to self-blame for thoughts you disapprove of as if they actually represent actions you have taken, and the belief, characteristic of selective abstraction, that because you are not *all* good you are no good at all, a belief that leads you to undervalue your true worth and overestimate the harm you are doing.

In conclusion, guilt reduction leads to healthy family growth and development because it enhances interpersonal functioning due to reduced fear of humiliation and rejection. Now all concerned, allowing themselves to be more realistic (about themselves and their son) than before, reduce strong negative punitive self-images and deceptively negative self-views and thus allow positive self-images to better emerge and become a source of positive energy, thus leading directly to accomplishing worthy things, thus meeting your own and your son's productive, creative aspirations.

Chapter 8

Communing with Your Son

Communing with your son productively consists of *communicating* with him effectively; giving him good *advice*; and getting appropriately and helpfully *involved* in his activities of daily living.

Communicating

While many laypersons and experts alike recommend that parents communicate with their sons, too few actually specify why they should do so and advise them on exactly how to do it.

Productively communicating with your son involves sharing feelings, airing problems, and exchanging information, all in a nonthreatening and affirmative way hoping to answer questions, his and yours; resolve differences; and meet relational challenges. The goal is to learn in order to change and grow into a more ideal family, one if not free of all problems then at least one on the path toward being joyful. Diminishing the distances between family members allows them to develop a true partnership between equals marked by mutual respect that leads to bilateral comfort. Now each participant, in the first place likely needy, gets some of his or her wishes granted, and some of his or her legitimate desires fulfilled, however much that requires simultaneously adjusting excessive expectations and relinquishing unreasonable demands by (if necessary) downplaying self-fulfillment in favor of altruistically meeting the needs of others. As a bonus, a united core family results that is a true team and mini-protectorate that as such becomes less permeable to destructive input from other family members because the family as a united coalition is now better buffered against "outsiders," particularly those outsiders who employ traditional ideology in order to negatively influence, or actually wreak havoc on, the thinking and actions of more liberal families and their more progressive family members.

Good communication does not:

- Refer to primitive emotions more than to intellectual basic principles
- Make every encounter an occasion to verbalize past (traumatic) experiences in order to repeat them with yet someone else
- Become rapidly, strictly, and overly nostalgic, fixed on a rosy (predisclosure) past however much that past is no longer relevant to the present, just because it is what worked for you once
- Humiliate your son for current or past "misdeeds"
- Interact sadomasochistically to get or give pleasure from ignoring, devaluing, rejecting, mistreating, and beating your son down, or proselytizing hurtfully, morally, in a way that involves putting your principles before his comfort (if you see your son as a disgrace to the family "on principle" because of his sexual orientation/gender identity, abandon this principle lest you wind up abandoning, and being abandoned by, your son, or at the least causing him—and ultimately yourself—so much pain that he acts out against you and abandons you, or acts out against himself and, abandoning himself, attempts suicide)

Some Rules of Style and Content in Communicating

The following rules of communicating are not absolute. Rather they change from time to time as parents, their son, and the parents' relationships with one another and their son evolve. That means that what parents say to their son must also evolve, that is, it must reflect growth as all concerned go through maturational stages, an important one of which is characterized by becoming more ready to hear something new that you weren't able, willing, or ready to take in before.

When communicating be *honest* enough with yourself and your son to accept and acknowledge some embarrassing facts about all concerned in order to properly deal with personal sensitivities and correct individual distortions by facing what having a gay son actually involves.

Think about all your statements and carefully plan your actions before you say or do anything important lest you say or do something you don't really intend/mean that you might later regret. Most family issues relative to having a gay son are sufficiently nonemergent to be handled leisurely, that is, without haste, short of impulsivity, and without allowing serious emotionalism to take control. Before you say much of significance, determine the full implication of what you are about to say. Be especially careful to first clarify your points in your mind so that you can make them in a way that avoids speaking thoughtlessly and creates misunderstanding resulting from speaking imprecisely, thus allowing your son to too readily be able to insert meanings that you didn't intend to into gaps left by your being vague.

Avoid thinking in terms of stereotypes that pigeonhole your gay son, forcing him to fit into a standard that he doesn't even begin to approximate.

Attain intrafamilial fairness through bringing to light pernicious secret affiliations, particularly a father-daughter (Electra complex) attachment originating not in compatibility, as the father might wish and claim, but in the father's sexualization of a daughter who has become for him "the other woman."

Never confound abreaction (getting feelings out by talking about them), especially when yelling is involved, with true communication. And never confound true communication with intimidation, which involves attempts at control associated with a compulsive need to have one's way—not because one is right, but out of a need to establish personal primacy.

Aspire not to full loving and closeness but to creating a functional family where all concerned meet basic obligations without either excessive merging or interpersonally destructive distancing.

Never use your son's being gay as an excuse for failing as a parent or as a reason you give to yourself to fail to meet your obligations to your family, and especially to your son, for example, when you pay your straight daughter's college tuition but not your son's after reassuring yourself that it's okay to withhold the money because "Being gay, he is such a loser."

Do not expect communication, no matter how good, to fully solve all family problems. Make your goal not perfection, but progress—especially progress in the direction of actively creating, rather than passively accepting, what happens next in your family.

Give yourself and your family time to adjust and make personal and course corrections. The only deadline is to never leave this earth (as many fathers of gay sons have done) on a sour note, as my father did when in the last months of his life still protesting that I was gay and that it ruined him—he cancelled a birthday party that some friends of his were giving for me just because I insisted on bringing Michael to the bash. A patient's mother ultimately said to her son's partner, just in time, on her death bed, "In the beginning I didn't like you at all; but as the years went by I began to see that you were just what my son needed, and without you he would have had a very different, and far less rewarding, life. Thanks for being patient with me." However, this patient's father never seemed to get used to the fact that his son was gay, and to this day he still harbors, and acts on, the defensive suspicion that his son's partner, having made him that way, "has got to go."

Respect diversity. Always make certain that what you say and do respects differences between you and your son. Make and embrace compromises between the old and contemporary straight and the au courant gay subculture, and fill in the generational gap between discordant/clashing/varied/idiosyncratic/disparate philosophies, personal ideals, personal identities, personality types, constitutional endowments, personal beliefs, and the various roles parents and sons traditionally, or by choice, play in any given family. Never imply or state that you view one person's needs and wishes as being of lesser value than another's. Especially do not view your son's personal needs and wishes as being of lesser value than yours. In particular, develop/retain the philosophy that in any given parent-son interaction, there is a place both for (more conservative) strictness/discipline and (more liberal) compassionate permissiveness.

Be *selectively* honest, always, without crossing the line that separates holding back from actually lying. Always balance being true to your thoughts and feelings with being considerate of your son's. Avoid being painfully honest where you openly express *all* your thoughts/beliefs/values/feelings about having a gay son simply because you believe that doing so is liberating for you and him. Instead seek a balance between your *constitutional* right to say what is on your mind and your *humane* and *moral* responsibility to treat your son compassionately by using constraint via not expressing any and all thoughts and feelings that could possibly hurt him. Only say something bruising if you simultaneously make it clear that, struggling within yourself, you are uncertain that what you feel is right, and therefore you are unclear about what you should say and what you should withhold. Temper being right with being kind and loving by withholding unalloyed negative statements, particularly those having to do with your son's sexual orientation. When there is no alternative to saying something that your son might find really unpleasant, at least counter what you believe to be necessary brutal honesty with compassionate reservation in your timing, for example, try to diminish the impact of your harsh words by saying them a few at a time. Also when what you have to say is not inherently soothing, make it less disruptive by saying it gently, that is, speak in a low volume so that your speech is emotionally contained although not necessarily less specific for that.

You can try to avoid hurting your son and avoid making yourself feel guilty afterward by putting all negative communications in as positive a light as possible, for example, not "I condemn you for this" but "You clearly are in conflict, and likely self-condemnatory, about that." Whenever possible, soften talk about what you have done *to* each other with reflections on what you have done *for* each other.

Lessen the critical impact of what you say by putting it from the point of view not of *your wish*, but of *your fear*—a fear that likely exists in association with your wish, as fear does behind every wish. For example, say not "You make too many demands on us for us to be understanding (and I *wish* you would stop)" but "If you don't stop, we *fear* that we will not be able to support you as much as we might like."

Also, to avoid being insulting, put things from the point of view not of *his* wishes but of *his* fears. Say not "You imagine we are angry with you"(accusatory) but, in essence, "It's clear that sometimes when you feel angry with us, you get so anxious that you turn your anxiety into a fear that we are annoyed with you then become so guilty that you fear we will get even angrier with you to retaliate. Then afterward you imagine your fears have come true and get upset with us as if that has actually happened."

However, not all bold negativity is inherently problematical and therefore prohibited. There are times when parents simply must say negative things and act in a less than positive fashion toward their son. And sometimes there can even be advantages to revealing negative feelings. Although your son might not like to hear them, on the helpful side he will perceive you as authentic, which is what he too wants to be, and he may, paradoxically, on that account alone, even feel more positively about you than he did before. This means that you at least have made a start in conveying to your son that you aren't ignoring, devaluing, or rejecting him; neither are you gratuitously beating him up, nor thoughtlessly putting him down.

In fact your negative feelings are unlikely to come as a surprise to him, for any sensitive gay son already knows on some level that you, his parents, are struggling with the belief that he is a problem for, even a disgrace to, the family. And he can accept that as long as he is clear that though you have these feelings, you don't necessarily fully support them in yourself. Your son will likely understand your being imperfect in the sense of not always having yourself under full control, and he will likely even forgive you for being excessively judgmental if he senses that you are being equally judgmental of your own feelings, including feeling that you are being more judgmental of him than you yourself would like to be. So rather than denying the obvious, ask your son to accept you as you are. Though in some respects you are faulty, you are at least trying to do better. For although you are foolish in some ways, you are wisely struggling within yourself in others so that you can remain caring and loving overall. (Although its name doesn't suggest it, homophobia/homonegativity almost never consists of purely negative feelings. For like many attitudes that at first appear to be uniform, it is in fact made up of mixed feelings. Therefore, homophobia should—at least theoretically in the majority of cases—be called not "homophobia," but "homoambivalence.")

Focus on the actual issues, not on other matters more valid emotionally than realistically. Certainly don't allow your own basic conflicts, especially those of a sexual nature, to influence your evaluation of your son and what you say to him.

Stick with what's important. Never belabor what is truly minor, especially minor criticisms you overstress to the point that you make them more significant than they actually are. Anticipate what you are about to say and listen to yourself as you speak. Say only what is really of significance and most likely to have impact. Your selectivity ensures that you at least leave some room to hear what *he* thinks about things, and where he stands on matters that are of consequence *to him*.

Seek feedback. As you talk to your son, ask for feedback so that you can learn about his sensitivities and so avoid carelessly touching upon his sore spots to the point of offending him and even starting an argument. You can clear up potential misconceptions as you go along by asking questions about how he is reacting to you and to what you say and do in real time. Perhaps you feel guilty about having provoked him when in fact you have done nothing to actually annoy him. Conversely, perhaps you feel you have been supportive of him when in fact you have seriously hurt him by actually being overly critical and in ways you didn't anticipate or couldn't even have foreseen.

Be apologetic (when necessary). If you feel guilty, and your guilt is appropriate, acknowledge that you have made mistakes. Both apologize for your errors and correct them.

Never say misguided negative things to your son when he is being an okay guy and his okay self, then say nothing at all when he is acting destructively and so can truly use your input/guidance.

Be aware of hidden meanings in what you say. Be alert to the different levels on which you communicate. So often what you say doesn't fairly reveal what you mean. Likely your words have deeper, often unintended, meanings due to nonverbal communications that contain hidden messages. For example, be alert to communication tics like repetitively sniffing at certain crucial points in the conversation. Tics like this actually represent an association to what you are saying and can be more telling about what you are thinking than anything you actually verbalize. Silence is also a form of (hidden) communication. More parents fail to set standards because they unduly fear being too controlling and so don't speak up, thus enabling their son to behave maladaptively because he takes nonintervention as active permission.

Be aware that different expressions have different meanings to different people. Be alert to and explain the nuances of what you say by being aware of and acknowledging the different meanings idiomatic expressions have for people who are from different generations and cultures. For example, your son might be unaware of the differences between a rhetorical and an actual question, and so the difference between asking him about and stating something to him. As a result he might misinterpret (along somewhat paranoid lines) innocent statements on your part as "prying and criticizing." To illustrate, are you aware that when you refer to a "gay lifestyle" you are in effect saying something both unacceptable and incorrect—that being gay is a choice, not of a way to live as a gay man, but of homosexuality itself?

When you do ask your son a direct question, make it clear that you are not being accusatory, but are seeking information, simply wondering about something you really want to know, neither condemning him for that exactly nor protesting too much by stating its opposite.

Avoid roundabout, especially passive-aggressive, communication. Particularly destructive to basic trust is passive-aggressive brutalization, which involves brutalizing by implication. An example is giving backhanded compliments such as telling your son that he can do better in a way that clearly suggests you are devaluing something good that he has already done. Avoid snide remarks, an example of which, in a personal communication on July 6, 2012 provided by the psychologist Raeleen D'Agostino Mautner, involves a gay man who was interacting with his child by giving him a "guess the color test." Whereupon the gay man's mother said to her son, "For this you need your PhD?"

Flag controversial opinions to distinguish them from facts. Consider flagging *all* opinions, even positive ones, as such. If you must express controversial opinions (certainly ones that are hurtful, and sometimes any at all) label them as "things I am willing to reconsider." That makes it clear that they are not "expert" opinions, for even you, among the most intelligent of parents, generally lack the necessary training and experience to have final unimpeachable thoughts on all significant matters, especially those involving being gay. That way you can mostly say what you think, however controversial and undesirable, for you have added, "It's not a fact, just my thoughts," that is, you have inserted a footnote—not only out of consideration for your son's feelings, but also because of the good possibility that, being personally involved and therefore probably excessively emotional, you are likely wrong. Specific qualifiers such as "I am not certain of the validity of what I say" can help soften harsh statements. So can self-criticisms, for example, for being overly moralistic, overly emotional, and incautiously blurting out things that you might, and probably will, later regret having said. Say "on the other hand" to take back words you regret having uttered, and if you feel you have expressed yourself in a way that has been unfortunate, take back what you said as quickly as you can.

Be especially alert to your son's identity issues. Always consider that he will interpret everything you say as a possible (negative) comment on his identities, which are (appropriately) sacred, and in the main consist of the following three basic ones:

- Sexual identity, which refers to the concept of oneself as homosexual, bisexual, transsexual, questioning, or heterosexual
- Gender identity, which is not about the concept of oneself as homosexual, bisexual, or heterosexual, but about one's inner sense of oneself as being either male or female (the term "gender role" refers to a related concept of living out of one's gender identity)
- Nonsexual identity, which concerns one's sense of self as it relates to non-erotic ideals, pursuits, and passions

Additionally many gay men have a "gay identity"—a cohesive sense of gay self that revolves around "what being gay means," often (but hardly always) containing an element of "free to be myself and to be sexually liberated." (Gay men often defend this identity passionately and not always rationally along more libertine lines of their own, as happened many times when my suggestion to "get married and thus live happily ever after" elicited a book reviewer's response along the lines of "You are clearly saying it's not okay to be gay.")

Parents who recognize, and speak as affirmatively as they can to, all these identities actually help their son create and develop a cohesive sense of self that will serve him well throughout his life. As an example of what not to say, my piano teacher failed to follow this rule. She was right to decry my overly percussive piano technique, but instead of suggesting that I soften my touch, she said that I "was banging." Thus she appeared to criticize not only my touch, but also my seriously entrenched masculine identity, one that arose out of my being "musically manly."

If you feel negatively about any of your son's identities and say so, at least subsequently try to come across as less negative by freely offering apologies and such disclaimers as "You are a good and valuable person; you do what you do well, and there isn't very much about you that needs fixing. However, let's look at some things that we would like to tell you, things that hopefully you could profitably learn from, perhaps in anticipation of considering changing accordingly."

Be especially cautious when referring to/discussing *gender identity*. You can feel disappointed in your son for being less than masculine, but you should never say so, even indirectly. So consider saying not "feminine," but "dreamy and sensitive"; not "If only you could have been a better little leaguer," but "Not everyone is athletic. God may not have given you a talent for baseball, but He gave you such fine fingers with which to play the piano that you don't need to be good at sports." Especially insensitive is being selectively proud of your son, that is, only for activities to which you assign what you believe to be a desirably masculine quality. My parents did this when, though they remained steadfastly unimpressed by my musical talents, they (much too intensely) approved of my ability to swim a quarter of a mile without stopping.

If you choose to deal with your son's gender identity at all, you must first determine how accepting *he* is about his uniqueness. Some gay sons are troubled by gender identity issues/conflicts and on their own actively seek to challenge themselves and change. Others are fine with the way they are. The first group seeks help, the second wants to be left alone. (Of course, because "what I want" can be either a true preference or a neurotic compulsion, parent-son interactions in this realm are full of enough traps to generally make passive watchful waiting a better idea than premature direct, forceful, impulsive intervention, which is likely to come across as being callous.) This said, gentle interventional trial and error over time exerting influence in a way that leaves open the possibility of making course corrections dependent on feedback and fallout can help minimize or avoid parental hovering and space invasions, and help you instead come across as a compassionate, if imperfect, person, one attempting, if not always successfully, to spare your son as many difficulties in life as you possibly can.

When discussing sex itself, tread particularly lightly. Have the discussion only in a deliberately supportive, consciously nonaccusatory way—without devaluing, humiliating, or embarrassing your son in any manner, thus causing him to resent you seriously and even close you off completely. Telling him to go straight is the rough equivalent of his telling you to go gay.

With those few exceptions where it might be a good idea to rehearse and borrow from others, avoid stilted speech that can be the product of parroting another's words exactly, mine included. Especially think twice before borrowing speech mannerisms from anyone else, including from a preacher, a psychoanalyst, or a book you read on how to interact with your son.

Soften your anger. Always try to keep your anger under control. Should a generalized blowout occur, apologize and say that in the future you will try to feel less angry/express your anger differently. Say that instead of flaring you will try to be more specific about what the problem is and limit your comments to what it is about your son that is making you mad (and what precisely it may be about you that is making him angry). If the former is the case, if he is making you mad, say that from now on before you express much of anything at all negative in response, you will first try to ask your son to let you know if your angry feelings are or are not justified, and second, if justified, then tell him you will try to discuss what you both can do to help all concerned avoid getting to this place again. And if the latter is the case, if you are making him angry, ask what you can do to apologize effectively and in the future change definitively.

Don't slip up and blurt out any of the following specific statements in anger. But if you do happen to do that, at least add a retraction, as follows:

- "I hate you and I never want to see you again." If you say such a thing, add something like, "Not for your being gay, but because sometimes we think you aren't sufficiently careful to try to avoid hurting us." Explain, if it's true, and it likely is, that sometimes when you feel angry you can't help but deal with your anger, however counterproductively, by striking out—but even then you are motivated not so much to hurt your son personally, but to get him temporarily out of your sight just so that you are not around each other to stir up even more anger, thus doing irreparable harm to your relationship.
- "I am disappointed about having a gay son." If you say such a thing, add "That's how we feel, but only sometimes, and it's not our basic feeling, and even if it were, we would try not to act on it."
- "You have ruined our lives." If you say such a thing, add "in a very few aspects only, and you might be able to help us put our lives together again by being gay in a better way—and here are some suggestions, from our heart, as to how to accomplish that."

- "I blame you for refusing to change." If you say such a thing, add something along the lines of "I do sometimes, but even when I do I know that's foolish, and so I really hope you understand that I am actually less concerned about your being homosexual than I am about certain aspects of your (homosexual) day-to-day life. So let's have a discussion not about your being gay and possible remedies for that, attempting to fix things that are not broken, but about your life and how you live it, and ways to make necessary repairs here. We do understand that your homosexual life feels entirely right for you—even though we can't actually see what you like about it so much. We do understand that there are compensations for not having children (if that is the course you choose to take). But we do ask you to specify what they are and show us how while being gay has its problems, it also has its rewards. In general, we are very eager to know far more than what you have actually told us so far."

How can you respond when *he* loses his temper with *you*?

Should he say, "I blame you for making me gay," respond by saying something like "Please don't blame us for making you gay. That only adds to our guilt, making us more defensive and increasing our tendency to blame ourselves, and then to blame, and take things out on, you."

Should he say, "You hate gays, don't you?" instead of responding, "No, we love them," which sounds like dissimulation and says, "You are wrong," something he will likely interpret/misinterpret as defensive, respond with your equivalent of "We don't approve of everything about some gays, but we are not homophobes, or at least we will try not to be as homonegative toward you as we have been to date." Also say, "We know we made mistakes in that area and if you tell us where you think we went wrong we can, or at least we hope we can, still make course corrections."

Should he say, "You are ashamed of me because you are just thinking of yourselves and your reputation in the adult community development you live in," respond by saying the equivalent of "We do care about what other people think about us and our family, doesn't everyone? But more than that, we care about what you think of us, and in that respect we will try to put you first every time."

Should he say, "I am going to punish you (by leaving)," don't beg him to stay. Begging, as by saying, "We are good people who love you and don't deserve that, we have tried so hard," will likely by being masochistic enhance his sadistic desire to hurt you. So instead say, "I can understand why you feel that way, and might even want to scapegoat us in a major way for something minor (or even major) we did wrong. But let's explore the specific issue you want to punish us for to see if we can tell the difference between what we deserve in the way of retribution and what, if anything, you are being unfair to us about—and so more punitive toward us than we, and the situation, warrants."

When possible change the topic to together explore, and share, your objectives both as individuals and as a family. Determine which of your goals are valid, that is, desirable, doable, and personal in the sense of being right for you and your son (hopefully) coming together as family. Avoid parroting the experts; thinking along one-size-fits-all lines; and parroting a society that tells you as a family how and what to think and act based on encrusted social norms that are derived from predetermined social standards of so-called incontrovertible inherent appropriateness, propriety, and decency based on something so arbitrary as "tradition." (A tradition is often difficult to distinguish from a long-lived mass psychosis.) Buying into misguided social input means you cannot be open-minded and flexible enough to develop a specific family plan that, right for you and him, can reduce overall tension, induce calm, and make the family joyful and successful—minimizing forced conformity while maximizing mutual respect through having jettisoned rigid irrational idiosyncratic standards, thus dodging making the bricks of being right out of the clay of seizing might.

Giving Supportive Advice

Each parent has to decide whether to actively approach his or her son to support and advise him, or to wait until he approaches them asking for their support and seeking their advice.

Even a gay son who may seriously need advice will likely balk at first and complain, "I would rather do things myself." But just as likely he will nevertheless secretly appreciate constructive guidance and in the future come to see, and admit, that he took your good advice and did so at least to the degree that it rescued him. He will likely also thank you for any guidance you gave that helped him achieve solutions to his problems with everyday living and without your being as intrusive and controlling as he feared you might have become.

Effective advice-giving involves concerned family members stating their positions and hoping but not necessarily expecting that their son will view them as reasonable and considered. Parents must never criticize their son ad hominem, particularly as personally "ill-advised," "misguided," or "stupid." Instead they should respect his essential wisdom along the lines of

"If you think and say something, it must on some level be valid, for if it seems right to you, it must be right in at least some respects."

So often parent-son advice-giving predictably seems as if it would necessarily be unhelpful due to differences across the generation gap. In too many cases the son himself takes the position that contemporary thought (his) should prevail over dated ideas that were held in favor years back but no longer apply (yours). Therefore, sons taking such positions often say that they are the ones in touch with reality while their parents are necessarily completely out of touch because they are from the old school. And so as sons they must by definition have the one (and the only) word and know the one (and the only) right way to be and do things. Most sons see their parents as outsiders in their (the son's) eyes, and as necessarily being unknowledgeable simply because (as the son believes) it is a given that as straight people, parents lack first-hand experience with what is going on in the gay world.

On their part, parents of gay sons generally counter that their might necessarily makes them right, so the inherent power imbalance in the parent-child relationship must certainly mean that by rights parents should always prevail as more knowledgeable and rational/unprejudiced, and, being of superior intelligence, must by definition have more sense than their sons. But each family member should strive not to defeat, but to help the others out without pulling rank on or refusing to understand the other person— instead always trying to be fair and open-minded, while avoiding misunderstandings based on false assumptions that typically accelerate to become hard feelings that invariably lead to interpersonal intrafamilial distancing.

Most families cannot reach full agreement within the family about how and to what extent to intervene when their son seems to be in real immediate danger. Disagreements tend to occur, persist, and take the form of "I think he needs more help" versus "I think we need to order him to go straight and do right " versus "Maybe if we ignore this, it will go away" versus "He is just being himself, and there is nothing we can or should want to do about it" versus "Let's compromise and find some middle of the road course to take" versus "Let's assign one family member to lead" versus "Let's just agree to disagree and move on."

Parents typically disagree about how to give their sons advice about coming out, especially about coming out in the best possible way. The alternatives involve coming out globally, coming out selectively, or staying in. Many parents advise their sons to strike a balance between freely coming out to others without ever dissimulating, and staying completely in to be safe in order to retain valued personal relationships that might not survive being removed from the protective cloak of reassuring personal reticence. I believe in purposeful disclosure, that is, disclosure that is not indiscriminate, that is, in disclosing not for itself but when there is a precise identifiable emotional or practical reason for doing so. That takes actually disclosing being gay to a new level, out of the impulsive and into the considered realm, so that disclosing becomes something functional—less resembling the morbid preoccupation that it can sometimes become and instead becoming an inherently valid part of the process of growth and maturation.

I believe parental advice should include advising a gay son to find and keep a loving partner, one who can enrich not only his life, but theirs as well. Of course, some sons chose to live a life solo, and that in the best possible sense. Some such sons find partnering/marrying stultifying and as such "so very not gay." That choice is a very personal one—meaning that you should take pains to respect it and not push your son to find someone to love when he is not so inclined. But so often the so-called inclination of the free spirit is in fact the compulsion of the emotionally shackled. If that is the case with your son, you might best be able to help him if you start by trying to help him resolve conflicts about closeness and hopefully, but not necessarily, in the direction of allowing a Mr. Right into his life.

Parents who choose to advise their son should always keep in mind the possibility that their son needs not advice, but therapy. This might be the case when he is suffering from that typical adolescent combination of paranoid fear, obsessive uncertainty, and social panic so commonly found in adolescents, gay or straight, which often when taken together amount to a discreet adjustment disorder of adolescence, if not to a generalized neuroticism.

Entering Your Son's Daily Life

Communing with your son in many cases of necessity extends to communing with his friends. As parents of a gay son, you should encourage him to bring his friends over to the house. You especially should make certain that he (and his partner) always has someplace to go for the holidays. Be particularly careful to not send your son a negative message by having his friends over only when no one else, like your extended family and your friends, is around, and otherwise exiling him when your relatives and friends are there with you.

You should fully educate yourself about his friends and their lives. Try to make some of their interests your own. Avoid being critical by becoming knowledgeable—about contemporary gay life and the particular gay sub-culture your son has chosen to immerse himself in.

However, never forget that you his parents are just one part of your son's life, and that what you think of and do to, and so with, your son generally counts for far less than what his friends think of, say about, and do to, and with, him. Also you should not try to be one of your son's buddies exactly, palling around with your son and his friends when you should instead be maintaining boundaries *and* setting limits. You should not willingly marginalize yourself in the sense of trying too hard to be "one of the guys"—trying so hard that you become unwelcome to him and within his group. And, of course, you should be selective about which of his gay friends you choose to meet and embrace. Likely only some of them ought to be your friends too. Others might be too personally unappealing or too dangerous to make suitable companions as much for you as for him. But decide which is which on the basis of preference not prejudice, reality not bigotry.

Unless there is danger your son doesn't know of and you must find out about, never contact his friends behind his back to get or give out personal information.

If your son's shyness means he doesn't have many friends, try to help him overcome his inhibitions so that he can actively seek out and develop new relationships. Encourage him to go out and meet people even, or actually, because that involves his breaking away from you. Never demand he be yours and yours alone. Vocally support his having an active outside life and even advise him as to how he can overcome any isolating inhibitions he may have. Is your son relationally challenged on the outside because he doesn't feel completely loved at home, by you, and as a consequence has become too uncertain of how worthwhile he is to feel up to/capable of relating productively to others? Is he living out specific problems he is having with you in the arena of his outside relationships—for example, making a bad choice of partner to parallel and perhaps resolve (according to the principle of the Freudian "repetition compulsion") problems he is having with you at home? If so, expect that improving your relationship with your son might lead him to improve his relationships with friends and potential partners outside the home. Then work toward that goal and, considering the possibility that time is quickly passing, do so as expeditiously as you possibly can.

Chapter 9

Handling a Difficult/ Defiant Gay Son

Being difficult/defiant is not the province of sons of one or another sexual orientation. Thus if gay sons are personally problematical, that is, hard to understand, tricky to cope with, and seemingly nearly impossible to manage, it isn't because they are gay; it is for the same reasons that all sons can be, and often are, challenging for their parents to handle. And parents who understand what makes any son, including a gay son, the way he is—in particular his anxieties and his guilt feelings—are in the best possible position to respond to their son not by feeling annoyed with him, but with genuine compassion not based on a view of him as obnoxious because he is gay, but based on a fair considered evaluation of what is troubling him because he is human.

Still, few parents find it easy to completely befriend a difficult gay son. Too many become irrational instead of even trying. Some turn from loving Moms and Dads into sadistic critics, harsh abusers, dominant and controlling jailers, and tyrannical martinets. Almost all seem to forget that every good parent-son relationship requires a joint effort—not unilateral tyranny but two-way loving, an endeavor consisting of a combination of speaking frankly and listening judiciously; allowing and forbidding; being close when appropriate and firm (if somewhat remote) when indicated; and offering empathy for their son that stops appropriately short not only of being enabling, but also of precluding empathy for themselves.

Many parents think that they should not intervene at all even when a gay son is being difficult. They fear that if they even try to do so, their son will accuse them, and rightly so, of being controlling, judgmental, and moralistic. What they forget is how often a son who is difficult gets into actual trouble and, should that come to pass, how they might wish they had spoken up promptly and forcefully without holding back due to having concluded that "Because my son is gay, I have to forgo following time-tested rules of parenting to passively accept everything he is and does; fully respect him (but not myself); and be guided not by my culture but by his—lest he brand me 'bigoted' and call me 'homophobic.' " Parents should never try to change a son's being gay or ever make their son's sexual orientation an issue at all. But when indicated they must step in if he is being gay in a bad way. They should focus on self-destructive living patterns that do not represent a problem with his being gay, but do suggest that he is having a problem living as a gay man.

Too often parents of difficult sons are concerned solely with whether by intervening in his life problems they are mistreating their gay son. Too infrequently they are too little concerned about whether their son, in affecting their lives, is mistreating them. Parents who discipline firmly will generally get abusive backtalk. But instead of backing off, they should stick with their position as if it is the right one. They should not silently take all of their son's negativity in without replying to it immediately by protesting. What they should always make clear is that they prefer not to be subjected to abuse of any sort, however much their son rationalizes that as politically correct and culturally approved. They should tell their son that they refuse to let him run everything his way and instead intend to quietly establish/reestablish their authority by insisting that they as his parents are entitled to be in charge as much as their son is, while making it perfectly clear that if they don't get respect, they intend to seize power by taking the initiative and indicated forceful action—not just saying "I *wish* I could compel you to be more respectful of me, but I can't, and I am truly sorry about that," but instead instituting real deterrents to bad behavior with the goal of keeping their son from disrespecting them personally by crossing indicated boundaries and disregarding sensible limits. In one case what finally worked was saying, "Straight or gay, you have no right to treat us, your parents, like a doormat or punching bag," only to then soften that with a more conciliatory, "We do care about you, so instead of letting our relationship sour, let's stop fighting, work things out, and come to some reasonable understanding."

Because time heals, be slow to respond in any way that involves no going back. Particularly avoid catastrophic knee-jerk reactions where—panicked—you commit yourself to a negative stance or action prematurely and thus permanently. There is rarely any rush to formulate fixed positional, let alone fixed *destructive* positional, responses. So consider and reconsider your first, more controversial words and deeds, certainly the negative and sometimes even the positive ones, before saying anything of great importance/taking definitive action. Show little of how you feel for as long as possible, always remembering that as the days and weeks go by, situations evolve and all concerned integrate/submerge/resolve many problems—either because changing reality means that the problems are no longer active or because, if the problems are still there, you have changed at least enough to make the problems no longer so pressing.

As parents you should try to understand *why* your son might require intensive discipline in the first place. Whenever possible learn why he is being difficult. That importantly includes determining if you are contributing to his being difficult—and if you are, as he (hopefully) agrees to change for you, you should also agree to change for him.

In particular determine if he is becoming defiant due to emotional trouble, as is discussed in the following paragraphs.

Gay sons with a *narcissistic* streak tend to resist negotiating because to them negotiating with = ingratiating others, which to them = self-abnegating. As argumentative individuals they generally go along with Mom and Dad only when doing so serves one of their particular purposes. As self-oriented boys and men they see others—particularly their parents—as primarily existing in their lives as sources of supply meant for their personal gratification. As omnipotent boys and men, thinking of themselves as all knowing, and additionally being very persuasive about claiming that, they too readily convince their parents of the validity of their (selfish) positions and the reasonableness of their (equally selfish) demands.

Gay sons with a *sadomasochistic* streak want to start a good fight with their parents even though, or just because, that leads to personal suffering all around. Their *sadistic* streak leads them to either consciously and deliberately, or unconsciously and almost in spite of themselves, set out to hurt their parents. As totalitarians they set ideational boundaries they expect their parents to comply with, live by, and respect as they detail the parameters of response they insist that their parents follow. Then if their parents don't do so exactly, their sons condemn them for being unloving/homophobic. So that they can view their parents as bad people suitable for rebelling against, they provoke them, which they often do passive aggressively through button-pushing, as when they bring home undesirable friends and lovers just to inflict them on Mom and Dad, hoping to gall and frighten them into taking, then failing, an important test. They do this simply because they actually desire to find their parents wanting. For equating growing up with moving out and being free and being me, and being free and being me with rebellion, they cannot simply leave home in good standing, but must instead go because they have been done a disservice and thus have been forced out. For if their parents provoked them to leave "because Mom and Dad have become intolerable," they can now leave with few to no guilty regrets. (A son's leaving home should be a joint decision in which his parents participate, not a unilateral act of vengeance whereby the son, engaged in an adolescent rebellion, feeling wounded, stomps out of the house.)

Gay sons with a *histrionic* streak are extremists who overdramatize complaints about their parents as part of their attempt to engineer an emotionally infused self-created reality that they go on to live out as if it is an actuality, which, being born as it is in purely dramatic purposes, often out of desperation, it is not.

Gay sons who are unduly *anxious* panic at the slightest hint that their parents might have lowered their status and defiled their identity, feeling not "My parents are imperfect, so what?" but "All is lost and I am in danger of no longer being able to be me unless I break off with them completely—to be free."

Sons with an *obsessive* streak are perfectionists compelled to chastise their parents for being but slightly imperfect, especially if and when the parental "imperfection" involves not being fully positive toward their son. For such sons, anything short of their parents' full acceptance of them constitutes full devaluation and rejection—an active and total siding with the homophobic enemy. Also for such sons, parents who are not all good (all parents) are not any good at all.

Bipolar sons are irritable across the board. A free-floating irritability results in their being upset by almost everything their parents say and do, with fights and temper tantrums a predictable result.

Sons with a *paranoid* streak, which is so common in adolescents as to be virtually normal, dislike their parents due to having irrational suspicions of them. Even though their parents love them and treat them well, they nevertheless still believe that, and even claim and act as if, their parents are mistreating/bullying them. For one son, his parents saying, "We have your best interests at heart and are trying to implement that" led him to think, "You are trying to control me." His parents saying, "We are just trying to set appropriate limits" led him to think, "You are trying to castrate me." For such sons actually positive/accommodating Moms and Dads become in the son's astigmatic eyes accusatory, controlling, condemnatory, and intolerant as the son misinterprets reasonable parental suggestions as unacceptable attacks, and kindly overtures by understanding, long-suffering, rational, parents as intrusive assaults. Such a son says, "I am going to give you, Mom and Dad, an ultimatum, and tell you 'I will live here with you until I'm ready to move out, but when I move out, you will not hear from me again for a month, then I will contact you, and if you still haven't stopped aggravating me by then, I will never forgive you, and I will cut off all relationships with you forever.' "

A son, being irrationally critical of his parents, read anything less than his parents' full approval of everything he said and did as their being disdainful of or bigoted toward him. This young man, just getting settled in the gay life, was, perhaps like any other new settler, hypervigilant about—and fixated on developing, affirming, and protecting—his emerging new identity. So to that end he (too) clearly delineated strict comfort boundaries he didn't want his parents to cross—meaning that he interpreted any parental advice/suggestion as an incursion/full frontal attack meant to dislodge him from a favored position. As an upshot, to keep his parents from breaching a defensive self-protective line, he maintained a barricade/protective wall that he forced his parents to retreat behind, a boundary he drew and considered inviolable. He was maintaining "his impenetrable self," which for him meant resolutely keeping his parents out of his intimate life due to a fear that they might try to deprogram him and bring him back into some homonegative fold. His parents, rationally, felt that their input could have made his life better. So they tried to help him live a better life through persuasion and other "reasonable" interventions. But that had the reverse effect. For all they accomplished was to make him so fully uncompromising that his way out was to become completely radicalized, as he put it, "just to get back at them and the society that they represent."

As a newly minted activist, this son acted out against his parents in an adolescent way (in the *troubled adolescent* sense of the term) long after his teen years had passed. He did so because he felt he had to have a foil to properly develop and retain his new, radicalized self—and his parents made the ideal candidates for being thusly cast, for they were people who both contrasted with his ideals and were right there on the spot as the convenient "enemy" for him to vanquish and triumph over. He cast his parents into this role so that he could make his identity creation and maintenance the centerpiece of his life—even to the extent that he would not attend his own twenty-first birthday party, one they were giving in their home in his honor, because he felt that to do so "was regressive" and far too "proestablishment." On the few occasions when he did visit his parents, he grabbed his computer and phone, and sulkily retreated to his old bedroom to text his buddies in privacy, refusing to talk to his parents or any of their friends, preferring instead to openly ignore them in favor of hatching further plans to rebel—plotting with the guys, people he considered to be his full accomplices/compatriots/only acceptable companions.

A paranoid son became unjustifiably suspicious of his parents' intentions and distorted their goals negatively due to projecting his inner thoughts and feelings onto them. His projecting led him to make his issues into his parents' issues, in particular, attributing his own self-hatred to his parents, to the point that he came to believe that his parents hated him. "You feel negatively toward me" was his belief, and that was simply the product of feeling negatively toward himself first, with outward displacement to them next.

His projecting, like any other psychological defense, was so "natural," so automatic, that his parents couldn't sway him by being fair by attempting to do a reality check to clear things up. No amount of discussion could correct his misperception that his parent's saying, "We love many things about you" meant "There are also many things we hate about you." If one or both of his parents said, "I don't mind having a gay son," he responded, "They are like Lady Macbeth, protesting too much. In denial they are hiding how they really feel about me (for otherwise they wouldn't have brought the topic up in the first place—that is, they wouldn't be so obviously positive if underneath they didn't as obviously feel so negatively)."

Dynamically speaking, paranoid blaming of his parents was his way to cleanse himself of what he believed to be his own wrong thinking and wrongdoing—his way to deny that he had thought, said, or done something bad that deserved his parents' disapproval, and to convince himself that instead he was a completely innocent victim of parents who had it in for him. As he saw it, since his parents were fully guilty of everything, he was not at all blameworthy for anything. He always considered anything bad he did to his parents not as first but as second strike, for it was what his parents deserved, and all he was doing was simply justifiably defending himself by attacking his parents *back* for their having attacked him *first*. Therefore, it was clearly his parents who needed to change their minds about and alter their negative behaviors toward him—and that meant they must say and do exactly what he wanted them to say and do, and along the lines that he had carefully predetermined. That came down to "My parents must be entirely affirmative about everything, and unconditionally advocate for me, their son, even when admittedly I don't necessarily think and behave in a way that merits anything like their full support and affirmation."

Not only did he view parents who actually treated him fairly as his adversaries and persecutors, unfortunately the more fairly his parents treated him the worse it was for them—because he had to work even harder to make them into the persecutors he so desperately needed for the full emotional release and conflict resolution that he so fervently desired.

A son became concerned that his in fact supportive parents were out to provoke, aggravate, hurt, deprive, mistreat, and neglect him because he was gay. For him Mom and Dad were adversaries and enemies, not people who loved him, as they actually did, but people who hated him, which they didn't, and hated him so much that he had no choice but to attack them back, blaming them for starting things, then further attacking them after they responded by claiming innocence in their own defense. Minor deviancies on their part, such as calling him homosexual instead of gay, became triggers for his angrily blaming them for almost everything. Perhaps his parents didn't get everything right, but most of their "wrongs" were trivial and no more serious than the "wrongs" participants in any interpersonal relationship do to each other. Yet he would regularly demand that they improve along specific lines or else, as he said, he would remove himself from them and never see them again.

To a great extent his anger toward them involved projection. That meant he was angrily asking them to make the very changes in their attitude toward him that he unconsciously held about, and knew he needed to make in, himself, toward himself. Making his issues theirs, he blamed externals to deal with/avoid dealing with internals. Instead of taking full responsibility for the fearful things he felt inside, he made his parents shoulder the full blame for what in fact he himself was feeling. Instead of viewing himself as guilty, he viewed himself as innocent never to be proven guilty, and his parents, the reverse, as guilty never to be proven innocent. Creating negative impressions of them out of his own negative impressions of himself led to self-fulfilling pessimistic predictions: doomsday prophesies of how they would think about and act toward him based on formulations of his own devising, in turn mostly reflective of what *he* would think under the circumstances. Thus "I hate myself for being gay" became "You my parents hate me for being queer." The resolution became not "I have to treat myself more kindly and give myself, then you, more of a vote of confidence" but "You must stop hating me and start treating me better, for since your mistreatment of me is what is causing me to feel bad about myself, that's the only way I can feel better about who I am." His view of Mom and Dad as people trying to deprive him of his rights as a son, and as a gay son, was based almost entirely on being unable to see himself as fundamentally okay, someone who can just accept what he desires and ought to have because he is fundamentally sound. Feeling inferior because he was gay, he blamed his parents for devaluing and depriving him—for that very reason.

Cognitively, he would rarely recognize those of their virtues that might soften his predetermined image of them as "losers." He rejected elements of their situation that did not suit his desired interpretation. He drew specific unflattering overall conclusions about them without sufficient evidence after cherry picking one or a few negative details and overvaluing the (negative) overall importance of those—while ignoring other, more important (and salient positive), aspects of his parents as total persons, severely distorting his overview of them and so devaluing his relationship with them significantly.

Predictably he came to dislike his parents completely when he found anything about them to dislike at all. Thus although they treated him well overall, he would remember, then emphasize, only those times when they had (inadvertently) put him down, or didn't give him things even though he did not desperately need, and they couldn't afford, them. And when they did give him what he needed and wanted, he accused them of something else: coming across with the things less rapidly and immediately than he, as "just a normal kid," was entitled to have, right now.

Constantly mining his parents' minds for anger on their parts (that wasn't there in them, for their anger was in fact only his own anger projected outward onto them along the lines of "It takes one to know one"), he read them as being inveterately nasty individuals. And guilty about his own sexuality, he saw them as criticizing him for being gay—and in every innocent look and gesture on their parts. In turn his negative views of his parents insulted them, for they were highly sensitive to what he was thinking. It also frustrated them because when they suggested he was wrong, not only did he disregard their viewpoint, but instead of making changes as they requested, he instead asked them to correct *their* view of *him* because *they* needed to be the ones to change, and in significant ways.

Predictably his parents ultimately became as negative to him as he had at first convinced himself they were. This was because allowing his expectations to guide his actions, he behaved in a way that did not merely anticipate, but actually created, his imperfect reality. And he could now blame Mom and Dad for causing his downfall, although it was he who had provoked his parents to act in a way that validated the pessimistic and angry assumptions about them that daily flooded his mind, further justifying his convictions that they were his adversaries—people who didn't care and who mistreated him in unimaginably harsh ways. Also, because he complained so much, the many negative things he complained about were of sufficient quantity to be of necessity borne out in impressive numbers by chance alone.

Overall he created an atmosphere where his fantasies about himself and his parents ultimately became rigid premises presumably validated by circumstances. That created even more negative everyday expectations that led to what he believed were reasonably pessimistic guideposts for him to live by.

Not surprisingly, all told he made life very difficult for his parents by rebuffing them completely, even though, or especially when, they tried to change their ways, even along lines *he* specifically laid out for them. It didn't seem to matter that they were trying hard to be as kind and helpful to him as anyone could possibly be, and to do exactly as he demanded.

Complicating the situation was the unfortunate truth that his parents, having long ago made mistakes that traumatized him, *had* actually treated him badly when he was young. But in many respects they had seen the error of their ways and had reformed. Still he continued to hold a grudge against them, as if they had neither seen the light nor changed accordingly. He remained frustratingly attuned to what his parents had been like way back when—even though that differed considerably from what they were like in the here and now. This contributed to the dereality that propelled him to behave as if they were his adversaries, and he theirs. His confounding the past with the present by itself gave him reason enough to see his parents as part of the adversarial "establishment" then to use this harsh critique of what they stood for and how they acted (as he saw it) as fodder to convince himself that he should break away from them. He needed to have something to feel outraged about to make their "straight, antagonistic" world a battlefield on whose terrain he could struggle to obtain what he felt he was not getting and would never get—justice and full across-the-board validation—code words he used for a much deeper desire for unadulterated unconditional approval.

Ultimately his relationship with his parents healed when they became full advocates for him. They began to march side by side with him, thus diverting him from the adversarial aspects of the relationship. Activism indeed had become a healing force for the whole family, for it brought son, parents, and the rest of the core family together, in large measure because it led the core trio to adopt a siege mentality where they were no longer against one another, but went hand-in-hand and asked the rest of the clan, and the world, to join them in turn.

As he said, "Mom and Dad's joining PFLAG to themselves become serious activists proved to me how they had recanted/reformed and, regretting their past behavior, were now doing everything that they could to make called-for amends." And, as he said, they were "even showing me they meant it by becoming outwardly oriented, publically demonstrative, vocally intimidating, seriously haranguing, threatening individuals who warned detractors of gay men of the potential for doom and disaster if they didn't shape up, and shape up immediately, and along lines we as part of the gay establishment had predetermined for them." The more his parents proselytized on a large scale, the more they formed and joined supportive cliques advocating a gay-friendly orientation, espousing gay goals, and affirming gay actions, the wider they disseminated homopositive beliefs, the more people they touched and got to join them in their cause of advocating reform, the more he saw them not as adversaries but as allies, and so the more powerfully in his eyes did they reverse the effects of all their earlier negative, presumably discriminatory, behaviors. As he went on to say, in essence, "True, at times their logic is questionable, their personal philosophy sophistic, and their principles slapdash, yet I am so impressed by the sheer force of their arguments/convictions, however specious, and their positive actions, that I feel that they have gone a long way toward their being able to undo their unsupportive misguided present and past attitudes toward me, and in a way that allows me to love them again."

Of course *social influence* contributed to his paranoid "me versus them" philosophy by encouraging him to be fully "me," and as a consequence to feel fully free to completely detach himself from "them," his parents. In a way this attitude on his part also developed in great measure from what one of his therapists said to him. This was a "therapeutic" formulation consisting of an unacknowledged rerun of the old and now disproven psychoanalytic concept from the earlier part of the last century that informed all parents that "what their sons needed to do to grow up was to grow out— to completely detach themselves from their overbearing castrative mothers and fully counteridentify with their passive wimpy fathers so that they could mature into authentic (gay) men full of self-assurance, rid of conflict, and able to self-realize without the burden remaining of being little reproductions of their own ineffectual sires."

Parents can help heal a son's paranoia by intervening supportively via gently challenging their son's adversarial thoughts. They can call his attention to distortions he can and needs to change, always doing so without making him feel guilty. They can do this not by telling him he is wrong, but by saying the equivalent of "You and we don't necessarily see things the same way. Let's identify our differences and explore the reasons for them to see if we can't bring them into focus, on the way to resolving them."

Additionally some parents do have to make certain course corrections related to reducing negativity to a gay son in order to enhance his pride, reduce his shame, and soften his anger. That might involve apologizing as well as making amends and reparations for any suffering they may have actually caused and are currently causing him. If they were once rejecting, they should now be more accepting. If they were once negative, they should now become more positive. If they were once remote, they should now become closer—fostering their son's *healthy* dependency by becoming more lovingly accepting of him. If they were once overly controlling, they should now become more permissive. If they were once excessively competitive, like the father who put his son down because he, his son, threatened to undermine his, the father's, supremacy as a parent, really as a man, they should step back and let/encourage their son to thrive by inspiring him to do better than Dad—selflessly cheering him on to grow well beyond his father's apparent limitations, and to develop capacities beyond those his father possesses. If they once failed to recognize and support his uniqueness, they should now view and treat him as at least *somewhat* special. If they once pushed him to be something and someone not for his but for their benefit, they should back off from their self-centered actions, stop wanting and trying to create a token son out of their own expectations, and reassess what will make him (as distinct from what will make them) happy. If once they bullied him, unless he is catalyzing their bullying by continuously and abrasively making them angry, they must completely stop what they are doing and instead do the opposite—jump to his defense. (All apologies must, however, stop short of parents begging a son to treat them better.)

Unfortunately because a paranoid son's negativity toward his own parents tends to originate in feelings of guilt on his part, his parents attempts to justify themselves by condemning him for mistreating them often make him feel even more sheepish about himself and his behavior, predictably intensifying his adversarial relationship with his parents. Therefore, handle complaints about you as positively as you can, which means free of disrespectful *blaming*. Perhaps, ignoring his negativity entirely, simply identify and respond positively to the things he does well.

Respond positively when he has succeeded, and certainly avoid responding negatively to the good things about him, and avoid putting him down for doing something wrong when in actuality it was something *you* did incorrectly.

Though he may meet your positive responses with negative (paranoid) assaults on you, your hope is that continuing positivity on your part will ultimately undercut his need to see you as an enemy/homohating adversary. Expressing positive feelings for him at the very least deprives him of some of the ammunition he needs, and is looking for, to pull further away from you. It helps him distinguish more clearly the difference between what you did (little to nothing) and what he imagines you to have done (everything). Your positivity also allows/encourages him to incorporate you into his identity so that you become an internalized force for his good—someone he wants to be like, not someone he wants to be as different from as possible.

Never argue with a paranoid son even when you are right and he does, or should, know it. For few paranoid sons are prepared to acknowledge, at least for the moment, that you have a point. And of course never try to argue him out of being gay or otherwise challenge any of his other legitimate core identities.

If you can't stop being critical of (or otherwise negative toward) him, try to understand why you must continue in this critical vein. It is likely that your criticism of him is really a self-criticism. As his criticism of you starts with a self-criticism, it is likely that your inability to accept your son as he is virtually always starts with your inability to accept yourself as you are. That makes your antagonism a projection onto him of the antagonism you feel toward yourself. It is also a way to prove to yourself how moral you are, and how by despising him you are different from him and so are in no way yourself like that immoral person he is (and who you so despise). Differentiating yourself from him (the devalued one), though it is a way to enhance your self-esteem, is also (and unfortunately) a way to lower his. It spares you some pain, but it causes him no end of intense suffering.

Chapter 10

Handling an Emotionally Troubled Adolescent Gay Son

Many adolescent gay sons suffer from two problems, often simultaneously: those primarily associated with being gay, such as difficulties that are the outcome of victimization by homohatred, and disorders of *adolescence*, such as adjustment disorder of adolescence, adolescent rebellion, ADHD, and conduct disorder. Therefore, parents must differentiate between the two sets of problems. This differentiation is especially needed when, as the Psychodynamic Diagnostic Manual (PDM) says, "relationships . . . become disrupted by the child's inability to attend to anything but [his] anxiety and [his] efforts to reduce it."[1]

Adolescent Narcissistic Personality Disorder

Narcissistic adolescent gay sons want their parents at one and the same time to treat them as equals, with equal rights as compared to their straight siblings, *and* to treat them as unique, awarding them special consideration/privileges. Such adolescents typically respond to necessary parental limit-setting as if setting limits on them is not only unnecessary, but also unwanted, being exactly the same thing as oppression. They want advocacy when they need boundaries. But when their parents set boundaries, feeling frightened, they become highly antagonistic and fall into a me-against-my-parents-the-establishment mindset to become no longer their parents' child, but their parents' rival cum mortal enemy.

Adolescent Distancing

Gay adolescent sons often distance themselves from their parents due to imagining that their parents are hopelessly antigay people who predictably favor and side with their straight children, giving their brothers and sisters the greater influence in the family, and more stuff. Some gay adolescent sons then go on to tell their parents, "I never want to see you again because you don't accept my gay life; you hate my gay friends; and you accuse me of taking drugs and having wild promiscuous sex when I don't do anything of the sort." Some leave home for the streets. Others flee to sympathetic relatives, if they have any. And still others create a fictive family out of close friends hoping, but not always with success, to enlist buddy help in separating themselves from their parents and overcoming the isolation that results from being without a family. Too many start drinking, using drugs, getting involved in compulsive bar hopping, and indulging in compulsive sex where multiple short conquests come to substitute for satisfying sustaining long-term relationships. Then they rationalize these behaviors as "just being my gay self" and "doing what all my friends do," although what they are doing is in fact misguided because it is a way to quell anxiety—anxiety about being separated from their family—by reassuring themselves that they are no longer alone and vulnerable, but are instead surrounded by a simpatico peer group that guarantees they will be physically intact and assures them they will be emotionally invulnerable.

While some of these sons need formal therapy, many of them need only more support at home to help them break through the firewalls they have erected against "these bad parents of mine." Conversely, unsupportive parents make the distancing worse by rendering their son less confident due to having lowered his already low self-esteem by becoming punitive toward, remote from, and critical of him. Thus one Mom and Dad, emphasizing their son's bad points, constantly reminded him of the deficiency in every one of his virtues, for example, "You may be bright, but still you are less a misunderstood genius than an ordinary misguided person."

Parents whose sons are distanced from them ought to try to help their son feel more comfortable at home—by devaluing him less and instead acknowledging his relational anxiety, identifying it as a problem, then analyzing what it is that is making him so anxious. After trying to exactly determine the cause of his anxiety, they should make an effort to act toward him in a restitutive/curative way. For example, they might try to become less intimidating by using what they learn about his makeup to scrupulously refrain from stressing him in areas where he has proven sensitive. Thus if he is sensitive to criticism, and it is their criticism that is making him anxious and depressed, they should reverse course, patiently hear him out, and whenever possible instead of calling him names like "irrational" acknowledge him as the opposite (e.g., "reasonable").

Adolescent Rebellion

Rebellious adolescents deliberately set out to make it difficult for the sincerest, most tolerant parents to fully endure them and/or successfully intervene when the adolescents refuse to stop acting the part of "the intolerable child." Such sons exhaust and demoralize their parents by discounting all their helpful suggestion as misguided, ineffectual, and/or intrusive until their parents completely run out of ideas as to how they can do better by their son and have no more suggestions as to how they can help. These sons tend to counter parental positivity with complaints about being enveloped. They likely offer up academic philosophical excuses for their own questionable behavior, particularly musings on the paralytic effects of parental discipline on their freedom—because, as they see it, parental discipline by definition lowers their self-esteem, and parental interference thwarts their objective of self-fulfillment—and so they have no alternative but to continue to behave as badly as before. Simultaneously they turn valid parental advice, especially that dealing with sexual issues and choice of profession, into power struggles about presumed authoritarian meddling, which they go on to condemn as being solidly homonegative. Should parents ask their son to think about his future by choosing a partner or selecting a profession wisely from the start, their son counters by insisting that he be allowed to go his own way "to be me, myself," even when he is too early in the process of developing an identity, or too seriously conflicted about what his identity is and should be, to "do his own thing" properly, that is, in a practical and creative fashion. Though such sons insist that they want a good life and to have it they must "do what I love," they must consider that what they love might not love them back.

(Adolescent) Conduct Disorder

Adolescents with a conduct disorder act out, often with substance abuse and promiscuity, not because they are gay and as such impulsive and unreliable, but as part of their quest to heal a deficient sense of self and satisfy/solidify/strengthen a shaky identity. Such gay adolescents often overshoot by emphasizing their "gay identity" to excess and to the exclusion of other identities that, while these currently seem to them to be less essential, are in fact immediately and in the long run just as important, significant, and meaningful. There is often a noteworthy "me-against-them" component to their "bad" conduct, as they view their parents as adversaries then protest against being persecuted by them along the lines of "You, being old, straight and homophobic, don't understand me, being young and gay" and "I *will* be gay all the way no matter what you say, and if you try to interfere with me, after calling you stupid I will never speak to you again." In such cases coming out may not be motivated solely by a need for self-realization, or even involve a self-satisfying, self-fulfilling confessional, but instead be propelled, at least in part, by defensive bravado meant to triumph in various, typical, adolescent parent-son struggles—making coming out not a way to grow, but an excuse to fight.

Adolescents with a conduct disorder lie to their parents, but they do so less because they are psychopathic and more because lacking in self-respect, they feel vulnerable to being discovered as defective. If they remain closeted to their parents, it is less because they are deceitful and more because they are holding back/hiding to protect themselves from "fatal discovery"—not so much that they are gay, but that they are in a general way more human than anything else. They often become deliberately provocative at home for the express purpose of self-definition through enhancement of their identity via oppositionalism. Often to get back at parents whom they disdain (and whom they feel disdain them) they stay out all night or become truant, running away from home to join with others whom they feel won't savage them—peers they perceive to be welcoming in a way that is exactly the opposite of how their parents have unfriended them. Some become seriously socially autistic, that is, they become insensitive to their parents'/everyone else's feelings in part because they convince themselves, motivated by reasoning that should be, and often is, obviously specious, that because their actions don't have outcomes, they can get away with anything. Making the "pleasure principle" their main guiding light, they do only what feels good, including taking drugs and having unsafe sex, with little to no concern for the consequences. (The pleasure principle, as distinct from the reality principle, emphasizes gratification in the here and how at the expense of being soberly concerned with the future.)

Sons with a conduct disorder put their parents in a classic double bind: between parental permissiveness (so as not to appear overly intrusive), and parental intrusiveness (so as not to appear overly permissive). I believe that parents should err on the side of strongly intervening in situations where their son is in immediate/serious danger, while remaining relatively passive (permissive) when not much is at stake and the sensible view is that things are likely even now to be better than they seem, and to improve on their own over time. I also strongly believe that intervening with sons who have a conduct disorder is not per se homonegative, even if it inevitably does involve some degree of devaluing and even moralizing along the lines of making such assumptions as "There is a definable right way and a determinable wrong way to do things."

When one parent favors intervention and another parent favors laxity, often a struggle over what to do ensues. Too often the goal becomes winning over the spouse ideologically when that should be secondary to another goal: resolving spousal differences to determine, and do, what's best for a son. For conduct disordered sons often get themselves into serious difficulties; and when a son is in danger, both parents owe it to him to put internal family struggles aside and do what is best for him, even though that may mean temporarily antagonizing the other parent. Hurt spousal feelings generally diminish or go away completely in the short or long run, but a son's hurt body doesn't always heal, no matter how long one waits for that to happen.

Properly setting limits in these situations starts with not confounding "understanding" bad behavior with actually limiting it, in effect thinking that one has exorcized it by having analyzed it, as if there is a practical remedial value just to scientifically determining what is going on. Recognizing that "He takes drugs because he is demoralized" or "because he is anxious and guilty about his sexuality" or "because he has an affective dysphoria (he feels uncomfortable and unhappy)," or "because he is valiantly attempting to feel real and involved again," is a means that by itself accomplishes no useful end. These concepts may be true, but ideas alone go nowhere unless accompanied by firm, rational, limiting/boundary establishing implementation/follow-through.

Parents whose conduct-disordered son has friends who encourage his bad conduct are generally torn between not intervening and thereby allowing bad-companions to go unchecked, and discouraging bad companions and thereby risking making them seem even more intriguing. I often recommend that parents so conflicted use modeling as the intervention of choice. Here they indicate how *they* handled/might handle friends who had/might have a bad influence over them. Conversely, parents with a conduct disorder of their own must not catalyze their son's bad behavior by showing and telling him how to behave badly, often defiantly, by exemplifying personal bad behavior/defiance. (However, this said, parents should take care in intervening through modeling because it can be condescending and insulting to assume that as a gay man your son needs you, or someone like you, someone strong and successful, unlike him, to be his role model. This is a put down because it implies that all gay men are sufficiently confounded to require an outside stabilizing force and suggests that, never role models themselves, gay men are instead always in need of someone to emulate, with almost anyone supposedly more solid than they are.)

In my experience, it is often a good idea for parents and therapists before recommending/giving a son suffering from a conduct disorder psychoactive drugs to first recommend and try psychotherapy. Psychotherapy with a son with a conduct disorder can profitably help him see himself and his situation in a new and better light. A positive relationship with a therapist can by itself diminish the negative effects of problematical relationships at home. It is especially beneficial for sons to learn how, when, and where they are projecting—blaming/scapegoating everyone else, from bullies at school to parents at home, for problems of their own—and doing that just so that they can continue to have fun without feeling guilty or concerned about the future.

Adolescent Depression

Gay adolescents often suffer from spells of depression. Sometimes these are precipitated by an external event, and sometimes they are endogenous, that is, they come on without an at least obvious precipitant.

Adolescent depression, particularly when of a less serious/pervasive nature, is often difficult to distinguish from grief/mourning. The presence of a loss is not necessarily a reliable differential criterion (favoring the diagnosis of grief) since, especially for adolescents, it is never clear what does and what does not actually constitute a "loss." When it comes to losses, all adolescents are especially vulnerable to fantasizing them, thinking they have had losses that in fact have never occurred, or viewing minor losses that have actually occurred as major.

This said, many gay adolescents suffer from real losses. These often involve breakups, which are particularly toxic when they are one way, that is, when the adolescent has been dumped. (As discussed later in this chapter, an adolescent who has been dumped may very well be in serious emotional danger.)

Symptomatically, depressed adolescents readily feel sad, easily become irritable, and regularly have outbursts of temper. Many experience fatigue and some loss of interest in life. Typically they suffer from feeling guilty and worthless. Suicidal thoughts are generally present, and as the PDM says, "depressed [gay] adolescent[s are also] at [special] risk for substance abuse."[2] Typically their personal negative self-evaluation/self-estimation leads them to view the losses that all adolescents routinely passively experience as ones they somehow irresponsibly, or due to "being a personal failure," actively brought on themselves. For as the PDM says, they believe, generally without foundation, that having brought them on themselves they "could have [somehow done more to have] prevented [these things] from happening."[3]

Depressed adolescents are often angry people whose anger is highly destructive not only to others, but also to themselves—the latter especially taking the form of using and abusing substances or of deliberately giving themselves a disease then rationalizing what they did, although it is in fact self-destructive, as "I do this in order to belong," as an "adolescent badge of pride" (thus revealing the real, compensatory, reason behind their acting-out behavior: "I don't feel welcome anywhere, and especially by my parents, for rather I feel ashamed everywhere, especially at home"). Under such circumstances parents often feel, and actually are, under attack from the "depression fallout." If this is the case, instead of retaliating parents should remain as supportive as they can throughout—no matter how tempted they are to do otherwise. Being supportive is generally facilitated by not taking what seem to be personal, but are actually impersonal, attacks personally and so viewing the adolescent anger not as a comment upon them, the parents, but as a self-revelation by him, their son. Seeing things this way makes it easier for parents to respond not vengefully but by intensified handholding and to continue to respond that way even though at first their son reflexively pulls/pushes them away.

Often a depressed son's denial defenses predominate, as depressed adolescents bury their negative self-estimation, as the PDM says, to give themselves and others "the impression that the traumata [of their lives have] not affected them."[4] Adolescents thus in denial tend to take the next step and frantically seek one relationship after another so that they don't feel completely relationally deprived. In particular they seek strangers to make up for what they believe they are missing/have lost in the way of partners/family/friends. Defensive attitudes often called "arrogant entitlement" that can drive others away often accompany their denial, as when they manifest gay pride abrasively or come out in a way that makes disclosure less a process of self-realization than a method for enhancing an excessively (inappropriately) low self-image through the devaluing of others. Defensive remoteness sometimes exists. It constitutes an attempt to avoid getting rejected, is a result of feeling mournful and despondent, and is a way to get back at parents (and other significant others whom the adolescent believes have both provoked and failed him) by shunning them. By being remote the depressive adolescent son nonverbally accuses others of not understanding and of being critical and bigoted toward him, and punishes them for having sinned—against him, and, more widely, against the gay subculture itself.

Unfortunately, insofar as a remedy goes, depressed sons generally do not fully appreciate the loving their parents try to give them and even pay their loving parents back by condemning them as being intrusive toward (e.g., infantilizing) them. Nevertheless, such sons, although at first they generally don't admit it, tend to quietly appreciate the parental offer of love and see their parents' efforts in this direction as sustaining. Conversely, parents who respond to their son's seeming refusal to immediately accept their love by themselves becoming permanently less loving/retaliatively unfriendly/ punitive forfeit the possibility of ever giving their son the support he is crying out for, diminishing the possibility that he will thank them in retrospect as in time he comes to appreciate their being there for him during this difficult period in his life. Even as your son rebuffs you he will likely be silently thanking you for having refrained from turning on him in response to his being difficult, and for instead having moved in with support and concern during his darkest hour. So instead of becoming impatiently unsupportive without compassion, stand by him and see him through what is likely to be for him, as it is for you, a very difficult phase of life.

Parents with a seriously depressed adolescent son should consider seeking help for themselves, and their son, beyond advocacy groups. Though advocacy groups provide someone to talk to, and offer support, that may not be enough. This, often a crisis situation, likely calls for someone professionally trained who knows not only how to listen, but also has the formal technique to respond therapeutically in a curative way.

Pharmacotherapy for a depressed son, and sometimes for his parents, is an option that should be considered. But it shouldn't automatically be the primary intervention unless the response needs to be radical because the problem is acute, serious, or even a life is at stake.

Adolescent Bipolar Disorder

Adolescent bipolar sons suffer from painful mood shifts, often seemingly unprovoked. Unprovoked episodes of rage typically occur and give such sons a reputation for being highly sensitive persons, however much they fundamentally lack sensitivity to others' feelings and needs. The anger outbursts are often accompanied by/alternate with frequent and prolonged periods of despair. These sons also seem "driven by impulses" due, as the PDM notes, to being "hypersexual and ... exhibit[ing] poor judgment"[5] in sexual and other venues. In a vicious cycle bad mood spins off negative thinking that cycles back to intensify the bad mood, ultimately unhelpfully affecting relationships both at home with a son's parents and outside the home, making the son globally relatively unmanageable and unreachable, creating interpersonal tension that then feeds back to put the son in an even worse mood.

According to the PDM, adolescent bipolar disorder puts the sufferer at an especially "high risk for harm to self or others." Because they are "highly sensitive, irritable, inconsolable," and at times "oppositional and disruptive," these individuals come to have a high risk for "self-mutilation, substance abuse, and suicide."[6]

Bipolar sons often become paranoid when they personalize others' mixed motives and behaviors as being *fully* homonegative. Typically they see a "half-full" compliment as a "half-empty" criticism. So when their parents say, "Some of my best friends are gay," they hear, "Only some? Is that because most gay men are your enemies?" They see hatred shadowing every expression of love, along the lines of others protesting too much, and they too clearly fathom the (unconscious) negative possibilities in statements at least in part consciously meant to be positive. Misinterpreting unconscious negative contaminants as primarily conscious negative positional statements, they make negative mountains out of neutral/slightly negative molehills. As a result, subjecting parental love to intense surveillance, they irrationally scorn their parents after having detected what are in fact their but minor negative trends and, seizing upon these, use them as "evidence" to justify finding Mom and Dad thoroughly contemptible.

Parents of such sons need to expeditiously reality test their son's paranoid misattributions. They can also try to prevent misattributions from taking hold by carefully explaining in order to mollify their parental position. While as parents you cannot always avoid making statements and indulging in behaviors that contain a hint of negativity, you can at least hope to minimize the effects of this negativity on your son by clearly stating that overall you do not intend to be, and in fact don't actually think you are being, antagonistic toward him.

Parents must always alter their approach to their son as his moods cycle—setting limits in his manic phase then doing an about face (as he does), offering support and personal validation (amounting to enhanced permissiveness) in his depressed phase.

Cautious parents should consider putting suicidal bipolar adolescents on a "parental suicide watch." At the minimum you might make a pact with your child that he won't attempt/commit suicide without first telling you of his wishes/intent, thus giving you a chance to intervene to prevent any such ill-considered action on his part.

You may have to take more stringent measures of control. Parents have to decide for themselves if monitoring a bipolar adolescent son's Internet usage to spot danger and intervene in a timely fashion creates more problems than it solves. Most parents of younger bipolar adolescent sons will want to monitor not only their son's Internet usage, but also, more directly, who he has for friends, identifying, and when necessary discouraging, problematical activities and relationships. This approach may not be immediately fruitful, and your son will likely protest. But his protests will generally be superficial and temporary, and mostly worth tolerating for now because a small amount of parental intervention can prevent a very large loss—of your son's health (and yours), or even of his life (and your life as well).

Adolescent Suicidality

Strictly gay-related issues rarely fully explain suicidality in gay sons. These issues may act as immediate provocative agents, but they are often less central than extant emotional problems of a general nature.

Suicidality can be a problem even for adolescent sons who are not unipolar, bipolar, depressed, paranoid, and in fact are not suffering from any emotional problem/disorder at all. For some "normative" gay sons can become suicidal mainly as the result of circumstances, and in particular as a result of being bullied. Generally being homophobically bullied, itself bad enough, becomes even more devastating for those who are vulnerable due to extant conflicts about being gay. The bullies make them feel more ashamed of themselves than before by giving them what they believe to be a new reason to lack pride in themselves, thus fueling the feeling that they are completely worthless.

Suicide often represents a way to escape from a difficult relationship with a parent/partner/classmate, one believed to be, or one who actually is, devaluing or rejecting the individual. The desire to escape through suicide is often fed by the need to angrily get back at those left behind—often those who having been bullies are as such felt to be deserving of being punished by being made to feel guilty along the lines of "Look what you have done to me."

Dynamically speaking, not a few gay adolescents become suicidal because they internalize their own aggressive wishes toward a parent or an intimate. This is particularly true for gay adolescents who are furious about just having been dumped. Those of us who have never been dumped, or are not particularly sensitive to a dumping that has actually occurred, have a hard time imagining how intense the response can be to, and how it can take months or even years for any man or woman, straight or gay, to recover from, the experience. Therefore, parents need to be especially alert after a gay son complains that a friend/partner has dumped him. As his parents you should neither ignore this event nor pull back from your son because of your own homonegative feelings about being gay and gay relationships along the lines of "We told you so. They never work." You can, and often should, intervene by serving as a substitute (transitional) object for your son, while also actively rallying the family around him, all in the service of reducing his loneliness and isolation. Simultaneously you might even be able to help your son find a new relationship/partner should he be ready for one. Conversely, your position should not be, "Give up, I told you so." Rather it should be, "Don't give up because you think that all gay relationships are unsatisfactory and that what just happened to you proves it's smart to forget about all of them before you get hurt again."

As parents you should always take any adolescent son's expressed suicidal fantasies seriously. It is never wise to minimize his suicidal ideation along the lines of "Think of all the other people worse off than you. There is no reason to get upset over such a small thing." For if your teenager gets upset over something, that thing is by definition, for him, not something small but something big, something important, not something trivial, something if not inherently completely devastating than at least quite upsetting. Calling real suicidal attempts "gestures" that are just a way to get attention is also dangerously dismissive. Because the consequences of overlooking/dismissing suicidality are far greater than the consequences of overreacting to a suicidal threat/act, overreaction should generally be considered the default action, even though the teenager protests along the lines of "You are messing in my life, making things worse, and should stop it right now"—and even though in retrospect you might legitimately feel "We could have let that pass" (but at the time how were you to know?).

Adolescent Grief

When your son seems troubled in any way, including being depressed and suicidal, try to connect his troubles to specific *losses*, both literal and figurative, that he may have experienced. For example, being bullied often results in several simultaneous losses: of high self-esteem, self-pride, self-reliance, and the strength needed to cope. If you are wrong about the losses and over-interpret their significance, it won't necessarily matter much. But it will certainly matter a great deal if you, overlooking a loss and its consequences, remain steadfastly implacable and callous in the face of your son's grief. Just because a loss seems minor to you doesn't mean that it's minor to him. As parents you should always avoid minimizing your son's plight by saying something like "You shouldn't react that way to something so trivial." Instead you should attempt to specifically identify what your son feels he has lost and how that troubles him, and help him cope with that issue exactly so that he can put the loss into perspective both intellectually and emotionally, while you try to make up for his loss directly by taking special care to be there for him, as much as possible, at all times, and whenever he needs you.

If his loss has the effect of lowering his self-esteem, start with helping him distinguish between self-esteem that is appropriately and self-esteem that is inappropriately low. If your son's self esteem is appropriately low, he needs you to set limits on him so that he stops behaving in self-destructive ways that leave him less than proud of himself. If your son's self-esteem is inappropriately low, for example, because he views being gay as the reason he has lost so much, or everything, do the opposite and give him support by making it clear to him that you love him for who he is and don't expect him to become someone else. Also hold him close and try to at least temporarily make up for what he feels he has, or has actually, lost. Never, sensing that he is down and relatively defenseless, use his temporarily weakened state as an opportunity to get through to him about/assault him for things you have always held against him because you think, "He is now too damaged to hold us off or to fight back."

A mother was taking care of her son when he was convalescing from an illness (a STD, or sexually transmitted disease) lasting several months (from which he subsequently fully recovered). Her son had few friends at the time because he had just broken up with his lover, and all their mutual friends went with his partner. (Indeed the breakup had simultaneously weakened his immune system and prompted him to act out sexually so that he became sexually compulsive and immunologically suppressed at the same time.) Inspired to greater heights by his self-blame over having "messed up," his mother moved in for the kill (she had always resented him for being gay) by making fun of him for not having any friends at all and thus humiliating him when he was feeling at his lowest over being all alone and friendless. Instead of criticizing him for being bereft, she should have offered him her companionship to ease his pain, along with philosophical and practical suggestions about how he could go about making things better for himself in the future. (Parents who temporarily substitute as transitional objects for a son's losses discover that though their son might at the time fail to fully appreciate what they are doing for him—because "You don't begin to fully approximate what I have lost"—they will likely discover that this, a time of enhanced vulnerability, is often a time of maximal positive impressionability and so a good time for parents to suggest life-improving changes that their son can implement to avoid a repeat of the same situation.)

Of course, no matter what you do and how well you do it, some grieving sons will see parental intervention as an unwelcome incursion into their personal lives and respond with disrespect by becoming critical of you—demanding that you stop trying to get too close and "Quit trying to get me to change because that way you are treating me as a passive and dependent person." Grieving sons will react especially negatively if they are too masochistic to accept help, too cynical to buy into being loved (especially from "members of the establishment" like their parents), too critical to identify with "someone as outdated as you," and too independent/rebellious to take advice from anyone, not even a therapist, with the possible exception of favored peers. In such cases parental attempts at getting close can have the opposite effect, inspiring an avoidant sadistic son to denounce his parents for not staying away and even for being gay unfriendly "because you haven't learned enough about gay life to appreciate how badly I feel, and, being too eager to help me, are clearly, stupidly, viewing me as being someone who by needing your help is therefore by definition weak and helpless." But you as parents should cut through these (generally unwarranted) protests and make it clear what you are trying to do, why, and that being helpful is hard enough without your son's invalidating the difficult depleting work you are doing on his behalf.

I have worked with parents who helped their son get over a loss simply by showing him how much they needed him. In one case a son got seriously depressed because he lost his lover. His depression cleared up almost completely when his mother got sick and asked him to take care of her. He felt useful, he felt involved, and he told me that the lynchpin of his recovery was discovering how much his mother actually needed and depended upon him.

Sons grieving over a partner's death often require special care and attention. Because my family never acknowledged how hard it was for me to lose a partner who died unexpectedly and at a very young age, I had to deal with four insults: my partner's loss, thinking his death was my comeuppance for how I treated him; having to weep alone; and, since it's hard to hide one's sexual orientation when grieving for a same-sex partner, having to come out to my extended family for the first time, and at a time like that.

If only because the majority of gay men view being gay as an asset, not as a liability, parents should not even think of trying to help their son get over the pain that "his being homosexual is clearly causing him." This is condescending and insulting, and will likely further lower his self-esteem by implying that since he needs to make major changes, he must in the first place have a problem of major proportions.

Adolescent Posttraumatic Stress Disorder

Most adolescents suffer from many adversities, of all types, but thankfully these usually fall short of being so unbearably traumatic that they result in full posttraumatic stress disorder (PTSD). Most gay adolescents experiencing crises/hardships become only temporarily destabilized, and act out at most moderately. But some gay adolescents after experiencing certain traumas— even traumas that on the surface seem more mild than severe—go on to actively develop PTSD. These adolescents do especially poorly when their parents further traumatize them by criticizing their sexual orientation/life while failing to give them the gentle encouragement they need to proudly face the world again and develop a new, healthier, trauma-resistant, even trauma-proof, attitude and functionality. Matters certainly turn ugly when one or both parents are sadists who respond negatively because for them their son's symptoms are the first blood they take as their opportunity to move in for the kill—or at least to wound him further. Sadistic parents take this as a good time to acknowledge a son's weaknesses but not his accomplishments. They angrily/vengefully deaffirm what is positive about him. In rare instances they even deliberately (if only unconsciously) set out to increase his difficulties by giving him bad advice along the lines of "When bullied, fight back, son, for being a peacemaker is being a sissy." Particularly devastating are parental infantilisms like temper tantrums over his being gay, giving him the silent treatment, and undercutting him passive aggressively, subtly, say by withholding needed positivity as their way to convey to him indirectly how they are basically uncaring and unloving. What their son needs at traumatic times is supportive parents who accept the gay life as a viable alternate to their own, ask few embarrassing questions, and withhold even indicated criticisms, at least for a while, just to avoid alienating their son at such a time which is one of great sensitivity due to so many raw painful feelings being ascendant.

Adjustment Disorder of Adolescence/Attention Deficit Disorder

Parents must distinguish adjustment disorder of adolescence from PTSD of adolescence. Both begin after a discrete trauma, but in the former the response is immediate (not delayed as it often is in PTSD) and, at least in gay adolescents, the majority of whom are more resilient than their parents think, and the literature suggests, usually self-limited/nonrecurrent. Parents should also differentiate attention deficit/hyperactivity disorder of adolescence from PTSD of adolescence. The former often develops after overstimulation, particularly of the kind that can occur when a gay adolescent son, enticed by the newness of gay experiences, gets too actively and deeply involved in gay life, overdoing it only to become excessively preoccupied with/enmeshed in the positive aspects of being gay without appreciating the downsides, particularly the severe disappointments and rejections that are so often the consequence of multiple relational attempts that, because of the sheer numbers involved, are for that reason alone likely to lead to serial relational failures that prove cumulatively devastating.

As parents you should not attribute any of the just discussed emotional states entirely to your son being gay. Gay men who act out may act out in a gay way, but their acting out is not pathognomonic (specific for/characteristic of) of being gay along the lines of "All gays are sexually compulsive." Rather it is more likely to be characteristic of a psychological disorder that just happens to exist in someone who also happens to be gay. Therefore, all acting out behaviors in gays should be primarily viewed and explained along familiar psychopathological lines, and only secondarily attributed to being gay in any way when specific identifiable gay-related provocations, particularly discrete losses of significant others, are clearly present and active. Especially, parents should never dismiss relational disappointments as par for the gay adolescent course—assuming that "All gay men have relationship problems" when in fact, as with anyone else, so many "gay relational problems" are instead either strictly part of life and the bad luck of the draw, or primarily attributable to unrelated emotional difficulties in ascendency at a difficult time.

Parents should certainly not focus on gay-related relational issues when other, often just as important, often equally painful, adolescent issues are active and need attention. These issues include relational difficulties with peers and teachers at school and are likely not limited to being bullied, but also involve the bullying of others. Difficulties with career choice sometimes also need attention, in particular the typical adolescent conflict between being true to oneself by following one's natural, if impractical, bent and being practical for oneself by following good solid vocational principles, including preparing for and getting a job that one might not fully love but will at least enable one to have a viable career and make some sort of a living.

Chapter 11

Establishing Boundaries/
Setting Limits

An Overview

Too many parents think that because their son is gay, he will be less likely to hear and accept their limit-setting on any or all aspects of his behavior. As a result they fail to properly supervise their son even though, gay or straight, he clearly needs their intervention. The son, effectively given permission to do what he likes or even to actually be defiant, accepts the challenge then enmeshes his parents in a sadomasochistic brawl where his greatest joy comes from being rebellious—striking out to score negative points against, and create hurt feelings in, people he should love—not only because of who they happen to be, but also because they happen to love him a lot. Perhaps to make a point, he becomes dangerously promiscuous, runs away from home, or provokes his parents to kick him out of the house. Just recently I emerged from a train station onto a gay thoroughfare in New York City at 7:00 in the morning to find myself in the midst of a dozen or so gay teenagers wandering aimlessly about, obviously having been out all night, possibly dissipating, and possibly underemployed or employed hustling to pay for hormones/drugs. One of my first thoughts was, "I believe that in bringing them up their parents *should* have been a little more judgmental." Then when I overheard them talking, loudly, I became certain of the fact. For some of them, clearly without homes, were announcing, almost proudly, that they had been kicked out of the house because they were gay. But I surmised that there might have been another reason besides, or in addition to, their being gay that led them to be kicked out. They might have been asked to leave because they were as difficult at home as they were in the street. They might have become less difficult had their parents brought them up differently instead of raising them too permissively and then giving up on them completely. They might have become less difficult if in place of withholding needed discipline, their parents had brought them up short with firmness that involved the timely establishment of sensible boundaries and the rapid setting of reasonable limits.

Setting limits on your son doesn't necessarily mean "cracking down" on him. What it does involve is:

- Being his colleague without being either overly accommodating or excessively controlling, and being his friend, while still remaining his parent. Giving him what he wants, needs, and legitimately should have, not unreasonably withholding these things in the name of properly firm parenting but—especially when true danger looms—still drawing the line when required, even if that means stifling select aspects of his personality and potential for self-realization and creativity.
- Being supportive and affirming without becoming pathologically enabling where in caring too much, you in fact lead him on to become careless.
- Giving him the freedom he needs to express and be himself without selectively imposing your own views/ideals on him and pressuring him to blindly conform—helping him accept guidance from you when it makes sense to do so, and/or is absolutely necessary to prevent his becoming the victim of his own immaturity and falling under the spell and influence of bad companions, thus protecting him, but doing so without shutting him up in a protective bubble.
- Giving him his freedom but asking him to respect the limits of how much freedom on his part *you* can tolerate.
- Helping him resolve problems that he seems incapable of handling on his own, without pushing him toward resolving them/succeeding in life exactly in the way that, though right for you, is wrong for him.
- Encouraging him to firm up his own identity but to achieve his goals, not yours.
- Encouraging him to be active while discouraging him from acting out that involves too much being "all me" and excessively "completely free."
- Being involved in his activities of everyday living, without being too active/forceful/overly involved in his private life.
- Allowing him to learn by doing, but without floundering, by allowing him to determine his own goals and objectives, and seek his own level of satisfying achievement by making his own mistakes, but not allowing him to make ones that are seriously irreversible because he is young and his judgment is not yet fully developed.
- Being ambitious for him without sending him off on journeys that he does not want to take, is unlikely to complete, and will be ill-equipped to survive.

No parent can always achieve a happy medium, always satisfactorily resolving dilemmas about how, why, and when to set limits. For some dilemmas, because they are built into the parenting process, are not always easily resolvable. The objective is to act as reasonably as you can in murky areas—to set limits benignly, but effectively, under what are likely to be the most challenging of circumstances. It helps if you as his parents make it clear that it's not "Listen to me, I know best" but "I am trying to help you be happier and more effective, not only for me, but also for you, so let's work together toward that common goal."

Consider sharing with your son that you know he needs to view you as part of the (hated) establishment—the arbitrary parents who always know best because they always know everything. Then reassure him that the authority that is vested in you as parents doesn't mean that you are by definition trying to be authoritarian and hence the enemy. Make certain he knows you understand that a degree of independence on his part is healthy, but that being independent does not require seeing your offers of friendly help as harassment; your desire to get close enough to share his joys while identifying his challenges as a wish to make him dependent on you; and your love for him strictly as part of your insidious plan to make him over in your own image. As you set limits on him, reassure him that you are trying to protect, not disrespect him; to educate, not hound him; and, fully aware that he does as many things right as wrong, are not, by focusing on his liabilities, thereby necessarily minimizing his assets. You are not looking to find an insidious method for asking him to mend his ways. What you are trying to do is suggest specific acceptable creative doable alternatives to things that need changing. You are not just issuing edicts, but are throwing out good ideas. Then, if he likes them, you want to help him implement them. Tell him that since you recognize he basically needs and even seeks your guidance, you therefore have sensibly chosen not to abdicate your responsibility to educate in order to strengthen him, however much he may protest. Tell him you are reluctant to withhold discipline out of excessive fear of being judgmental, for without being judgmental you can't offer any guidelines at all, since even asking your son to "use good judgment" requires being judgmental! At the same time, reassure him that you are not in any way, at least not intentionally, devaluing him as a person. Rather you are narrowly directing your attention to what he is, and is not, doing right—specifically focusing on defined human problems that you hope to help him solve, while not judging him as overall being a problematic human being.

Tell him that though you will try, you recognize that you cannot always avoid fealty to your own values. You understand that personal beliefs/

morality, especially around sexual matters, will always creep into parent-son discussions. But even when you are moralizing, you will try to put him as a person before impersonal principles. You will not put your intrinsic logic before his actual happiness and will not make political less important than scientific, uncompassionate correctness. Also make it clear that at least consciously you are not trying to set limits/prohibit actions to resolve your own problems through him, saying that you want to help him live a better life as a guise for helping you live a better life yourself. You are trying hard, as Jennings says, to "separate your issues from your child's,"[1] that is, to avoid "project[ing your] ideas on to your child"[2] and so to avoid having your limit-setting be strictly a response to your, not his, needs and situation. Specifically you are trying to tell him "what I might do if I were you, though we are, of course, different people." Remind him that you are trying hard to distinguish your personal beliefs from gospel. And make it clear to him that even if your personal opinion, even personal prejudice, does get into it, he still retains the right to challenge you and to keep his fondest values intact even when they differ from yours—as long as his values basically remain rational, not stubbornly anarchistic. Your principle is, and has always been, to hang not only with people who agree with you, but to learn, through discussion and confrontation, from those who disagree with you and so from your son, even when he strongly challenges what you stand for and offers a reality that is different from yours.

Some Basic Principles Involved in Properly Setting Limits

Always remain contemporaneously gay-aware so that you can correct for cultural disparities and generational differences.

Keep the focus away from lofty principles and onto earthy ventures, and in particular onto your son's earthy misadventures, that is, on things you can reasonably spot/fairly identify as mistakes he has made, and is making, and ought not to repeat.

Avoid obvious ploys such as attempting to introduce him and his friends to women, or after a family dinner turning off the gay TV channel and turning on the game so that you can indoctrinate him along "sensible lines" (that consist more of common bigotry than of common sense).

Do not overworry that your son will necessarily respond to rational discipline by becoming annoyed, put off, or devastated. He might, but as long as you don't criticize him for being gay, and criticize him only, if need be, for being gay in a problematic way, and still remain proud of him throughout in spite of any flaws he might display, though he will likely protest, he will as likely eventually calm down and think about what you said. Then as he grows up enough to appreciate where you are coming from, he will likely begin to view your input not as interference, but as helpful direction that he can in the long term act on by accepting the boundaries you set forth as positive interventions that can lead to being a happier and ultimately better son to you, and result in himself being not less of a man, but more of a survivor. In short, don't withhold limits because he, like most sons, is unlikely to accept them immediately and fully. For many sons will accept them if not now then at some time in the future after thinking things over—and hopefully in time for the limits to do some good (and in time to report back to you how helpful you have been to him).

View all his (inevitable) protests not purely as a sign of resistance, but also as a recognition of need and a cry for help along the lines of his protesting too much. Instead of backing off, keep calling a halt to the acting out behavior that he already knows is not in his best interests, doing so even more firmly as you get comfortable knowing that on some level he himself is aware that while he is sincerely trying to navigate a difficult world, he doesn't yet have all the equipment he needs to do so adequately—and you basically hope to supplement his lack of equipment with gear from your own supplies.

Do not get discouraged when your son doesn't respond immediately in a positive way to a point you are trying to get across, or when you disagree with him and have to tell him so insistently. If you are on the right path, continue to pursue your contentions with vigor, and when necessary, repeatedly over time. Face down your son not by being authoritarian, but by being strong. Though he will predictably complain about you being excessively intrusive, controlling, and uncomprehending, consider pushing your way past his protests and continuing to attempt to do what you believe is necessary to ensure his well-being. Say something that is important more than once—until he hears you enough to finally realize the difference between helpful limit-setting and damaging attempts at control, and setting limits and criticism, to the point that he stops responding with an insurgency cleverly rationalized as inherently necessary to his independence and maturity. Many adolescent sons are moving too quickly, leaving one shore before even spotting the next port. Many are doing so because they are rebellious. You hope that at least before taking off on a dangerous journey, he will slow down and more healthily develop his identity, individuality, personality, strength, and intactness—differentiating himself from others in his community while remaining one of the solider soldier citizens of the world.

Keep in mind that the risk involved in taking a stand—if your stand is not arbitrary, irrational, and inapplicable—is likely to be less than the risk involved in saying nothing at all.

Always remember that being accommodating is not the rough equivalent of being loving. Supporting him in whatever he does (including promiscuity and drug usage) just to get him to like you can seriously ignore the downsides of his, and the gay, life—not of his sexuality per se but of related activities of his daily living. Also don't go easy on him just to reassure yourself that you are not being "overly parental" when in fact you are just doing your parental job. Avoid feeling that because you in your own growth and development were oppressively stifled, you must avoid doing the same thing to your son. For you will just be doing one bad thing, depriving your son of your support and protection, to avoid seemingly doing another, being smothering. In my opinion, there is a thin line between guidance, limit-setting, boundary establishment, control, intrusion, and smothering, but it can be worth crossing at least a little during that pivotal period of adolescence where lapses in judgment are frequent and serious enough to lead to a tragic loss of self-control that could end up with an even more devastating total loss—of life.

Make it clear that by setting limits you are not implying criticism or intending to brand your son as stubborn and resistant unless he accepts your limits.

If you get a negative response, keep open to the possibility that it may not be because of what you say but because of the way you have said it—in a disparaging way, raising your voice, being sharp and cutting, or being passive-aggressive, as when you withhold compliments as a subtle way to be disrespectful or critical.

Avoid buying into and going along with his overly general/clichéd ideas that arise out of currently popular trendy thinking, such as his saying, "I want to be true to/embrace myself and never be false to myself," for such a statement on his part can both represent a simplistic solution to complex problems and may not actually in itself be a good idea. For example, it is possible to be true to oneself only in those rare instances where there is only one self inside, meaning that the self inside is not divided, that is, selves are not in conflict with themselves due to mixed feelings about who one is and ought to be, making self-realization difficult because—with many "me's" inside, each longing to come out—the selves are jostling with each other for recognition and incorporation into an overall superordinate "self" or "identity." Here what is required is instead of grasping only one self and sticking with it pigheadedly, synthesizing the many selves inside to make a workable superordinate self that represents a compromise formation that walks back to create persuasive inner harmony where identities based on a desire for self-expression and individuality coordinate with identities originating in a proper need for self-control and social sensitivity so that activism is modified by assimilation, challenging society is modified by cooperating with the establishment, taking risks is modified by remaining safely (and productively) behind in some shadows, close-fisted aggression is modified by open-handed abdication, and too little sex mollifies the extreme of sex having become too much of a good thing.

Also remind your son that it is not a good idea for him to even attempt to be himself when his favored self is not a sanguine but a sinister one. Too, remind him of how risky it is for him to firm himself up (no going back) and secure his identity (no changing) once and for all during the formative years, especially in adolescence when things move so quickly that loyalty to any one self is, and should be, ephemeral—like that tattoo at age 18 whose message has become passé at age 21. Also ask him to determine if his desire for self-realization is more defensive than primary/authentic so that he really wants to be this because he fears being that, making identity establishment the product not of wish, but of anxiety and guilt about actually allowing oneself to be who one is, leading to an uncomfortable, unworkable, jerrybuilt resolution of the conflict between "what I prefer to be and what I fear actually becoming." When the desire to "be me" and to "be free" is constructed more out of passion than out of principle, it becomes not a proper goal, but a symptom of emotional illness, often one characterized by a compulsive need to attack and rebel. This was the case for one son whose "being himself" consisted of standing on a street corner loudly bragging to his friends and even passing strangers how many young boys he had seduced the night before, making his "being the real me" not just a cliché but also a very bad idea.

Focus not on his sexuality, but on issues related to his nonsexual identity. Help him develop his nonsexual identity by assisting him to resolve conflicts about who he is and what he does. Also, as the *DSM-IV* notes, parents should avoid trying to influence a son's basic total personality organization and rather stick with trying to help him sort out specific issues related to "multiple matters such as long-term goals"[3] as well as matters related to "career choice, friendship patterns . . . moral values, group loyalties,[4] and nonsexual relationship issues involving partnering/marriage.

Make certain that the limits you set are appropriate in the sense of being achievable. For your goal is not to help him function perfectly, but to achieve an overall functionality (however imperfect that may be).

Take as reasonable positions as you possibly can. Examples of setting unreasonable/inappropriate limits involve condemning his self-affirmation as stubborn rebelliousness, damning his creativity as serious eccentricity, and demeaning valid social compliance as pathological passivity. Be as rational as you can about such controversial matters as those involving coming out; attending events to which a partner is not invited; living with or separately from, or staying with or leaving, a current partner; and monogamy as distinct from polygamy. Sons often warn parents who jump into these areas that they are being "too forcefully opinionated and attempting to control how I think." But I believe that the real risk lies in parents, especially those with a satisfactory marital relationship of their own, *not* sharing the wisdom that comes from their own years of experience—experience that they can use to help their son bypass unnecessary catastrophes arising out of greenness that too often propels an adolescent son to make serious irreversible mistakes early in life.

Generally it is safe to set limits about matters that are controversial if you as his parents—cautiously distinguishing opinion from incontrovertible fact—qualify your limit-setting by clearly flagging your ideas not as dogma, but as somewhere in between personal opinion and personal prejudice. Limit-setting about controversial matters is best kept flexible by being presented as merely a talking point. Certainly too firm ideas about which path your son should take through gray areas should yield to framing options about which road *might* be a good one for your son, as an individual separate from you, to *consider* traversing.

In assessing his situation, distinguish things your son is not responsible for (e.g., events that occur due to bad luck) from self-induced problems that he needs to resolve by undergoing true called-for personal change.

A conservative approach for parents worried about their son's seriously mistaking their limit-setting for control or criticism involves finding out what your son is thinking and how he feels about certain matters at hand, then gearing your response according to the feedback you get from him. Is he also worried about the outcome of his life; concerned, perhaps overly, that all will not be well; and alarmed about the possibility that his future will not be bright? And so is he likely to basically want help from you in these areas however much he may at first seem to be reluctant to seek and accept it. Does he mean it when he says not "Thanks," but "I want to be left alone?"

Parents who feel especially uncomfortable even just broadly outlining recommendations/setting limits/setting boundaries (as if that necessarily amounts to unilaterally issuing stifling edicts) often feel more comfortable doing these things through modeling. Here their hope is to have a son identify with them as they make an effort to openly display admirable traits, traits they wish to have their son emulate, such as those involving self-control. By showing—not just telling—they hope that their son can by mimicking their actions benefit from their experience. However, if you are teaching him by example what you want him to be like, you must first make certain that you make a good role model who is setting a good example, one that leads your son to *want* to be like, not to have to be as different as he possibly can be from, you.

Don't assume that if he resists, it means that he is being stubborn. For given the possibility that you yourself are not a paradigm of excellence, it just may mean that he is being sensible.

Reassure yourself, and your son, that you are not being hypocritical just because you don't follow your own advice. It's okay to say "Do as I say, not as I do" as long as you recognize the disparity between your goals and your actions, and make it clear that you are trying, as should your son, to do well, and better in the future, by living up to your own standards.

Recognize urgent need but never condescendingly imply that because your son is needy that means that he is in dire straits to the point of requiring emergency intervention/special care.

Feel free to try to set limits on his not meeting *your* legitimate needs. As his parents you can, within boundaries, encourage him to do what *you* would like him to do because it benefits not him, but *you*. If *you* really want grandchildren, consider encouraging him to adopt or to use surrogates. If you don't like his plan to move too far away from you, tell him you feel he may not recognize he is hurting you and ask if he would be willing to reconsider. If you don't like how his partner behaves toward you, explain what it is that you don't like about that, and why, then consider intervening directly, of course in a positive way, by helping him resolve problems involving his partner. If he is alone, consider fixing him up with a guy you know is also looking for someone wonderful. Don't, thinking his love life is necessarily off limits to you, hesitate to intervene in selected relationship problems he might be having, especially if he is suffering through a bad romance. I believe that the best advice you can give a gay son is to find/pick a lifetime partner who will simultaneously enhance not only his life, but also yours. Then (from the background) supervise the results in a generally nonjudgmental (but, if need be, in a controlled, helpful, judgmental) way, remaining actively—but always creatively—involved in this aspect of your son's life, and for as long as is necessary.

If he needs a therapist and you know of a good one, tell him who that is. If you yourself are seeing someone who is helping you, consider the possibility of inviting your son to join with you in family sessions. Never make therapy an occasion to continuously complain about what his being gay has done and will do to you, ranging from embarrassing you with the extended family to depriving you of the grandchildren you want.

Always embed any negativity on your part in a problem-solving matrix. Any negativity should be both narrowly focused and preliminary to resolving specific difficulties he may be having. Thus any negativity should refer to given problems exactly while avoiding such general name-calling as "You are ruining my life by being queer."

If you must express your anger, consider expressing it as concern, not censure. For example, instead of criticizing your son for being excessively wild, say, "As I see it, the problem is that you are keeping late hours. Therefore we are *concerned* that you are not getting enough sleep to keep up with your graduate studies and might even be ruining your health." That helps you set limits and draw boundary lines with respect, boosting, enhancing, and augmenting his life supportively and lovingly, not blocking it deaffirmingly.

Always tailor all disciplinary actions to fit your son's personality type/personality problems. *Anxious* and *depressed* sons do best with parents whose discipline avoids being condemnatory. Help an anxious/depressed son reduce guilt by gently trying to talk him out of his gloomy thoughts and suggesting alternatives to his self-destructiveness. But come down hard on *psychopathic* sons who are self-serving troublemakers and who, finding ways to escape feeling as distressed as they ought, need less in the way of understanding and support and more in the way of control. Here the absence of limit-setting along the lines of "Do what feels right for you" is destructive because such sons' judgment is not good enough to align what "feels" with what "is" right. For what feels right to such sons can be precisely what is wrong for them, you, and the society in which they live.

In an emergency, that is, when your son is in danger, move in definitively without undue concern for whether you are being adequately affirmative, too controlling, or excessively arbitrary. Then carefully monitor the effect you are having on your son. Afterward, when indicated, continue to get directly, if selectively, involved in his life without feeling that you are being underhanded—as if you are not ensuring his safety, but disrespecting his privacy.

Parents who have a good relationship with their sons, especially parents who do not disrespect and mistrust them, can most effectively monitor them and intervene when necessary. A son who knows you love him will accept more discipline, even discipline that is misguided, from you than one who doubts your affection. In the latter case, no matter what you say or do, he might still think you don't have his best interests at heart. And he just may be right.

As discussed in Chapter 8 on communication, there are times when honest communication consisting of a productive discussion with openly exchanged useful ideas is truly the best approach to monitoring, supervising, and intervening to prevent acting out. My mother, doing the opposite, never discussed anything that might have been helpful to me. She gave me no useful formulae to follow. Instead she just passively observed my behavior, neither complaining about it nor contributing anything substantial to my life; neither criticizing my failures nor complimenting me for my successes; but instead always leaving me with the burden of her silent disapproval without the benefit of her wisdom and experience. On the other hand, my father, going to the opposite extreme, was a harsh, strict critic and disciplinarian who had no compunction about wildly and often randomly viewing me through the screen of his personal condemnatory philosophy of my life, where his basic principle was, "Moral is what I define morality to be." He would pounce on me like a gang of one, an at-home schoolyard bully, leaving me first feeling chastised and second feeling helpless and all alone. Both parents were in effect bullying me. My mother was doing so subtly by not being there for me, and my father was doing so openly by not hearing my side of things and never allowing me to be me or to defend myself against not being him. Hence I acted out restitutively. I constantly felt that I was neither respected nor loved and always believed that that was a crisis requiring immediate relief. So for years I sought to gratify my immediate needs and soothe my most pressing fears without concern for an overall life plan. For the latter required postponing seeking pleasure until tomorrow, and—at that stage of my life—waiting for tomorrow felt like having to wait forever.

Don't let a stubborn son manipulatively intimidate you. Many sons will attempt to do this by citing the generation gap, telling you, almost reflexively, that you are too old to know what is going on with youth and so what is good for them. But while you as parents don't know all the latest terms and about the most modern of trends, you are likely very well versed in the important underlying basic principles. Your experiences, though not fully contemporary, are still apt to be basically up-to-date enough to warrant passing on. If somewhat "outdated," they likely need only minor modifications to become appropriate and relevant to your son's generation. As an analogy, the details of what I learned in medical school no longer always apply today exactly, but the basics of what they taught me remain sound. How you accomplished having a good, responsible, creative life may no longer apply precisely, and the details may no longer be entirely relevant to what your son should do to achieve the same goal. He is unlikely to want to emulate you exactly because to an extent your time has passed. But no doubt there will be contact points where information from you serves him well—especially that involving outlining generalized admirable character traits fundamentally worth his emulating without their being discordant with his more modern, generation-specific ideals and attitudes. You probably had many of the same problems when you were young that he does now. And knowing how you solved them can be invaluable when he is as young as once you were.

Adolescents like to gang up on their parents. One way they do that is to tell them they are no longer relevant based on minor deviations from contemporary thought. This is partly rebelliousness (bad). But it is also partly maturational (good). Many adolescents do, and should, find a way to perceive their parents as their foil—someone they can contrast themselves with as an aide for developing their own ideal identity. But the truth remains: old school is not necessarily unschooled. For the old rules, many of which are both universal and timeless, still apply and supersede generational differences. And asking your son to follow what very likely have become standard operating procedures is encouraging your son to use your valuable guidance on how to relate to others (which starts with learning how to relate to you). "Current" is cosmetic, and cosmetic is soon enough passé, and besides if you stick to your once "outdated" positions long enough, they become new all over again. To illustrate, sound philosophical positions embracing traditional values are no longer as out of touch in the gay world as they once were. Today the old-time gay promiscuity is not as vibrant as it once was, and monogamy, with long-term/permanent loving coupling and having/adopting children, is "cool" again. Ten years ago a critic complained that my book *My Guy*, in its emphasis on gay marriage, was out of touch with the gay sensibility. Now his complaint is out of touch with the gay reality. (Almost every gay man I have spoken to wants on some level to get married. And many of these gay men, no matter that they want it, want to deny it.) "Dumb" parents who were deemed out of touch just yesterday for saying, "Just find someone to love" are the wise men and women of today, and for saying exactly that same thing.

Of course, if you are too resolutely from the old school, you should update your ideas to make them newer, and become less provincial by incorporating changing mores as you modernize ancient rules and laws via becoming more knowledgeable about what it means to be gay in today's world.

Always be flexible, altering your input according to your son's response. Sons rapidly grow and change as they mature, so their current will not necessarily turn out to become their entrenched positions. The way things are today with a son is rarely a certain measure of the way things will be with him tomorrow. And that is certainly true of his relationship with you.

PART III

Therapy

Chapter 12

Indications for Seeking Treatment/An Overview of Therapy

Indications for Seeking Treatment

Therapy might be indicated for parents who tend to overlook (go into denial over) how their specific parenting problems are causing serious difficulties for themselves, their son, the rest of the family, and ultimately even for society as a whole, or who rationalize these problems as minimal, inevitable, or readily excusable. These parents need help breaking through the refutations that have led them to believe that all is well when it isn't, and that they aren't actually struggling with having a gay son when in fact they are. They need to stop making flimsy excuses as they try to keep their problems and hang on to their difficulties. They need to stop rationalizing not being accommodating to their son by saying, "Since my son isn't married and doesn't have children he as a single man won't require what our other children, who are family men and women, must have," thus giving themselves a reason to award preferential treatment to their son's brothers and sisters guilt free—without shame or regret—as they award their other children more quality time, more affection, and more financial support than they give to their gay son. They need to stop rationalizing their malfunctioning, for example, "It would be hard for anyone to parent a gay son," which sounds like just another of their attempts to normalize what is excessively hard for them by thinking and saying, "No parent-child relationship goes smoothly, so it's not surprising that our relationship with our son is no exception." Although on the positive side denial and rationalization help them feel better about their "situation" and thus about themselves, on the negative side such denial and rationalization likely keep them from discharging many of their primary parental responsibilities toward their son, depriving him of things he needs and withholding things he should right-fully have.

Therapy might be indicated for parents who blame their son for who he is and what he does when instead they should be retroflexing their finger of blame at themselves for what they have done and continue to do to him, including provoking him to do the very things that they complain about/find unpleasant and off-putting, viewing him not as their victim but as their perpe-trator just so that they can continue to criticize him as being the "bad" one.

Parents who are generally vindictive toward their son should consider therapy for themselves. Homonegative parents tend to feel that if they are causing difficulties for their son, these do not go beyond what they believe he deserves, for "Clearly he has made his choice to be gay, and to maintain himself that way in the face of our protesting, stubbornly hanging on to his unconventional attitude about what constitutes a good life no matter what we say or do, thus defying norms that have been established in our family for years, and verified by the culture in which we live, and for longer than he has been alive."

Parents who are excessively homonegative should also consider therapy for themselves. Unfortunately, few parents enter therapy primarily to deal with their homonegativity. Most deal with their homonegativity, if at all, reluctantly, secondarily, and if that, obliquely. At best, they start by explor-ing their neuroticism in a general way, and only later are willing to try to determine if it contributes to their homophobia/takes a homophobic form, and to delve into the unconscious reasons for their homohatred. As an example, a father abhorred and figuratively washed his hands of his gay son because of a sense of moral superiority that was less the product of his conscious philosophy (as he believed it to be) than the product of his unconscious sexual guilt projected outward (as he failed to recognize). With him I had to deal with his difficult, homophobic relationship with his son not by focusing specifically on his antagonistic bond with this child, but by focusing on the sexual guilt behind his negativity. That did, however, free him up to become less removed from and less critical of himself over his own sexuality—which translated directly into his becoming less critical of, and less removed from, his son.

Parents who are ashamed of their son should consider getting into treat-ment. Ashamed of their son for being gay, they show no pride in his actual achievements. He accomplishes less. Then he becomes depressed and does less. And then his parents feel even more ashamed of him. Their lack of pride in him diminishes not only his self-esteem, but ultimately theirs as well. Feeling devalued, they act even more vindictively to him than they ever did before, and that leads them to become more ashamed of themselves and then, retaliatively, ashamed of him.

Parents who have unduly low self-esteem should consider consulting with a therapist. Parents with unduly low self-esteem have few expectations in life for, and from, anyone, and perhaps especially for, and from, their gay son. Because they don't feel they deserve any better, they too readily conclude that a "fully satisfactory relationship is impossible." Then they rationalize that belief as "Anyway, what difference would it make?" Then they take few or no steps to make adjustments/improvements in their relationship so that it can become more satisfactory and uplifting.

Parents who are serious sadomasochists should think about therapy. Parents who are primarily *masochists* too resolutely put the needs of their gay son first to the point that they completely ignore their own needs (and those of their other children). Parents who are primarily *sadists* can become so hurtful to their son that they actually enjoy seeing him suffer, an attitude which they rationalize as "It's his punishment for being gay" (and often, as well, his punishment for everything else that they believe he has done wrong in life and to them). They criticize and disapprove of him precisely to hurt him. They deliberately hurt him not only for his being gay, but also, and often, for something else distantly related/unrelated, such as his personal choices, especially the profession he selects for himself. More often than not they even actually threaten him—to cut him off financially or to throw him out of the house physically. Parents who are *sadomasochists* provoke an adversarial relationship with their son beyond what is to be expected in run of the mill parent-son relationships. They do so in the hope that he will act in an adversarial fashion toward them so that they can fight with him—both to make him suffer ("as he deserves to for being gay") and to hurt themselves in the process (as they deserve to be hurt for making him suffer).

Therapy may be indicated for parents who are unduly pessimistic. Unduly pessimistic parents fail because their pessimism leads them to actually achieve the failure that they fearfully anticipate. Moreover, they don't seek to improve their relationship with their son. Instead they give up on him entirely, and prematurely, because they believe that given the specific, serious, nature of his problem it's impossible for them to do any better.

Therapy may be a good idea for parents who are too easily swayed by what others say (and especially others' negative comments). As excessively

impressionable individuals, they tend to buy into their community's validation of their homonegative beliefs. They hold as valid the belief that by
being negative to their gay son, parents are actually enhancing, rather than
destroying, their son's life by inspiring him to positive action (to go
straight). They also believe they are enhancing, rather than destroying,
their own lives by improving their reputation within their community—
as a family possessed of true, traditional, family values. Such parents need
to recognize how by being homonegative they are likely not enhancing,
but actually damaging, their own reputation, not merely with their gay
son and ultimately with themselves, but also within their community—
and often with the very straights—family and friends—whom they are trying to impress and win over. As for their reputation with themselves, how
can a truly moral, deeply religious parent preach compassion and love for
all then make exceptions based on sexual orientation without on some level
feeling guiltily hypocritical? How can presumably logical parents of gay
sons wear T-shirts that say, "How can a moral wrong be a civil right?" without wondering if they are mistakenly comparing apple "wrongs" to orange
"rights?" And as for hurting their relationship with others—the straights in
their extended families and their straight friends—"All the world loves a
lover" so that, at least in my experience, even some peers/cohorts who seem
to approve of and publicly encourage parents' antigay stands recognize, at
least in the privacy of their own rooms, that homonegative people, and
especially homonegative parents, as disapproving people are harsh individuals whose ideas and behaviors signal the presence of a sadistic bent that
ultimately puts others off because it leads many more people than even
they realize to ignore them as friends, to make sure that their sisters marry
into another family, to associate socially with someone else, and politically,
if they are running for office, to give their vote to another candidate.

   Parents who are so scrupulously moralistic, and have to be so "morally
right all the time," that they have lost sight of what is important—which is
people, and more specifically that person who is their son, should consider
entering treatment. If this is you, you are minimizing/destroying the personal
gratification that you could be getting from your son, depriving yourself of his
love, and missing the potential satisfaction to be gotten from rearing him up
from a happy child into a sturdy man—not only for his benefit, but also so
that he can become a lifelong companion to, and source of support for, you.
What you as such parents gain in the way of fighting sin and maintaining a
smug morality you lose in the way of a potential friend and helper you could

otherwise have had and enjoyed. For as you only see him as you want him to be, you never get to know him as who and what he actually is.

Therapy might be indicated for parents who are overly distanced from their son. Some sons don't want to participate in family life much or at all. They want to be left alone even to the point of becoming pathologically isolated. This might be because they are very private people who choose not to communicate a great deal; because they are such sensitive people that they regularly anticipate criticism that they believe they won't be able to handle; or because they have something to hide from their parents, like gauges in their ears residing invisibly under their hair, and know that if Mom and Dad found out about them they would brutally savage and discipline them. In other cases, it only seems that a son wants to be left alone when in fact he doesn't. It seems that way to parents because that is how they see things—through the scope of excessive expectations of how close a good parent-son relationship should be—so that in fact their son wants a relationship with them but not one that is as intense as they think it ought to be. In still other cases, a son's distancing himself from his parents is not his but his parents' problem. For distancing is his response to how you, his parents, are actually treating him. If he doesn't introduce you to any of his friends it may not be because he is too shy to share, or too ashamed to show you who his companions are. It may be because when he did introduce you to his friends you didn't respond positively/didn't like them at all—and were both vocal about it—condemning decent people (that any other family would be proud of knowing and willing to accept) and prohibiting him from seeing his friends again, not for good but for questionable reasons, and not for his benefit but for yours.

You might seek therapy if you feel that you don't love your son as you should in any, most, or all respects. You don't even look forward to his being around. You don't look forward to his coming home for the holidays. And when he does come home you feel unhappy about his being there. Indeed if he has moved away, the tension level within you, and even within the entire family, seems to increase when he comes back, only to subside once again when he departs. Perhaps too you have become excessively secretive with everyone, including your own friends and family, who are even complaining that you, hiding something, are no longer the people they once knew and loved.

A therapist might help parents who detect that their son seems to be courting danger and they don't know exactly what to do about it. For example, you get notices of moving violations coming to the house in your name after you have lent him your car. Or you spot suspicious entries on a computer he has given you permission to log onto. The situation becomes even more alarming if you suspect your son is getting into trouble to be oppositional just to hurt you and doing so completely without justification—because you have done little to nothing to merit that.

A positive indication for therapy is that you suspect your homonegativity over his being a homosexual/his homosexual practices (although they are between consenting adults and no one is getting either physically or emotionally hurt) involves your being neurotic in the sense of being over-involved and overconcerned with his being gay, although he is fine at least for now, and his life is not the pressing concern of yours that you make it out to be. Perhaps you are even becoming punitive, for example, using his being gay as an excuse to totally abandon him "just because there is nothing I can do to change anything about him anyway."

You might benefit from treatment if you are in a state of serious grief, especially one severe enough to appear to be an emergency. If grief is less severe, before seeking therapy consider seeing if the tincture of time is an adequate remedy—that is, if your grief diminishes over the coming weeks or months as if spontaneously, or because you have worked things through in your own mind. If your grief is a response to special traumatic life circumstances related to your son being gay, as when he has left home because he feels unaccepted and unacceptable there, consider trying to lessen your grief by improving your circumstances—and that through improving your behavior.

Therapy might help you if you feel depressed and as a result are drinking too much, having temper outbursts, or are experiencing crying spells over problems related directly, indirectly, remotely, or not at all to your son being gay. Because of this depression, you become ineffective as parents not only with him, but also with all your children. You even become a difficult, blaming, finger-pointing spouse constantly having so many arguments with your husband/wife that your marital relationship is threatened. (Often this is because one of you is positive and the other one is negative to your son, and the negative parent, in spite of pleas to change, does nothing to improve his or her attitude.)

Consider seeking therapy if you aren't challenging/facing down homonegative extended family/friends but rather are letting them determine your attitude/behavior toward your son—as you put them and what they think first, making impression management count for everything. You may even be doing this with people who shouldn't count for much in the first place, even letting virtual strangers come before your relationship with your son, who is, after all, family, doing so perhaps even to the extent that you don't allow your son to invite his partner to family affairs because his coming to your house as part of a gay couple might embarrass you and put others off.

Consider speaking with a therapist if you find yourself excessively controlling what your son does based on what you want him to, not what he himself wants to, be and do. Or, going to the opposite extreme, you have become too passive, leaving him entirely to his own devices when he clearly needs your participatory help.

Consider seeking help if you feel poignantly confused about how to raise up your gay son. Recently there has been a great deal of controversy about whether parents should let their younger/growing sons watch certain TV shows/read certain books/take certain classes that extol gay behavior. Parents don't know whether to buy into the argument that watching these shows can cause a child to deviate along an undesirable gay pathway, or into the argument that even the shows that present being gay in an alluring light have no effect whatsoever on a son's sexual orientation. No one, including your therapist, can completely decide how all parents in all cases should respond, and often therapists disagree with one another. Thus one therapist told parents who were his patients, "Children do identify with what they see and though these identifications won't definitively change sexual orientation, they might change superficial behavior along related lines. Therefore, my advice is to set limits through prohibitions, although he will likely resent and defy them, and go behind your back to read and see what he wants." But another therapist in disagreement said, "Hands off, TV messages can't tip a child from being straight to becoming gay, or even change how your child lives his life as a gay person."

Finally, consider treatment if for any reason you need help with parenting your son as revealed in his reasonable specific, and justifiable, complaints about problems he is having with you.

Who Should Go

Hopefully the needier more troubled parent will be the person to at least start the therapeutic process. But when he or she won't go, the other parent should schedule sessions and discuss one of two possibilities: putting pressure on the spouse to seek treatment or making it less necessary for the spouse to seek treatment by becoming more therapeutic oneself with one's partner, thus reducing the pressure one's spouse is under.

What Kind of Therapy Should You Seek?

Parents of gay sons who choose to enter therapy should consider eclectic psychotherapy, a form of psychotherapy that consists of a judicious parent-centered combination of insight-oriented psychotherapy, cognitive-behavioral intervention, interpersonal therapy, therapeutic education, and therapeutic support. As Oldham says, "[V]ery often a therapist will combine many different approaches to achieve the optimal treatment for his or her patients."[1]

Developing *insight* involves parents discovering what having a gay son means to them both on a conscious and on an unconscious level. This discovery starts with asking and attempting to answer such questions as, "Why do you feel the way you do about this?" "What exactly, if anything, bothers you about your son being gay?" "How exactly does it affect you?" "Precisely how do these troubling things trump your ability to love your son if not unconditionally than at least sufficiently?" "Where and when did your negative thinking start, that is, how far back does it go?" "What about him and his being gay triggers your present negativity?" And, considering your assumptions and fantasies, "How exactly does your son being gay resonate with your goals and expectations for him, as well as for yourself?"

The *insight-oriented therapist* is particularly interested in discovering whether specific no longer relevant ancient issues persist to make for contemporaneous problems that don't realistically need to be there—that is, in discovering how long-dormant inner forces have been aroused and rearoused to become awakenings as the product of disclosure. To this end he or she asks parents to go back in time to uncover unresolved conflicts and anxieties that have persisted over the years to contribute to present-day troubled responses to having a gay son, and in particular how disclosure might have intensified any unresolved personal problems parents are struggling with related to unconscious belief systems/conflicts about personal sexuality and identity. For example, insight therapy often uncovers how homophobia is in fact erotophobia because parents deal with their own sexual guilt by compulsively proselytizing against who their son is and what he does, making "He is an embarrassment" and "Gay marriage is unacceptable" as much statements about their own sexual reticence as they are comments on their son's so-called immorality. Parents are thus helped to explore why they are so involved with the issue of having a son who is gay, why they seem to be so threatened by that (often to the point of hysteria), and why they waste so much time and energy creating and upholding morality when they are not strongly affiliated with a religious institution, and touting antigay laws when they do not work for a law enforcement agency. Hopefully as a result they will stop emulating my patient's parents who received a flyer for a gay sexually oriented book in the mail and could not simply throw it away and forget all about it, but instead had to get involved in endlessly protesting to their son and to the authorities about the lax laws of today, until I had to question their true motives and point out that this was an obsession, for their need to crack down on one or more aspects of their son's life clearly originated in their own compulsive need to crack down on the immorality that they perceived within themselves.

The *cognitive* therapist explores illogical ways parents think about themselves and their son, as well as their and his current and future situation. A goal is to diminish negative feelings by learning about the faulty logical assumptions upon which these are based, and to then employ that knowledge correctively—specifically (but not exclusively) against parental antagonistic behavior.

The *interpersonal* therapist conceptualizes family members as part of a team, all of whom need both equal validation of their assets and equal scrutiny of their liabilities. Likely all have interconnecting problems requiring resolution that can best come both from exploring the nature and effects of family coalitions and the modes of interaction of individual family members within those coalitions through identifying interconnective sources of tension, all so that specific antidotes can be determined. (Therapy that involves only the parents is likely to be called couple therapy.) Hopefully the family will learn the wisdom of favoring people, their son included, or especially, over principle as they learn to make the well-being of actual individuals in the family, their son mainly, more important than fidelity to some abstruse philosophy/membership in a given social or religious affiliation.

The *educational* therapist teaches family members what exactly they need to know in order to survive. This therapist also challenges myths about being gay and having a gay son so that all concerned can do a reality check to identify incorrect assumptions about the world of gays, myths that go on to color parental impressions of what is actually taking place in the gay world.

The *supportive* therapist gives positive feedback based on the assumption that the individual(s) in therapy are not bad people, but good people behaving questionably. The therapist says and does little to nothing to embarrass or humiliate the parents. Rather, he or she emphasizes positive over negative motivation, avoids being critical and fault-finding, stays away from embarrassing the parents in the guise of understanding them, and instead of arguing with the parents/putting them down affirms their essential wisdom before going on to suggest that what is required is more in the way of fine-tuning than in the way of radical change. The therapist freely dispenses empathy along the lines of "I understand how you feel" and as freely offers reassurances such as "Your son being gay is not your fault because it isn't a fault and anyway, being inborn, it is beyond the realm of any method of influence." The therapist acts supportively in a paradoxical way—by *not* being *excessively* reassuring. Instead he or she, being fair, identifies any counterproductive destructive parental contribution to a son's life that might be causing their son to have difficulties in living (which difficulties feed back to become problems in living for the parents). A supportive therapist also deals with excessive parental guilt both by reassuring parents that they aren't bad people and have done nothing much to be guilty about, and by (again paradoxically) *withholding* reassurance if the parents are actually in the wrong, making it clear that they need to stop doing things wrong, without delay, and instead start doing things right, and right now.

If therapy is necessary, the choice of what therapy to undergo depends in large measure on family characteristics/dynamics. Individual therapy is likely indicated when it is mainly one parent who feels negatively toward a gay son, while couple/family therapy is more likely to be indicated when both parents are united against a son who is gay.

Here are some important issues parents of gay sons looking to get the most out of their therapy should consider. Parents should take their therapist's advice only after filtering it through their own good judgment and deeming it right for them personally. For example, advice from Jennings, who says to give every gay child "that validation from his parents [that] says to him, 'You're OK. I love you just the way you are' "[2] or from McDougall, who says to "keep telling your child that your love for him ... is the most powerful force in your life"[3]—while generally valid—may be invalid for parents who have a difficult son who needs tough, not unconditional, love.

Parents should avoid a therapist who focuses exclusively on psychopathology to the detriment of giving any reassurance, encouragement, and comfort at all, that is, he or she fails to offer sympathetic listening and positive feedback through consensual validation, and withholds soothing and gentle reality testing. Instead they should seek a therapist who reduces stress by countering negative alarmist thoughts with sobering reassuring realistic notions, for example about what having a gay son actually involves—which is generally not as much as some parents make it out to be.

Before getting involved in prolonged therapy, you should carefully consider that Oldham says, "maybe you're fine the way you are"[4] and that you can work out your problems without outside help. Also consider that instead of helping, treatment can sometimes make things worse.

Prognosis

The most favorable prognosis exists for families motivated to resolve problems by looking at themselves and accepting responsibility for at least some of their difficulties; for families who view disclosure as only one aspect of family life with a gay son, not the central or only issue that needs to be addressed; for families possessed of intellectual curiosity, psychological acumen, flexibility and openness to new ideas, and a willingness to try new approaches to solving problems; for families who accept having goals that are realistic, doable, and based on a desire to help rather than control; and for families who listen to the therapist rather than seriously resisting him or her, especially by constantly replying to therapeutic formulations not by esteeming the therapist and learning from his or her interpretations, but instead by devaluing the therapist and giving him or her an argument.

Chapter 13

The Psychodynamic Approach

The psychodynamic approach focuses on developing self-understanding as a method for reducing anxiety associated with psychological conflict. This approach recognizes that parents who wish to improve their relationship with their son can profitably start the process from within, that is, by first improving their rapport with themselves by resolving personal conflicts to achieve the inner harmony they need to fully develop a healthy relationship with their son. Since having a gay son means different things to different parents depending on the parents' individual personality structure and any extant emotional difficulties that they may have, the important question then becomes not only "What is having a gay son all about?" but also "What are you all about that determines your unique, personal response to having a son who is gay?"

The scope of the analytic investigation must include not only excessively negative, but also excessively (defensive) positive positions—such as being too much the advocate less as a way to express a favored homopositive position than as a way to deny one's own, personally unacceptable conflict-inducing homonegative stance, that is, a homonegative stance that you yourself view negatively and wish to alter.

Examine the Past

Parents' current response to having a gay son does not start in the here and now with disclosure, or even with predisclosure. Instead it goes way back to the early years of their own lives and to the beginnings of their relationship with their son. It is generally fruitful for parents to discover what long-standing issues, if any, give the reality of having a gay son a graver and more emergent caste than it actually warrants. With this in mind, parents should try to uncover relevant information about their early relationships with their own parents, and their own brothers and sisters. For example, because one of my father's brothers drowned at a very early age, my father wanted me to be straight partly because to him that meant being masculine, and for him that meant being invulnerable. So, otherwise ashamed of me, he came alive with pride only when I managed to do something that didn't make *me* that proud—only *him*: when I managed to swim nonstop a quarter mile at summer camp. But even then he wasn't so much proud of me as he was relieved that he wouldn't have to worry that I might drown, just like his brother.

Visit Your Defense Mechanisms

Parents who are having problems accepting having a gay son should examine their defense mechanisms whose presence, by generally rendering their relationship with their son less forthright and direct than it ought to be, tend to complicate, and typically worsen, their relationship with their gay son. These include:

- *Projection*, where you make your issues into his issues as you take your personal aversion toward homosexuality/sexuality out on him, turning him into someone who is, in your view, as personally abhorrent as you deem homosexuality to generally be.
- *Identification with the aggressor*, where you bash him back as you believe he has bashed you first, thus, "I'll fix him for doing this to me (being gay), for one thing by refusing to openly acknowledge the good things about him, including, or especially, that he is, and can ever be, happy in a long-term relationship."
- *Displacement*, where you recast other, gay-neutral, issues to become gay issues, as when your dislike of "gay flamboyance" represents a shift from a fear of expressing any and all emotion, or when you turn a generalized erotophobia (consisting of guilt and shame about everything sexual) into disgust with gay sex and then into an abhorrence of gay life in general, and your son's gay life in specific.
- *Denial*, where you become his too-full advocate as a way to suppress critical or even hateful feelings toward him, in effect "laughing" about his being gay to avoid "crying" about it.
- *Dissociation*, where you decouple your spiritual and practical sides, thus working around your distaste for certain aspects of, while retaining your love and advocacy for, the whole person, along the lines of "I will stick to my antigay principles and continue to love the sinner, but never, never, come to love his sin." For some parents this defense is a good way to deal with any negative messages that are part of their religion, for example, "Your beloved son is an abomination." For others it is a bad way because

though defensive, it is inauthentic and as such doesn't spare your son your antipathy so much as it models for him how to be disingenuous.

- *Rationalization*, where instead of ignoring/suppressing the Bible's homonegative passages, you reconcile your love for your son with your love for your Bible in its more homonegative pronouncements by spinning the overall importance/impact of the Bible's seemingly homonegative remarks. You admit you know that the Bible says negative things about gay people, but you emphasize how for you these are but a small aberration of little importance in the Bible's greater, more loving, scheme of things.

- *Passive aggression*, where the goal is to mollify your anger (and so your guilt about being angry and the impact your anger has on your son) by expressing your anger toward your son not openly and directly, but subtly and indirectly, yet still provocatively, for example, as "disappointment."

- *Masochism*, where you handle your anger by degrading yourself. You take anger directed at your son out on yourself then beat him over his head with your bloody body, asking for pity and absolution as you too willingly and inappropriately offer to change for him—when he needs to be the one to make many of the changes for you.

- *Depression*, where your goal is to reduce anxiety by feeling guilty and sad, for example, "because I haven't matched up to my own ideal of what good parents should be." So you condemn yourself for wanting your son to go straight, and instead of accepting this as "just being normal," harshly hold it against yourself then see yourself not as a loving person overall with exceptions, but treat yourself as an overall unloving, rejecting individual, with nothing positive to make up for that.

Examine Your Personality Structure

As noted throughout, disclosure often relights parents' ingrained personality characteristics that in turn help determine current parental responses to having a gay son. For the *dependent* parent thinks that "Somehow his being gay means that he will abandon me"; the *controlling* parent thinks that "His being gay means that I can't get him to mind me, stop this foolishness, and get married"; and the *competitive* parent thinks that "As a gay man he won't be as valuable as I, his straight father, am or as any other straight man is—which in a way is a good thing for me because it means that I can win over him, just as I want to win over everyone else."

Parents with a *narcissistic* streak take their son being gay far too personally. They believe that a son being gay, and everything else a son is and does, is somehow relevant to (and a pejorative comment on) them. They make a son being gay not at all their son's, but solely their own, business, personal concern, and source of negative self-evaluation. They then try to control and influence their son to make him over in their image not as a way to satisfy him, but as a means of elevating themselves. In particular, if their son favorably touts any aspects of his gay marriage at all, they view that as a negative comment on their own straight relationship and on straight marriage in general. Using themselves and their own leanings as the litmus test, they believe that their being "straight like me" is pure and that being "gay like you" is foul. They thus guide their relationship with their son accordingly, and absolutely, in terms of what is good and true according to their on-a-scale-of-1-to-10 reasoning. They then back themselves up by viewing such of their homonegative "truths" not as arguable, but as givens—and thus primary, and so noncontroversial—for example, "Everybody knows that if you want to be successful in life, you must not live with another man," and "Life should be an uneven playing field where straights have (traditional) rights and privileges that gays don't deserve." They accept no input and brook no disagreement from others, not only their own son but also their ministers, teachers, and therapists. Instead they respond to others' more sanguine views not by listening and becoming more rational and compassionate, but as if others are assaulting them with their beliefs. Thus they dig in and simply, and often angrily, repetitively restate their cherished homonegative credo along the lines of "I know it to be so and therefore it must be so, and if you disagree with me, you're stupid." Overidentified with their (generally highly conservative) positions and principles, they hear contrasting (generally more liberal) input not as a statement of reasonable if debatable alternatives, but solely as a vicious attack on their person, not only on their values and beliefs, but also on their very bodies and souls.

Making it especially difficult to argue them out of their beliefs are their own feelings of superiority based on their statuses as parents, as straights, as older adults, and as more scrupulously socially and religiously correct than thou—for they are people who in every way espouse, and who in no way deviate, from the one and only acceptable orthodoxy.

Narcissistic opportunism also prevails based on the (irrational, self-serving) belief that straights are and should be the only ones to get all the stuff. Thus when they say, "Keep gays out of the army," they can selfishly mean, "I, and those like me, want to be the only (straight) ones chosen to serve my country—but, of course [they aver] only for legitimate, for example, for moral, reasons," even when (as they rarely admit) financial considerations on their part pertain equally, if not primarily.

Narcissistic parents owe it to their sons to be skeptical of their own (self-proclaimed) expert status and instead become more modest, unassuming, unpretentious, and meek about who they are and what they believe and know so that when it comes to their ability to evaluate gays, gay life, and their gay son, they come to recognize that they are amateurs with little or no firsthand experience or knowledge in such matters and so hardly are possessed of the universal and solid wisdom they believe they have. Instead they are just expressing their personal opinion that is not backed up by "credentials," motivated to a great extent to enhance their own self-image by contrasting themselves with their son—as if he is not a person different from them, and in a good way, but, like everyone else with a same-sex sexual orientation, is a lower form of life, and certainly below the level of what they, his parents, believe they are on.

Parents with an *obsessive-compulsive* streak view their son through the distortive lens of a harsh conscience. For such parents a gay son is the spot of dirt they simply must wash off their hands. They in effect marginalize/exile their son so that he doesn't contaminate the field in which they exist. Furthermore, as rigid perfectionists they view their son as falling not somewhat but completely short of their (excessively) high ideals and expectations, and so to be properly condemned for being unsatisfactory, inadequate, and damaged. As a result they come to see their son being gay not as a parallel life venture, but as a flawed and sullied example of the deviant life and the so-called abnormalities that characterize it.

Parents with a *phobic streak* are true homophobes in at least one sense: they spiritually resemble a dog phobic who fears the dog as a stand-in for another, primary, inner fear. So they view their son's being gay as a symbol of their own fearful unbridled perversity—figuratively, as if being sexual means being poised to get out of control and "bite."

A father, instead of criticizing himself for his own forbidden sexual longings, shunned his son as someone whose behavior epitomized his own unacceptable sexuality. By doing so he could thereby avoid feeling that he was in any way condoning those secret "perverse sexual desires" his son made him aware of in himself. Thus his homonegativity was a true homophobia, less "condemn and attack" than "fear and avoid." His cry, "Don't let gays be a pastor in my church" or "a scoutmaster in my district" or "get near my children at all" was for this father, as it often is for such parents, the approximate psychological equivalent of the dog phobic's cry of "Leash it, and don't let that beast anywhere near me."

As with other phobics, such parents secondarily rationalize their fear and avoidance as being an appropriate response to an actual external danger along the lines of "It *makes sense* to avoid your son because he is defective and really does do disgusting things." As a result just as those who fear flying claim to "fear it only because planes do crash," they claim that they are rational, good citizens acting responsibly and doing their social duty because gays *are* a dangerous menace to society.

Parents with a *psychopathic* streak retain/use homonegative imagery/bigotry as their way to achieve some specific concrete end/accomplish a certain, often political, goal. They commonly use bigotry to enhance their credentials/standing in life so that they can ensure entry into a certain social group, or get a specific job appointment/win a certain election by developing a reputation within their (conservative) circle as "gay bashers for good." The challenge for such parents becomes to stop using their son to achieve their own nefarious ends through employing destructively antisocial but personally rewarding and socially remunerative mechanisms. This is especially necessary when an entire family's selfish ambition encourages them to use shared homonegative passions for their own benefit without much caring how their son feels—as long as they get what they want.

Parents with a *histrionic* streak are excessively involved in both the positive and negative aspects of their relationship with their son. They make that relationship everything as if nothing else in life counts. They focus excessively on their son but not necessarily truly on his welfare. Flattening their perceptions, they overlook the difference between minor and major, and they react with an intensity that is inappropriate given a specific reality. They view unlikely possibilities as likely. As alarmists, they sound warnings, keeping all concerned (not only themselves but also their son) in a state of constant agitation about being gay—seeking a cure for being gay when there is no disease, redemption for being homosexual when there is no sin, and absolution for being queer when there is no need to apologize.

Parents with a *passive-aggressive* streak are angry people whose anger is provoked by specific issues belonging to one or more of the familiar triad of basic human concerns—thwarted *dependency* and hence fear of others' excessive distancing ("By being gay you are pulling away from us, and you don't love us enough to stop it"); fear of excessive *control* ("Your being gay is taking over our lives"); and concern about *competitive* loss ("Your being gay makes us look like losers compared to the other parents on the block").

Basically, passive-aggressive parents are sadists who, like other sadists, are inspired by first blood. They either passively long/wait for it to appear on its own, or they provoke it to actively draw the first drop. Wanting to maintain both their relationship and their distance, they avoid being openly harsh in favor of being still hostile—but in a way that they can later excuse/deny. So they both express and take back their negativity to their son at one and the same time, continuing to make their negative points but now making them in a way that keeps their son from condemning them, his parents, as readily identifiably nasty/villainous people. They ask their son loaded questions that are in fact negative assertions, such as, "Don't you think that you are ruining your life by moving in with a male lover?" Or they protest too much that they love their son's friends, and they do so in a way that seems to imply that they would love them even more if they were straight. They wreak subtle havoc by giving a straight daughter and her husband a joint gift at Christmastime, but their gay son and his partner two separate ones. Or they introduce their son and his partner as, "This is my son, and this is Bob." Or their hostility takes the form not of what they say, but of what they omit. Thus a father told his son that he was too broke to buy him a birthday gift—without telling him that the reason he "had no money" was that he was depositing all his overtime pay into his daughter's child's college fund. Typically they precede their condemnation of their son with a diversionary compliment generally accompanied by a weak smile for cover-up, for example, the much-overused and patently obvious "I still love you, my son the sinner, though I haven't changed when it comes to hating your sin."

Passive-aggressive parents often angrily blow up when their passive-aggressive defense, yielding to internal pressure, fails to fully contain their anger. To avoid this, passive-aggressive parents should consider either saying what they mean right from the start openly and honestly so that all concerned (they and their son) can deal with it directly, or not saying anything at all so that they (and their son) do not have to continue concerning themselves with their negativity. Of course, they might best try to avoid disruptive blowups directed toward their son by reducing their anger to the point that they come to feel less adversarial in the first place.

As the *son* of passive-aggressive parents, you should use your own responses to Mom and Dad as the key that unlocks the true parental message. If you feel devalued, your parents have quite probably (subtly) actually devalued you, so don't think "I am hypersensitive" or "paranoid" as if you are incorrectly reading negativity into a neutral interaction when in fact you are reading things correctly and drawing the right conclusions. However, simultaneously try to correct for any paranoid distortions you are making where you imagine your parents are being hostile to you when they are not because, having projected your anger onto them, you are in fact being hostile to them first, and to the point that you come to (rightly) fear their retaliation. In other words, read your parents accurately and hear what they are saying exactly. As you would want them not to make their issues yours, you should also not permit yourself to make your issues theirs.

Parents with a *sadomasochistic streak* on some level want to make their sons uncomfortable or to actually hurt them. Such parents might become dangerously physical to their son to "beat sense into him to teach him a lesson." Or they "merely" act sadistic intellectually—by putting principles before people—what they consider to be good, right, and moral before what would be better, that is, being loving. Because generally sadists are also masochists, they simultaneously hurt themselves in the process, as when they banish their son if not literally than figuratively by exiling him emotionally in a way that results in their, as much as his, experiencing loss.

Begging or ordering sadistic parents to stop being sadistic is generally not effective. Mostly the best sons can do under these circumstances is to patiently wait until they grow up and can leave. Or in an emergency they can, and perhaps should, call in third parties/outside organizations to first protect them and then help them seek specific appropriate remedies.

Chapter 14

The Cognitive Approach

Parents often think illogically about having a gay son. Typically they distort both what being gay involves and the role they play in having caused their son to become "this way." And then they develop idiosyncratic notions about how to view, cope with, and handle the resultant "problematic situation."

Fortunately parents who both identify and challenge their illogical belief systems about having a gay son can reduce or eliminate the chilling effect that their cognitive distortions have on their sons, on the parent-son relationship, and ultimately on themselves—especially necessary when these cognitive distortions create unwarranted negativity that leads parents to bully their gay son, perhaps to an even greater degree than any bullying that their son might otherwise be exposed to outside of the home. Also, a *son* who understands and corrects his *parents'* erroneous beliefs will likely experience enhanced emotional comfort. For the son who can recognize and subject his parents' cognitive distortions about who and what he is to a reality check can, at least intellectually, understand how his parents came to their misguided notions about him, discount what they say as logically wrongheaded, and thus come to feel better both about himself and about his family situation. For example, the son who is depressed about being gay because his parents tell him, "You, my son, are sick and so need to be cured" will likely feel less despair if he recognizes that his parents in coming to this conclusion are making egregious cognitive errors, two of the most common being:

- *Selective abstraction*, where parents register only the troublesome (outlandish and self-destructive) "gay behaviors" that they read and hear about, and that do admittedly exist in some gays and in some parts of gay society. They then take these behaviors out of statistical context, apply only these to their son, and come to assume the worst about him and his life.

- *Part = whole*, which makes one or a few aspects of a thing into the entire matter, turning the partial into the whole (entirely negative) view then applying that to their son exactly to view and devalue him accordingly, striking fear into his and their hearts about his prospects—not because of what he is and will certainly become, but because of how they incorrectly evaluate who he is and his potential in life.

Cognitive errors do not always lead to falsely *negative* perceptions of what it means to have a gay son. They can also create falsely *positive* perceptions—due to *positive* irrational thoughts leading to excessive *loving* no matter what, even when what is indicated is "tough loving" comprised of setting indicated limits and establishing workable boundaries. Overall positive illogic can in its own way be just as destructive as negative illogic, for while excessively negative parents abuse sensitive sons by being cruel to them, excessively positive parents abuse insensitive (troublesome) sons by being excessively supportive of and permissive toward them. In the first case, the son needs love but instead gets disdain/hate. In the second case, the son needs education/control, but instead gets the go ahead. While in the case of excessive negativity, the tragic result might lead to expulsion from the home, in the case of excessive positivity enabling can encourage disruptiveness to all concerned: the parents, their son, and often, as well, to the rest of the family.

In addition to identifying distortive thoughts, it is helpful to understand their origins, generally multiple and mainly emotional. Cognitive errors can be profitably understood from two perspectives: the *developmental* and the *psychodynamic*.

As an example of the *developmental* origin of a cognitive error, according to some classic psychoanalytic thinking, an Oedipal son desiring to "eliminate" his father so that he can "marry" his mother might, using selective abstraction, deem his father as all bad to justify his own murderous desires toward him. When he grows up this Oedipal son becomes himself an Oedipal father. Now if he happens to have a gay son, he continues to use selective abstraction to form the, for him, utilitarian fantasy of gay = ogre so that he, this new Oedipal father, can now extrude his own son from the fold in order to deal with what he considers to be the competition, that is, "so that my own son won't take his mother, my wife, away from me." (He then defends his selective abstraction by rationalizing it, as in "I am right to view him negatively/exclude him because a gay son doesn't belong in my respectable, and self-respecting, traditional family.")

The *psychodynamics* of cognitive errors include causative idealism, guilt, compromised ability to control one's instincts, moodiness where affect drives and rules ideation, and the passive uncritical absorption of society's distortive ideas and false values—the latter being the ones found in that politically incorrect world that characteristically first makes slanted authoritarian pronouncements then demands that others buy into, and base their personal reality upon, them.

Also such cognitive errors as the belief that being gay = sin owe their persistence to two cornerstone *defensive* intellectual maneuvers: (1) *rationalization* so that one first makes the error and then speciously supports it as legitimate, that is, not as distortive but as the product of water-tight logic, however sophistic that logic may be; and (2) *projection* where one disavows having a personal hand in thinking distortively by claiming that the thinking reflects reality. Thus "I don't have a problem thinking my own sexuality is sinful, my observations of the gay world have led me to inevitably conclude that being gay does definitely = a sin." Thus one father in decrying his son's gay marriage by proclaiming that "In reality the only valid marriage is between one man and one woman in a union blessed with children" was defining marriage this way, his way, out of a personal need to condemn himself for his own secret wishes to defy family tradition by striking out on his own to rebel against what he considered to be the overly harsh strictures that his family of origin and society had placed upon him. And one mother who flatly asserted that gay marriage = a violation of the holy sanctity of matrimony thought this way so as to quash her own conflicts about rebelling against her parents' values. She in effect proclaimed that out of passivity, guilt, and love she had "decided to carry on the family tradition because my neediness left me no choice but to submissively accept my parents' idea of what was the right thing to do, and what was the wrong, immoral, way to act." For many parents the idea that all, not just some, gays are promiscuous expresses the projection of a personal erotophobia—a need to condemn gay men for being sexually wild by proclaiming one's innocence to keep one's own similar, similarly forbidden, and similarly wild sexual wishes under control.

Cognitive errors often originate psychodynamically in pressure from the ego ideal, that is, in that part of the mind that dictates how parents *should* think and what parents *should* believe regardless of the reality that they consciously truly know and themselves accept. They can also originate in the "ego" in the form of an ego deficit consisting of an inability to synthesize tumultuous conflicting wishes and fears, primitive feelings, lofty aspirations, self-indulgent longings, and self-punitive regrets into a healthy rational whole creating a view of what being gay is truly about and thus what it legitimately means to have a gay son. In such cases the result of this synthetic inability can be stereotyping, the product of defensive oversimplification in order to avoid confusion by forcing closure, however truthful that closure may be.

Mood or affect also spins off specific cognitions, particularly pessimistic versus optimistic thinking. Thus pessimistic parents think the way they do because they are depressed ("Alas, with my luck my son's gay life will be problematical and entirely unrewarding"), while optimistic parents think the way they do because they are hypomanic as epitomized by a quote in McDougall from a mother in Perth, Australia: all "gays are gentle, kind and caring people."[1]

Specific Cognitive Errors

Here are some specific characteristic (overlapping) distortive thoughts (cognitive errors) that color the reality of having a gay son, with therapeutic correctives either stated or implied.

Now = forever

Parents who make this cognitive error reasoning emotionally assess an issue's/event's durability according to the nature and intensity of its present impact on them, then thinking "now = forever" come to believe that a momentary harsh unpleasantness will last a lifetime, and so feel that "all is lost now" is the same thing as "all will be lost from now on." As a result if their son's lifestyle is demonstrably problematical, they become excessively fearful and depressed because they view it not as the product of transient adolescent turmoil in a son who happens to be gay, but as an ominous portent of things to come due to their son's current "deficient lifestyle" no doubt, they assume, the direct product of his being gay, becoming persistent and fixed. As a consequence, they feel helpless, suffer from panic attacks, get depressed, then take desperate often irreversible "corrective" action—giving nonexistent, trivial, and transient problems imprimatur that imparts a significance to these problems that they don't have/warrant, and an imputed aura of perceived permanency that is unlikely to realistically exist. Parents next make things worse by overreacting and becoming alarmist and then making unnecessary contingency plans that lead to their taking irrational, excessive, often destructive precautions, thus intervening in a controlling straight-jacketing way that risks perpetuating the very behavior (their son's and their own) that they originally set out to eliminate.

In reality most gay men change over time, and many change for what their parents consider to be "the better." In particular gay men often become less promiscuous after their adolescence (actual or prolonged) is over as their relationships broaden and deepen. So if not certain, it is at least highly likely that your son will eventually dedicate himself to a partner who enriches his, and hopefully also your, life. And if you as his parents plan on that instead of being convinced of some negative alternative, you are in a better position, at least emotionally, to actually help bring exactly that about.

Common = normal, rare = abnormal; different = bad/worse

This view equates exceptional (in the sense of "unusual or extraordinary") with deviant (in the sense of being "off-kilter") so that parents view that which is not statistically common not as incomparable and thus as outstanding (and that in a good way), but as "anomalous" and thus as standing out (and that in a bad way). For such parents common/unexceptional (heterosexuality) = normal (good), and less common/exceptional (homosexuality) = deviant (bad).

In fact being different merely = being dissimilar, without implying "better" or "worse." Thus being untraditional is different from, not better or worse than, being traditional, just as being gay is, at least in some ways, different from, not better or worse than, being straight.

Parents who think along such distortive lines naturally make value judgments due to assigning a value on a scale of 1 through 10 to being gay and to their gay son's "lifestyle." They pit "good, traditional marriage, 10," against "bad, untraditional marriage, 1," as they bemoan gay marriage in general and their son's partnership in specific as being less meaningful/sacred than the liaisons that their straight children have formed, or will form.

The belief that different = worse is often associated with the belief that different = traitorous. Parents who believe that assign a very personal motivation to their son being gay. For them it is as if he is being not only personally immoral, dishonorable, and unethical, but also being deliberately antifamily, as if he became gay just to spite Mom and Dad.

All or none (dichotomous) thinking

In a general way parents who think dichotomously divide the world into black and white, good and bad then—too readily pigeonholing their sons—compartmentalize them as devils versus angels, although most gay sons are mere mortals somewhere on a continuum between the two extremes. They also establish a dichotomy between gay and straight where gay = bad and straight = good. Then what they want is an angel (one who is an *all* good son, which to them = one who is straight) not a devil (an *all* bad son, which to them = one who is gay). Given this excessive expectation of what a son should be, they go on to treat the son they have as falling short of their ideal and so as a complete loser.

Parents who feel *completely* guilty about having any unloving thoughts at all about their gay son also treat *themselves* shabbily. They treat themselves as completely bad people, as if anything less than fully accepting their son = totally rejecting him, and not being entirely supportive of their son = being fully unsupportive of him. They also fear that any incompatibility between them, the moral ones, and their son, the gay wastrel, means that their son is completely immoral and hence has fully abandoned all constraint and, having become a libertine, given up on embracing any admirable, especially spiritual, values.

In short, because dichotomous thinkers are in essence perfectionists, for whom anything less than 100 percent = zero, serious disappointment in themselves and their son becomes predictable, as does the potential both for self-punishment and for taking punitive action toward their son.

Disagreement = dissent/attack

Parents often believe that a gay son who disagrees with them at all is attacking them personally and especially assaulting their traditional family values. They also often believe that any form of dissent = abandonment more than just of family values, but also of them and of the entire family as well.

Evaluation = comparison

Parents who think this way fail to assess the value of a thing on its own merits. Instead they look only to how it measures up in alignment with something else.

Sometimes their motivation in making comparisons is not a negative, but a positive one. Thus some parents desperately try to forge a positive link between success and a homosexual orientation to reassure themselves that their son will, though gay, be okay, or even better than if he were straight. They also do this to reduce their guilt about what they have created in, and done to, him. The method they use involves aligning him favorably with flourishing gay men of the past and present. Thus they reassure themselves that "He's going to be all right" by reviewing a list of famous figures of yore who were gay, characteristically Oscar Wilde, Lawrence of Arabia, and ancient Greek luminaries. Although their motivation seems positive and the results seem sanguine, the thinking nevertheless remains distortive—for it is still the product of incorrect notion driven by, and shot through with, ideological partisanship.

Parents like this generally define "success" in their own, again comparative, terms. They equate it with fame, being married, never being divorced, having good (standard) children, being a professional with a steady remunerative job, making a good living, and having a certain lifestyle that marches to the rhythm of a certified heterosexual drummer—as they see it, all things that gay sons compared to straight sons supposedly don't and won't have, and will never do. They next convince themselves that there is a negative relationship between being gay and being successful by instead of measuring their son's success in terms of his personal satisfaction and individual happiness, measuring it in comparison to their heterosexualized standards of what being successful entails. Such parents should abandon preconceived notions about the good son. They should, if necessary, help their son do not what they approve of because it is standard issue or ideal for the parents, but what is suitable for him and so a measure of success within his own gay parameters, which can be unique. They can now better accept compromise between what is ideal and what is practical, as they evaluate their son's situation on its own, honestly and dispassionately, without indulging in stereotypical comparisons that fail to take into account their son's personality, capacity, and individuality—except insofar as it aligns with what *they* believe to be best.

Sequential = causal

Often for reasons that are more emotional than intellectual, guilt-driven parents create arbitrary/forced and hence false linkages between events according to their belief that if one thing occurred before (or in some other significant proximity to) another, then these two things must of necessity be somehow related. For example, they become convinced that "I caused my son to be gay by what I did to him" first by identifying problems of their own then by blaming their son being gay on these problems simply because their problems occurred first and their son "became gay" next. Not surprisingly such parents are prone to buy into such beliefs as the one that being a passive father and being a devouring mother cause a son to become homosexual. And they believe this even though what they are like had nothing to do with their son turning out to be gay, or even a certain kind of gay person. For plenty of passive fathers and devouring mothers have straight sons, and plenty of gay sons had fathers who were tyrants and mothers who were too passive to do anything to move in to protect their son from a tyrannical Dad.

Ad hominem reasoning

In ad hominem reasoning, irrelevant linkage is established between the so-called quality of the product and the assessed value, generally based on a distortive *negative* valuation of, the producer. That paradigm predictably leads the parents to an equally distortive/negative evaluation of themselves because they produced a gay "product," their son. Parents who think this way, like most of society, also judge their son's professional acumen by a preinstalled negative opinion of their son's sexuality. In psychoanalytic terms, they are equating ego with id—their son's "higher" intellectual with his "lower" instinctual behavior—and judging him accordingly, along the lines of "What can he possibly amount to if he is gay?" They then, for example, conclude that "Because he's gay [his sexual identity], he can't be a soldier [his nonsexual identity]." (Society often does the same thing then rationalizes it, e.g., "Gay men shouldn't be inducted into the armed services because by definition they will make bad soldiers.")

Selective inattention/selective abstraction

Many parents create/retroactively justify negative assertions using selective inattention/selective abstraction (also discussed later in this chapter). In one example—the belief that a gay soldier is a bad soldier—this thinking proceeded as follows: It is conceivable that a gay soldier might try to seduce a bunkmate, that attempt will demoralize certain bunkmates, and the next bunkmate may not materialize in anticipation/fear of being seduced. But in reality this is only infrequently the case and happens only with some recruits. And as an issue it is hardly as important as another consideration: the loss of a few potential bunkmates is not a bad price to pay for gaining many recruits, thus building up one's manpower, something that is possible only if one doesn't exclude able men due to their "being disabled because they are gay."

Parents who make the error of selective inattention/selective abstraction after overlooking how many gay men are in fact happy and successful conclude that only being straight can ever possibly lead to a flourishing life. They then convince themselves that by definition their gay son is going to be a failure not because of who he is and what he can do, but simply because he is gay. They often overlook statements in the Bible that could if they so chose lead them to feel even more loving toward their son. Instead they focus on the statements that express and justify their own negative feelings about homosexuality, proving that an idea becomes a conviction only when there is a preexisting fertile field in which it can grow. A motivation here is to avoid having to take responsibility for their negative feelings by shifting blame. For now they can assign their negativity to this external source, the Bible, thus allowing them to whitewash their negative attitudes toward their son and so to steadfastly maintain their view of themselves as personally innocent of irrational hatred.

Thinking = doing

Parents who make this error think like shamans who, believing that they are omnipotent, feel that they can defy natural law. Parents who think this way believe they can simply make being gay go away either by not thinking about (ignoring) the facts of the situation as if it will somehow thereby pass on its own, or by actively, often ritualistically, wishing it gone. Generally reparative therapists think like this—then offer up a form of therapy that amounts to little more than an ongoing, prolonged ritualistic, virtually magical, soul cleansing.

Wishing = accomplishing

Along similar lines, parents of gay men often confuse having goals with achieving them and the value/intensity of their goals with their actual viability. Again, parental omnipotence/magical thinking confers imaginary power and capacity for influence upon parents, leading Mom and Dad to believe that if they wish it to be so, their son will change—along the lines of "Because it is desirable, therefore it is possible, and so can and will be."

Catastrophizing

Parents who catastrophize turn the reality of having a gay son into an event of life-changing significance—not something they can integrate and coexist with, but a complete disaster for all concerned. Unable to take their son's being gay in stride, they instead view everything about his being gay, and him, as calamitous (or as a debacle) and, at times coming close to being delusional, even worry that "Since being gay is inherited, it can be passed on to my grandchildren even by my straight children, creating even more monsters in this world."

A component of catastrophizing consists of the flattening of the response curve to the point that even minor meager stimuli create major responses. Thus parents with many sons, only one of whom is gay, respond as catastrophically to having one gay son as do some parents whose only son is gay. This was the case for the mother in a family with five sons, four of whom were straight. She nevertheless still felt that because she had one gay son, she would never have (enough) grandchildren.

An important component of catastrophic thinking consists of selective abstraction (as discussed previously) where parents see only the negative aspects of having a gay son, obliterating from their consciousness such positive elements as the advantages of diversity, and of homosexuality itself, both of which as considerations could lead them to have pride in, not be ashamed of, their son being gay.

Characteristically, catastrophizing parents suspend their sense of humor, become excessively gloomy, and progressively lose perspective about their "situation." This happens when depressive feelthink replaces neutral/optimistic logical thinking, as when parents fail to make subtle or gross distinctions and see extant differences, thus allowing unfavorable assessments to form and negative responses to completely take over.

Parents who catastrophize miss the opportunity to learn exactly what their son is like. Instead they feelthink their way into his gay world, which they create out of the stuff of their own fears arising out of taking their son's being gay much too seriously. That makes it hard for them to perceive their son as he actually is and difficult to see his future in life as it likely will actually be.

Activists often harness catastrophic thinking for their own social/antisocial purposes, consciously employing it not only to justify their own views, but also to create a specific advantage/get a competitive edge/impress and convince others to change. Controlling narcissism also ultimately factors into catastrophic reasoning along the lines of "Because I think you need to change *completely*, therefore you must do so, and for me, and whether or not you happen to agree with my (extreme) position about what direction you should take."

Inexact labeling

According to Ursano and Silberman, inexact labeling consists of the "tendency to label events in proportion to one's emotional response to them rather than according to the facts of the situation."[2] Self-justifying rationalizations firm up the emotional view intellectually, underlining plausible (however false) ideation, predictably leading to taking unnecessary and often inappropriate negative action.

Tangential (slippery slope) thinking

Thinking tangentially involves using minor, incremental logical distortions that string part concept after part concept together to crawl rather than to leap, and not to where the thought processes go naturally, but to where the thinker's own emotions long to take them. These distortions of logic are each so small, the resultant falsifications each so gradual, and the logical shifts each so imperceptible that the process as a whole disguises its overall irrationality by stealth. A series of semilogical baby steps starting small but ending big melds into one large major single (generally negative) dyslogical leap, spreading anxiety, often culminating in serious panic consisting of a "that's how it starts" and "one thing leads to the other" depressive mental state that goes something like this: Being gay is unacceptable because it breaks the social mold; that means my son is breaking with tradition; that means my son is a nontraditionalist who will be part of a nontraditional society; that means my son will overthrow the little world of our old established family; that means my son will make it hard for us to relate to our old friends and extended family—and will reject us and the rest of the family completely; that will lead to total family anarchy; and he will even found a movement that when it gains traction will lead to catastrophic widespread social upheaval where society accepts gay polygamy, child marriage, child rape, and bestiality, for, if you give gays a finger they will take an arm so that gay rights will lead to gay marriages, gay marriages will lead to a violation of the sanctity of the family, and a violation of the sanctity of the family will lead to the downfall of propriety and society, thence to a downfall of the human race so that there will never be peace, and the end of the world will be near, and soon upon us.

Such slippery slope thinking, and its cleverly slow-but-sure off-course deviations overall ignores two commonsense considerations: first, the idea that because something can conceivably occur doesn't mean that it is likely to actually happen, for common things are common and rare things are rare, and commonly things somehow work themselves out, and only rarely do events develop such a life of their own that they lead inevitably to Armageddon; and second, that most times most things stop somewhere short of the bottom of the so-called downward slippery slope.

Blaming/scapegoating

Blaming parents believe that such natural occurrences as being gay cannot and do not occur without someone having to be responsible for their having happened. Some parents blame themselves for making their sons gay; some blame their son for refusing to go straight for them. Some therapists blame being gay on a castrating father's imploding his vulnerable passive son, others on a predatory mother for turning her son off women. Many parents alternate between guilt and blame, now attributing their circumstances to divine punishment for the sins they themselves supposedly committed, and now blaming their son for the sin of punishing them—not for something they actually did, and so deserve to be punished for, but undeservedly, because having done nothing, they are actually completely innocent of everything.

Scapegoating is often the blamer's convenient way to avoid self-blame by other-bashing. We hear, "The reason I am not a good parent is that I have a difficult son," when in fact it can be equally or entirely true that the reason parents don't have a "good" son is that he has difficult parents.

Hypocrisy

Hypocritical parents who overlook, or dissociate away, glaring inconsistencies that subvert their own fondest contentions condemn others for doing or being something that they themselves also happen to do, or are. If their son wants to get married, they condemn gay marriage as unnatural because it is against nature, yet they defy or improve on nature every day—in small ways, as they walk with a cane, or in big ways, as they force themselves to be monogamous when they would really like to indulge in one or more of the alternatives (or the reverse).

Stereotyping

Stereotyping is a complex cognitive error consisting of a number of contributory suberrors, some of which have already been discussed.

Parents who stereotype homogenize gays simplistically even though gays are in fact a highly diverse population/group. They then evaluate (and judge) their gay son, rarely positively and mostly negatively, not as an individual but as a member of (some) fantasized cohort with supposedly overarching distinguishing (again, generally negative) characteristics. Stereotypes may hold because the ones doing the stereotyping subsequently actually validate their venality by influencing their victims in the direction of the stereotype.

Parroting/echoing

By osmosis, parents *learn* stereotypes unique to a homophobic society, such as "You can spot gays by their effeminate ways and unmanly interests." Intelligence does not always protect them from such learning. This is because stereotyping serves a psychological function that facilitates those intellectual processes that are supported emotionally. (Individual and social stereotyping can to some extent, but not entirely, be conquered by organized activism consisting of challenging the stereotypes logically, emotionally, and, when need be, legally.)

Condensation/symbolization

Stereotypes are simplified condensed products consisting of important personal issues expressed symbolically. For example, making the gay man a symbol of evil incarnate, parents stereotype all gays as promiscuous as their way of referring to their own thoughts and fears about their own sexuality.

Displacement

In like manner, due to displacement many complaints about one's gay son are really less complaints about a son being gay than they are (though couched in gay-specific, often gay-unfavorable terms) more relevant to and so potentially translatable back to important non–gay-related fears of the parents/innate in parental life. Thus a parent signals that he or she is "concerned about *losing* my son (to homosexuality)" by referring to all gays as nontraditional people who reject family values. Often parents expresses *control* issues of their own by viewing all gays as excessively passive, or, conversely and paradoxically, as hopelessly stubborn, along the lines of "You can't tell them anything, and especially you can't tell them to get the help they need to get over this and return to some sort of sanity." Also parents express *competitive* fears and wishes in the form of value judgments that invalidate gays out of a fear that gays represent a competitive threat to their parents. For example, they express fears about their own not winning/losing out as the reassuring belief that being gay is personally inferior (less worthy than) being straight, and that the gay way of life, as compared to the straight lifestyle, is necessarily second best (to their own).

Sublimation

Sublimation consists of rechanneling socially unacceptable (often "dirty") into socially acceptable (often "clean") ideas and desires. Concerns about gay sex ("disgusting") are often channeled into other parental concerns we hear about being gay, such as complaints along the lines of "I wouldn't mind his having gay sex as long as he didn't do it *so often.*"

Sophistry

Webster defines sophistry as "reasoning that is superficially plausible but actually fallacious."[3] Dynamically, sophists intellectually justify emotionally determined (even delusional) premises after the fact, often for personal, typically utilitarian, purposes. To illustrate, to maintain complete loyalty to an extended family out of fear that otherwise they will be completely shunned by the relatives, parents of gay sons argue speciously (but convincingly) for the traditional lifestyle by falsely emphasizing how nontraditional gay lifestyles, all being from some imagined underground, and so all having distinct downsides, are therefore regularly substandard. (Typically sophistry precedes and prepares the sophist to be intimidating along the lines of "You better believe it, for I know it is so because I happen to know it exactly." Thus the sophist avers, "Openly gay men must not be in the military because it's clear to me that their mere presence in the armed services *will* disrupt morale and discourage recruitment.")

Paralogical predicative thinking

In this type of thinking, according to Bemporad and Pinsker, "the slightest similarity between items or events becomes a connecting link that makes them identical."[4] The (false) reasoning is that if A can be meaningfully equated with B in any respect, and C can be meaningfully equated with B in any respect, than A = C. The oft-cited example of this kind of thinking is, "I (A) am a virgin (B). The Virgin Mary (C) is a virgin (B). Therefore I (A) am the Virgin Mary (C)." Parents think this way about their gay sons in order to create favored stereotypes that, however irrational, they can use to condemn their son for being gay. Accordingly, some parents think, "Some gays are pedophiles, you my son are gay, therefore you, like all gay men, are a pedophile." In like manner, parents stereotype their gay sons as making inferior military men by using the slightest (justifiable, or in this case, unjustifiable) similarity forced into a connective link, concluding that gay (A) = feminine (B), girl (C) = feminine (B), so gay (A) = girl (C) (and girls can't fight).

Too often parents judge their gay son's overall professional potential on the basis of their own (devaluing) assessment of their son's sexual performance when they reason that work is a performance, sex is a performance, so therefore sex = work, and bad sex = inferior work (and therefore all gay men lack professionalism). They also reason that sex involves seduction, homosexuals are sexual people, and therefore homosexuals seduce other people, and, what is more, are all promiscuous child-abusers. And they further conclude that homosexuality is unique, sick people are unique, and therefore homosexuals are all sick. Typically parents who believe that a few shared characteristics make disparate into identical individuals assume that all gays just by virtue of being gay are sissy boys, effeminate, personally passive to the extent that they will allow themselves to be bullied without complaining or resisting, but instead swooning, and certain to be professionally effective only in those "gay" professions where "It's not required to be forceful, or masculine, at least not enough to fully take charge."

Part (truth) = whole (truth)

Parents often stereotype after overlooking how most things—being imperfect—have both a good and a bad side. For example, they seem to forget that there are merits comingled with the so-called demerits of being gay. They devalue all diversity completely because some of the disadvantages of cookie-cutter sameness are lost on them. Or they come to feel alienated from or antagonistic toward a beloved child simply because they believe that *all* (not just some) gays as outsiders are thereby by definition remote from and unavailable inside, to their parents.

A related erroneous belief, one that entirely overlooks the overwhelmingly genetic component of homosexuality, turns "raising" (a part concept) a child into "fully creating" (a whole concept) a child, making "influencing somewhat " into "forming completely," leading to full self-blame for being entirely responsible for a son's having become gay.

Or the part truth "It's good to communicate with your son, to honestly say what you are thinking" omits consideration of the known negative consequences of saying everything that comes to mind, leading to the (dangerous) belief that "Since honesty is the best policy if it's honest it must be good/acceptable, so *never* hold anything back."

Parents who reason this way make and promote unwarranted extensions from the specific to the general. They learn about a negative aspect of the reality of gay existence and then view that as its entirety so that they come to view rare, uncharacteristic, and exotic behaviors on the part of gays both as more significant and more widespread than they actually are, and as (stereo)typical not just of a few gays, but of the whole class "homosexual."

In the view of some parents, because some gay men are sinners, even their beloved son is a sinner, and possibly a child molester. Having thusly defined the whole class according to one or a few of its assumed unsavory aspects, they create the false picture of a gay son as renegade, a picture that at first exists only in their minds, but ultimately determines significant aspects of their parent-child relationship (as well as any subsequent social action on their parts). Such parents often make globally negative judgments that are typically based on using the sexual yardstick as the sole measuring instrument by which they assess their son both personally and professionally. They might judge their son as globally disabled due to his being a sexual compulsive, and his being a sexual compulsive due to his having more than one partner at a time. Then, having concluded that a "disability" in this one area is a disability in all, they fail to recognize that gays, like anyone else, compartmentalize so that gay sexuality, coming from a different part of the brain from professionalism, is unrelated to the ability to do one's work/value as a worker.

Selective abstraction

Selective abstraction, also discussed previously, is related to part = whole thinking. According to Beck, this reasoning leads to making stereotypes by drawing full conclusions about a situation or event based on "a [single] detail taken out of context ignoring other, more salient features of the situation, and conceptualizing the whole experience on the basis of this element."[5]

Parents who think this way stereotype by magnifying a point, thus creating the entire picture out of just one of its parts. They then evaluate their son's overall attitude toward them/his overall behavior based on only one or two aspects of how he actually values them/behaves. Now anything less than his full acceptance of them = total rejection of them; not being completely supportive of them = full mistreatment of them; and not being fully traditional in one area (heterosexuality) = being fully untraditional overall and thus a disgrace to the family. In turn such parents, equating anything short of completely affirming their son with having fully deaffirmed him, develop serious parental guilt. Now they come to think that they are bad parents because they aren't fully compassionate, having failed to embrace their son's gayness completely and to advocate for him absolutely. Then anything short of their being all good means to them that they are all bad and therefore bigoted. Stereotyping themselves, they now come to feel that they are sufficiently homophobic to have hurt their son's chances of growing up good, strong, and successful. And as a consequence they become anxious or get depressed.

Because of gay marriage's admittedly para-traditional subelements, these parents see everything about gay marriage not as para-traditional, but as antitraditional. They also view all gays as sick just because, like anyone else, some have developmental lags and unresolved dynamic conflicts. They dub these as causal, not incidental and as significant, not trivial. Simultaneously they overlook the many true values of having a homosexual son because they overlook the many observable values of being a homosexual. To cite a few examples, homosexuality can be an advantage for some psychotherapists and for activists hoping to help minority groups avoid/cope with prejudice and discrimination. Such parents also don't acknowledge that much so-called typical negative/undesirable gay behavior is in fact situation specific—thus representing an acquisition of the moment—perhaps according to whim and passing need, or existing solely due to having been specifically provoked. Overgeneralizing this way, these parents make predictions and draw conclusions about all gay sons based on a few examples of behavior in some gay men—those whose behaviors prove a negative point they wish to make. Then, tarring their son with that same brush, they conveniently forget that out-there raunchy underworld gays who recruit and molest children are very few compared to the (many) gays who love and have children. They see only the baser aspects of gay sex up close, unsoftened by the loving, erotic bath that covers more primitive/animalistic behavior with positive, even ethereal, emotion.

Conversely, parents can overuse this error not only to overlook positive behaviors mixed in with the negative, but also to overlook the occasional downside of behaviors that are otherwise positive. For example, they can wholeheartedly advocate activism in the belief that "nothing ventured = nothing gained," overlooking the possibility that "nothing ventured also = nothing lost."

Similar = the same thing

Parents who make this error believe that being gay = being gay in a certain (stereotypical) way. Thus for them, all gay men constitute a collective, one generally typified by its (however atypical) unsavory members, all of whom, as they see it, can predictably, and correctly, be typecast as being promiscuous, impulsive, and unreliable.

Guilt by association

In this form of faulty reasoning, homonegative parents stereotype all gay sons by putting them in an excessively negative light after grading them based on the people who do, or presumably will, surround them: friends, a partner, or the partner's parents. Parents who think this way—believing in human osmosis—assume that if their son is gay, he will necessarily absorb the tenets of, and so be an integral part of, the gay underground. Therefore, the son already has, or soon will have, pierced nipples and eyebrows, and a preoccupying foot fetish. (And even when that *is* the case, they see it as a serious problem without recognizing how often it is temporary and/or if permanent accompanied and softened by other, neutral, non-exploitative, loving behaviors.)

Circular reasoning

Parents who think this way stereotype homosexuality as an illness because it is not mainstream. They then stereotype homosexuality as not mainstream because it is an illness.

Personalization

Parents who think this way (narcissistically) stereotype gay sons as the family adversary by design. Assuming that everything their son says and does is somehow relevant to them—and thus their business, their concern, and a proper source of their anxiety—they come to believe that their son has become gay to spite them or that he has married a partner they disapprove of to retaliate against them. They see sons who "disagree with me in any way" as being thoroughly and deliberately disagreeable, and complain that any difference a son has with them is not a divergence from, but an attack upon, their values.

Zero sum

Parents who think this way stereotype gays as immoral because they presume that there is a finite amount of morality in the world, and it is quantifiable. Therefore, they believe that if they accept gays as moral, they will simultaneously have to reduce the quantity of morality left for straights. The most familiar example of this is the belief that gay marriage doesn't simply stand side by side with, but somehow—in ways that nobody can definitively define/prove—diminishes straight marriage.

Ignorance

Ignorance, which can be not innate but motivated, can lead to stereotyping due to getting the facts wrong. Ignorance differs from psychopathic dissimulation for effect through the deliberate creation of illogic to gain specific practical advantage—for example, the psychopathic stereotyping of a gay son negatively to provide his parents with a rationale to not financially support a son they disapprove of for being gay—along the lines of "I don't do it for practical reasons—to save money on him so that I can give all my wealth to my (straight) children—I do it because it is so writ."

In conclusion, stereotyping leads to flat assertions both too broad and too narrow, where opinion supplants facts and irrational supplant rational arguments, leading to the theme with variations that having a gay son is a very difficult, harsh, unrewarding experience. By implication, parents instead of stereotyping where "It becomes obvious" and "Everyone knows that" should focus on rational multifaceted views about having a gay son and both drop or keep their irrational one-dimensional opinions to themselves while remaining sufficiently flexible to stay open to arguments to the contrary.

Therapy

Correcting cognitive errors can alter the parent-child relationship sufficiently and for the better by enhancing loving cognitions and thus reducing gay bullying/bashing at home. But by itself understanding and correcting cognitive errors rarely gets at the root causes of parents' relationship problems with a gay son. Other root causes, especially of a deeper/psychodynamic nature, have to be exposed if one is to help create change that turns out to be more than superficial and temporary.

Behavioral remedies that accompany correcting cognitive errors can often be helpful, though again they are rarely fully curative by themselves. Thus proudly saying, "I have a gay son" not only to strangers but also to family can elevate self-pride yet still be inadequate to bring about full healing unless the underlying basic reasons for feeling shame are simultaneously explored, understood, and rethought to the point that shame can be at least suppressed in favor of allowing pride to come through, and prevail.

Chapter 15

The Interpersonal Approach

Toning Down Negativity, Harnessing the Power of Positivity

Negativity almost always creates and sustains parent-son relational problems that turn a potentially rich, rewarding, productive relationship into one that, at best, is characterized by perfunctory pleasantries, and, at worst, is marred by distancing characterized by shifting between complete silence on the one hand and having serious and frequent arguments and blowups on the other. For example, parents who cajole, nag, and criticize their gay son to tell him that he simply has to go straight both for their and his sakes may think they are being constructive when in fact they are instead putting him off by conveying to him how ashamed they are of his being gay. Parents who complain, "How could you have gone straight if lying around your bedroom I still find pictures of that boyfriend of yours, the guy I ordered you to get rid of?"; who say, "You should stop what you are doing to give yourself away as being gay, like the way you dress and that earring of yours ('by itself reason enough to exclude you from family functions and even from the family as a whole')"; and who complain about their son's professional choices, as in "I am disappointed in you because I wanted you to be an architect but instead you chose to get a job in the theater, and it seems as if you won't ever find real employment"; who bounce from punitive accusations of wrongdoing to open threats of punishment along the lines of "Here's what Dad is not going to leave you in the will because as a gay man you don't need a rifle collection" and "Here's why Mom prefers your brother to you and what she's going to do about it" collectively leave their son feeling hurt and cause him to become so defensively resistant/stubborn that he turns unreceptive to anything Mom and Dad legitimately need or want from him. He also feels tempted to give them exactly the opposite of what they hope for, that is, a hard instead of an easy time, and a good deal of resistance instead of a great deal of cooperation.

Perhaps the real tragedy of negativity is that it keeps Mom and Dad from knowing who their son is and why he is the way he happens to be. I spent so much time arguing with my parents that I never got to really know them, or they me. Meaningful communication ceased and years went by in polite (or impolite) superficial interaction, with all concerned overscrutinizing even the simplest most innocent appearing words and deeds as likely containing hidden negative assumptions. This then necessitated negative interpretations of thought and action and required the defensive adoption of an arm's length parent-son relationship that hampered much of my growth by depriving me of my parents' knowledge and experience, thwarting my development by keeping me from making their good attributes my own, and progressively eroding mutual admiration and trust, thus reducing chances that I would ever healthily identify with them while increasing chances that because my shame was enhanced and my self-pride was shattered due to having bought into the mean things they said to and about me, I would develop considerable guilt about who and what I was, having become absolutely convinced that if they were so down on me, I must have done something terrible to deserve it.

In contrast, *positivity* toward a gay son can prevent and heal parent-son relational problems. Positivity consists of expressing favorable, while mostly suppressing and not expressing unfavorable, thoughts and feelings about a gay son sometimes even when his behavior strongly merits a critical response. As an approach it bypasses, and sometimes actually leads to solving, parent-son relational problems. Instead of being preoccupied with blaming along the lines of "Who is doing what to whom, who is going to wreak what havoc on whose life, and how can we as parents most effectively punish and get revenge against our offending son?" positive parents put all these things aside to, among other things, disrupt vicious cycles of strike and counterstrike. For now fights don't start, self-perpetuating destructive parent-son interactions diminish or actually cease, covert and overt resistances subside, and compliance is enhanced as all concerned remain silent when they find they cannot be minimally respectful to one another (if they don't stop struggling with each other altogether).

Parental positivity can also actually reduce/cure some of a gay son's specific symptoms and symptomatic behaviors, almost as if by magic. These include acting out by picking unsatisfactory partners, indulging in unsafe sex, using illicit drugs, allowing/provoking bullies to harm him, and making impractical professional choices. That is because many times such "outside behaviors" tend to start at home due to feeling unloved by one's parents, which leads to desperate, wrongheaded misfiring characterized by desperate attempts to enlist others to help enhance one's self-esteem and create a greater sense of self-fulfillment, no matter how poor the odds, and how grave the necessary sacrifice.

Positivity is not the exact equivalent of permissiveness. Parents who are positive don't abdicate their right to rule entirely. They can still set needed standards, enforce proper limits, lay down sensible rules and regulations, and demand that their son respect them, as long as their motivation is to help and they present themselves not in an abrasive, but in a soothing, way.

Realizing positivity effectively does, however, require that parents have and exercise considerable skill. Parents must avoid giving the impression that their positivity really involves being calculating and manipulative, forcing a closeness that they do not feel, and acting, particularly play acting, not in their son's best interests but in order to gratify themselves. Properly done, positivity takes into account a son's individuality, adjusting and read-justing itself according to feedback from him that does or should make his parents aware of how what they have said and done has affected him so that they can, and will willingly, make indicated course corrections as they yield when they have said or done something upsetting, changing direction from having been unreasonable to instead becoming rationally supportive.

Parents/families with different personalities/personality problems will, and should, implement their positivity in different ways, that is, in ways that are in character for them. Positivity will take a more subtle form in an avoidant than in a hypomanic family. Some families find that what works best is the opposite of blaming: not blaming your son for much or anything at all, but instead readily, and willingly, taking one's share of the blame upon one-self. For example, not "It's not us, it's you" (or, more specifically, not "We are not ruining your life, you are ruining ours") but "Clearly we are doing something to upset you to the point that you seem to be getting back at us, and we would like to stop it if only you would let us know what it might be." Other families find this approach unacceptable because to them it means caving in, and doing so in situations in which they sincerely believe that their son's, not their, faults are clearly the problem. To these families, then, this approach is an undesirable capitulation that they see as being the exact opposite of the tough love that their son clearly needs and that his behavior actively merits.

A family I once treated illustrated the benefits of positivity and the unhelpful aspects of negativity as follows. This family learned the hard way that the quickest method for helping a difficult son become less so was to be positive toward him whenever possible, and that, conversely, even a modicum of negativity between Mom, Dad, and their son created vicious cycles of hurting and retaliating that could have been prevented if only the father had been a little more supportive of his son, and the mother had urged the father to do just that and to do it in a timely fashion.

The father never even hinted to his son that he loved and respected him; never showed the slightest interest in what his son was doing, even when the son was being highly creative; never identified problems the son was having in preparation for helping him solve them; and never made any attempt to reduce the tension between him and his son in any way, certainly not by admitting that—if only on occasion—he, the father, was the one at fault. Rather, he regularly increased the tension level by constantly concerning himself with who was doing what wrong by and to whom, who was going to wreak havoc upon whom, and who in turn should properly seek revenge upon whom for having done this or that. Though the father was himself a very difficult person, he saw himself not as being problematic, but as being the innocent victim of his son's acting in a deliberately fractious manner. So he constantly upbraided his son, ultimately reducing his entire relationship with him to "Are you, or are you not, going to stop being gay, and being gay in a bad way?" The result was arguments without enlightenment, and power struggles without resolution. Though the son asked his father to at least sometimes trust in his essential wisdom and goodness, and allow him to be the one who at the minimum made the important decisions about his own fate, and did so on his own, the father nevertheless continued to constantly tell his son that he was going about living his life wrongly while commanding him to change and giving him specific roadmaps to follow as to how to do just that.

This son sincerely both wanted and needed his father's guidance and affirmation. He even told his father that that was the case and that he, the son, would have responded more positively had the father given him those things. But not once did the father let up on being controlling, or apologize for being that way, not even saying "I'm sorry" to the extent of making a general comment along the lines of "Fundamentally I love you, and just the way you are, and so don't mind me so much, I know I am an irascible guy with a temper who doesn't really mean some of the bad things I think and even say to, and about, you." So ultimately the son had no choice but to respond to his father's obdurateness by retaliating, at times with stubborn silence, at others by giving his father an argument, and ultimately by threatening to leave home and actually disappearing from the house for a few days at a time.

After some months the mother, finally, and just in time, took over and told her son that "We love you no matter what" and that "Your father has problems. Try to see that and excuse him for behaving in a way that seems, but isn't, unloving." That was all the son needed to hear! Now in what appeared to be a miraculous turnaround, the son, within a few weeks, became cooperative-to-loving to the point that he no longer needed to destroy himself as his way to destroy his father. Instead he turned his life around precisely so that he could please both Mom and Dad, both of whom he now saw as two people who had his best interests at heart and were doing their utmost for him, although they both (and perhaps Dad in particular) in many respects fell short of perfection. Next, as if miraculously, Dad in his turn responded positively to his son's positivity by becoming far less negative to his son than he had previously been. The rule of positivity now began to work for the father too. For the father, himself feeling less ill-treated by his son, did what was virtually an about face and himself began treating his son in a better, far more positive way, even confessing something that for him was actually remarkable: "I admit it, I did you wrong, and I am glad I saw the light before I behaved badly in a way I could never reverse."

Avoiding Being Passive-Aggressive

One specific way parents can come to feel and act more positively toward a gay son is by avoiding being passive-aggressive toward him. (Passive aggression is also discussed in Chapter 7.)

While parental passive aggression never causes a son to become gay, it can cause him to become gay in a certain, unproductive way—to live well below his capacity simply because he doesn't feel good about himself, and to act out self-destructively simply because though he can't put his finger on why he feels his parents hate him, he nevertheless is certain that they do and that he deserves it. Passive aggression toward a gay son is certainly often responsible for the underperforming so often (incorrectly) attributed to a son being gay. For living is a creative proposition that, like anything else creative, flourishes with parental support as it borrows self-pride from feeling "Mom and Dad are proud of me." Conversely, in the absence of parental pride in a son, or in the presence of its opposite, parental shame of their son, a son's self-pride withers due to creative blockage, leading to the development of diminishing functionality. A son thus treated fails to thrive as a gay man because without his parents on his side he can never fully give himself the vote of confidence he needs to be maximally effective. Like anyone else, for gay sons congratulations, almost always in order, are routinely welcome; conversely, as with most people, a son's functionality decreases when few to no best wishes are forthcoming from Mom and Dad.

Still, too many parents of gay sons are angry that their son is gay and deal with their anger toward their gay son by expressing it in a roundabout, subtle, dilute, way, that is, through passive aggressiveness. Such parents feel hostile toward their gay son. But they do not become openly hostile to him. They do not threaten to shun, punish, or banish him. Instead, expressing their aggression in a restrained and indirect fashion, they become "gently angry." For example, they constantly pout. Or they become "helpful" by pointing out reasons their son should go straight, doing so less abrasively than, as they see it, politely, nicely, subtly, and in a refined manner, as if they are actually providing him with a beneficial resource. But though they think they have successfully covered up their gay bashing with tender prodding, all they have in fact done is to set vicious cycles of strike and counterstrike in motion where their anger, however "politically correctly" expressed, nevertheless leads to their son's retaliation, leading to further parental provocation, leading to further retaliation on their son's part.

Thus one Mom and Dad, very angry with their son for being gay, said so indirectly by the way they framed their annoyance. They expressed their criticism of their son as worry. They favored one thing to disfavor another, for example, a series of informal partnerships ("the best way to avoid getting hurt," they said) to disfavor ("throw cold water on") his impending gay marriage. They devalued their son being gay by praising the alternative, which for them was asexuality. Instead of discrete temper tantrums, they displayed constant irritability over time. For example, for years they spitefully took the gay unfriendly side in ongoing straight-gay controversies such as the one about the acceptability of enlisting openly gay men in the military. They would *think* about taking a favorable proson (not an unfavorable antison) family position instead of *actually taking* one, and *contemplate* gay negative imponderables nonassertively, intellectually, and always reluctantly, as when instead of openly condemning their son's being gay they ruminated about whether his being gay was a choice he made ("You brought it on yourself") or was selected for him genetically by his (and their) biology. Instead of making overtly homophobic statements, they asked questions with clear homonegative implications like "Do you like to cook?" and "Do you understand football?"—queries intended not to seek information, but to convey approbation. They often indulged in meant-to-be humorous comments that were in fact nevertheless quite piercing. For example, once their son heard his father tell a buddy, "For Christmas

I gave my son a pink poinsettia to acknowledge how that is the right color for a queen." They would offer help when it was not needed (since now they could anticipate he would reject it) but withhold help when they determined he could clearly use it. Thus for years Dad would typically worry unnecessarily about his son's physical condition, for example, constantly warning him about catching such obscure diseases as a fungal infection from the back of a movie theatre seat, and taking him to one doctor after another when he was perfectly well. But when his son actually got sick, with a real ailment, the father seemed not to see, understand, or care, for example, that his young son was wheezing from an asthma attack or had a severe second-degree sunburn the father allowed to happen by refusing to drive his son home from the beach before exactly eight hours ("a full day of pleasure") was up. Both Mom and Dad would selectively ignore most of their son's real needs, letting him flounder in the guise of "not being intrusive and controlling." And they would actually advocate parental nonintervention when in reality he needed parental guidance, doing so just because they didn't want to be bothered and waste their time "with someone (so hopelessly gay) like him." They would *affirm* their unconditional love for their son only to add, "We do so even though he is second best, but could easily be first rate, and even more loveable, if he went straight." They said they accepted their son's friends, but in fact they never allowed him to bring them over for dinner on the holidays when other family members were present. Playing favorites within the family, they singled their son out for neglect while giving his siblings preferential treatment, for example, financially putting his sisters through school while making their son work to pay his own tuition, then rationalizing their behavior not as being "based on prejudice" but as being "according to need."

They would devalue their son being gay by giving him backhanded compliments along the lines of "Some of the best people in the world are gay" or by taking the (currently laughable) position, one that however at the time they nevertheless wholeheartedly embraced, that "Some of our best friends are gay." When they actually complimented him, they did so only for something that didn't count for much, thereby implying that that was the best they could do because that was the only one of his qualities worth noting.

They would offer fairness and love in situations where it didn't count for much, for example, "To show you how much I advocate for gays, I will boycott the Boy Scouts, fundraiser at the mall." They would side with almost anyone but their son after finding some reason to do that. For example, in a typical example of passive-aggressive heterosexism reflecting the mother's subtly negative attitude toward gay men, her son, an experienced professional, told his mother that one day at work he was testing a baby for breathing difficulties. He complained that the baby's mother had asked him, "How long have you been doing this?" and that he had perceived the question as an implied insult along the lines of her accusing him of inexperience. But his own mother, instead of supporting him, defended the baby's mother in no uncertain terms: "You don't understand her at all. That's because as a gay man you aren't, and never will actually be, a parent yourself."

They regularly justified their homonegativity by saying that they "were entitled to their opinion." Also they would express their homonegativity in the form of pseudo-realistic strictly theoretical *concerns* along the lines of "We are worried that gay marriage will undermine traditional marriage" without, however, saying (or realizing) exactly how that might happen. They claimed that their negative feelings were in fact entirely rational, for, they insisted, they were only making "proper sensible good-bad distinctions" that in fact turned out to be distinctions without true differences along the lines of "I love you, the sinner, I only hate your sin." They would attempt to whitewash all their negativity by claiming positive motives for their off-putting positions ("I am just trying to protect you from having a difficult life"). Or they would try to hide their negative feelings under the aegis of claiming reasonable uncertainty ("I just *wonder* if as a gay man you will have as good a life as you could have had if you were a straight").

They often also provoked others to dutifully do their own (hostile) work for them, typically by passing on information that the rest of the core family, their extended family, and their friends could use to attack, or to ignore and isolate, their son. Thus they regularly provoked their son's brothers and sisters, as well as members of their extended family, to act out their negativity toward their son for them by passing on what their son said to them in confidence in one of his unguarded moments, never thinking that Mom and Dad would pass his remarks on to his siblings and relatives. This predictably caused the latter to feel offended and act out retaliatively against him.

Too often when they could no longer contain their anger, it all came rushing out and they became highly vocal about how their son's being gay traumatized and depressed them. They once actually said that his being gay was so terrible that they did not regret attacking him verbally, for, as they noted, "You deserve it because of what your being gay has done, and still is doing, to us."

Dynamically, as with other passive-aggressive parents, the goal of their passive aggression was to reduce their own guilt about feeling angry ("I am a loving parent, not a homophobe, an altruistic person longing to be nice to, and do good for, my son"), while still getting their angry point across without completely undermining its significance and validity by having become openly mean-spirited. With this in mind, they found ways to proclaim that their passive aggression was simply "diplomacy," though they were just fooling themselves to spare themselves recognition of how hurtful they were being to their son, and at a very large cost to him. They also worked to convince themselves that though their passive aggression was unrelenting, since each individual incident wasn't doing their son much harm, they had no reason to stop. They said that they believed that their son, like anyone else, clearly would be able to accept covert better than overt criticism. But what they overlooked was that overall direct aggression would have been less disturbing than passive aggression. For their passive-aggressive hostility in the long run was far more devastating than any overt aggression could be because overt aggression involving actually getting mad meant getting it over with, thus making it easier for their son, the victim, to take and handle their aggression because he would at least know exactly where he stood and what he had to deal with. (Conversely, when a parental attack is covert, its lack of focus and clarity enhances its potential for negative impact simply because it increases the likelihood that the son will make generally correct half-empty negative interpretations of what his parents are trying to disguise as half-full positive statements.)

Overall, their passive aggression was particularly difficult for their son to manage because it was so hard for him to identify. All he knew was that he felt uncomfortable, without quite knowing why, causing him to wonder if he, not his parents, "had the problem, for since they were being so measurably rational, something must be wrong with me. For if I were a better son they wouldn't feel this way about me. And if I weren't so paranoid I wouldn't think that they didn't love me/hated me. And if I weren't so sensitive I wouldn't react so negatively to what Mom and Dad implied or said. So since I am the one with the problem, I am the one who needs to change, to love Mom and Dad more, not the other way around. Now if I am nicer to them, they will recant and be nicer to me. So perhaps though they aren't actually coming out and saying so, I really do need therapy in order to be a better person for myself, and, as well, by going straight, to be a better son for them."

This said, it is not always entirely a bad thing for parents to express their anger covertly (not overtly) in a less (rather than in a more) abrasive way, in a passive-aggressive (rather than in an openly aggressive) way. Passive aggressiveness helps parents directly diminish if not their anger itself then some of its harmful effects. But there are better ways to do this. They can speak softly, never yelling, while at the same time referring to their anger as obliquely as they possibly can and diluting its impact with simultaneously expressed self-criticisms such as "I wish I were a calmer person who didn't get so upset about things, but I'm not." They can also displace their anger onto other topics, topics more neutral than those directly involving their son's being gay. For example, instead of complaining about his being promiscuous, they can question him about the late hours he is keeping. Or they can use defensive internalization, which involves turning their anger around on themselves, blaming themselves for being too sensitive instead of blaming their son for being overly insensitive. They can also turn the focus from feelings and onto issues, thus pouring their rage into an honest, rational, responsible, dispassionate statement of valid concrete matters worth constructively observing and discussing and into problems worth resolving, turning negative feeling into creative idea—as they think things through dispassionately to avoid feelthink where feeling becomes reality, however delusional that reality turns out to be. These are *positive* yet essentially non–passive-aggressive techniques for expressing anger. For as such they allow parents to express some of how they feel in a healthy way, while still sparing their son, their target, the full brunt of their negative feelings.

Reducing Your Anger toward Your Son

This said, it's always better for parents to try to become less angry with their son. A first step involves parents trying to determine why they feel angry with their son in the first place. And that step begins with developing intrapersonal insight that starts with being honest with themselves. This is a step that often requires deep psychological introspection with the goal of discovering the psychodynamics of their anger so that they can determine if any of their concerns are valid, or if instead their angry responses are mainly or entirely emotionally driven.

Parents should consider the possibility that much of their anger toward their son is the product of irrational *fear*. This fear is likely to occur over internal issues involving dependency, control, and competition. In the realm of *dependency* fears, parents feel anger because they fear that their son being gay means that he will abandon his family because, as they see it, no gay man will have the feeling of obligation toward and ties with his family that (again as they see it) all straight children have. They fear that "In associating himself with the gay lifestyle, he will predictably dissociate himself from us." Should they in actuality be dependent on him, they will likely fear losing him even more along the lines of "There will be no one to take care of us in our old age." Therefore, some parents who say, "My son is sick and needs to be cured" may be expressing as much a wish (for him to be sick) as a concern over his being ill. For if he were truly sick, he might be more dependent on them and so be more malleable and thus more easily influenced to bend to their will.

In the realm of *control* fears, many parents feel frustrated that they might lose power over their son because he is gay. They become annoyed that he won't turn straight for them on command. They become fixated on winning or losing the battle over who is going to prevail in that arena, along the lines of "Why must you insist on having a man over a woman sexually? Have you actually tried sex with a woman?"

In the realm of *competition* fears, many a father views his gay son as inferior to straight sons, perhaps as a "cripple" due to being "sexually retarded" along the lines of an old psychoanalytic belief that "Being gay is a regression from being straight." Such fathers come to feel angry because as they compare themselves to other fathers whose genes didn't produce a "defective offspring," they begin to feel that their son (by being what he is) makes them ashamed of themselves because they are defective as fathers. But the disappointment in not having a son who is "good and strong like me and can compete with me in sports" comes with another, paradoxical, secret, feeling: "At least that means that he won't outshine me, so now I can easily best him. For his lack of masculinity removes a threat, particularly an (oedipal) threat to my exclusive relationship with his mother, my wife." Such fathers are actually happy to have a gay son, but they can't accept that. So instead they hide that wish under an expressed outrage—"My son is somehow defective." Yet they secretly continue to wish that "He will never become less so, to the point of showing me up, and even taking his mother, my wife, away from me." But instead of acknowledging that they welcome having a gay son, they acknowledge only their (safer) unwelcoming feelings, for example, "That son of mine pisses me off by being queer and refusing to stop it."

Reducing anger may also require developing *interpersonal* insight that involves understanding how negativity is an aspect of one's personality/ personality disorder and one that has clear implications for parent-son relationships. You as parents can diminish your anger by altering the following aspects of your personality should these lead you to become angry with your son over his being gay. Anger about having a gay son may be the product of:

- Being an *obsessive brooder/compulsive worrier* where morality matters excessively as your son being gay gives you qualms in principle and leads you to long to, or to actually, implement moral strictures, even though these having only a theoretical relevance won't help calm your rage and will instead make your son feel bad; and being such a *perfectionist* that you refuse to accept anything less than your son's being flawless. You see his being gay as his being imperfect, as you feel that your being perfect (not just good enough) parents is what is desirable, however much it is impossible.
- Being a *depressed pessimist* who sees only the bad in people and situations and thus strongly believes (and so says) that the worst case scenario (all gay life) actually represents the most likely outcome.
- Being a *histrionic* who reacts to trivial prompts as if they are momentous provocations, thus turning minor issues into major concerns as alarm drives alarm until worry becomes certainty that all concerned are in big trouble.
- Being a *paranoid* with a tendency to project so that you make your into his issues. In particular you furiously criticize your son for the many things you criticize in yourself. Now you form an angry adversarial relationship with your gay son around imagined slights you come to feel head your way directly out of his being gay, ranging from his being a traitor to family values to his having joined "some foreign society" you don't condone, understand, or have anything in common with, and so to which you feel you don't even remotely belong.
- Being a *phobic* whose anger is an avoidance mechanism.
- Being an *avoidant*, for anger reassures avoidant parents (parents who fear their positive feelings are shameful and embarrassing) that closeness is unlikely and so won't become a source of anxiety and worry. Avoidant fathers welcome their anger because it protects them from becoming too emotionally involved with their sons, thereby becoming flooded by overly strong feelings, especially those let loose by disclosure. Anger also helps avoidant fathers contain their fear that the slightest stirring of positive emotion might cause all positive and negative emotions (with all emotions being forbidden) to spin out of control and overwhelm them, leaving them no longer in charge and in control of themselves or of their situation, causing dissolution of the self (ego). Anger also helps avoidant fathers draw boundary lines and set/enforce limits to deal with personal erotophobia intensified by the fear that loving their son too much is somehow forbidden because it is, in a way, by itself inherently homosexual.

- Being *masochistic*, for masochistic fathers and mothers—being afraid of success—fear getting what they want, in this case a loving son "who is too good for me, the bad parent." As a consequence, masochistic parents (needing to condemn the good things that happen to them as bad things) view the best of times, such as good joyful family events with a gay son, as the worst of times because joy is unacceptable and happiness forbidden. So they actually welcome disappointment over having a gay son so that they can go through life suffering over having such a child—simply because they feel that that suffering is their destiny
- Being *narcissistic* so that anger is the product of the egocentric view that your son's being gay is not only a negative occurrence but a pejorative comment on *you* and what *you* are capable of producing.

Interpersonal anger is also often the product of making cognitive errors about having and parenting a gay son. It follows that correcting these cognitive errors can lead to becoming more rational, that way lysing the parent-son antagonisms that arise out of such distortive thinking. Therefore, parents who feel angry should search for causative relational cognitive errors such as *personalization* that leads them to believe that their son is criticizing them as individuals just because he asks them to change toward him in some way; *some = all* thinking that implies that just because their son has *some* complaints about them, his parents, for example, for being less than accommodating in *some* ways, that necessarily means that he hates them *completely*; and *catastrophizing* that commonly results from the flattening of the response curve to the point that as parents they can hardly modulate the tone and amplitude of their responses to make them fit the actual intensity, severity, significance, and importance of their stimuli, so that they now create high drama that has little basis in reality as they divide the people in the gay world into protagonists and antagonists, and indulge in calamitous slippery slope—"For want of a nail the ship was lost" thinking along the lines of "Since my son, the antagonist, challenges me about some things, he will of necessity go on to disagree with me about everything, and that means that he will soon enough hate what I stand for, and me completely." Parents with this form of chain thinking, believing that giving a finger predictably means losing an arm, leap pseudo-logically from one negative association to another without in each case determining the significance of/the validity of the linkage. Thus they fail to recognize the likelihood that the progression they fear will of necessity go from A to Z may very well stop at B. For them gay life becomes predictably as troublesome and dangerous as they, as catastrophizing parents, believe it to be, although in truth most gay sons are not nearly as deserving of parental disappointment in, and anger toward, them as many parents believe. For example, they feel that because a son is sleeping around a bit (A) that means that he has become hopelessly promiscuous (Z) to the point that he will never change and have a good, calm, creative, productive life. Yet chances are that one day, and sooner rather than later, he will settle down (B) with someone he loves and who loves him (and even, hopefully, someone who loves you, his parents, as well and just as much).

Parents should carefully search for cognitive errors that constitute oversimplifications that are the result of *removing* levels of complexity, particularly the optimistic possibilities that generally reside among negativity, making pessimistic interpretations of reality the product of rigid, one-sided, overly personal selective interpretations. Parents who do such a thing create pessimistic passion due to contradicting their positive theses by processing information in a way that disregards heartening facts that do not fit with their negative fears and, on occasion, negative yearnings. Conversely, some parents *add* unnecessary levels of complexity to simple interactions by reading something sinister/alarming that is not there into a benign situation then overreacting so angrily to their self-created malignant precepts that they completely lose all perspective about what their reality actually is.

You as parents can also reduce your angry feelings over your son being gay by refusing to view him as a transference object. You should especially not view him, like you would view a Rorschach inkblot, through the distortive lens of your own past experiences, particularly those with your own parents and siblings, and do this to the point that you fail to see him exactly as he is now. Parents in a strong transference reaction to their son make their relationship out of a repetition of old feelings/recurrent traumatic occurrences that they newly revive to recycle as if fate necessarily is repeating itself. For example, my father was angry with me for being *different* because to him my being different from him was a liability, not an asset. In the main, this was because it reminded him of how his own father found my father wanting simply because he, my father, chose not to go into my grandfather's business. That meant that any of my achievements that were at all unique fired up old unpleasant experiences related to my dad wanting to be different from his own dad, and did so with catastrophic effect. The upshot was that my reviving feelings of how disappointed his own father had been with him made my father even angrier with me.

When you feel angry at your son, try dealing with your rage by utilizing *empathy*. Empathy involves putting yourself in your son's place to see that likely he is not a bad person, only someone trying to live his life as a good person, which isn't always so easy for every gay man. Empathy avoids making life even harder for a gay son by your reframing "Life is hard for him" into "His being gay makes life harder for us." At the same time empathy respects his limitations, which are due not to his being gay, but to his only being human, and so, like you, imperfect. Fortunately it's not necessary for your son to be perfect; for imperfection is the norm, and many imperfections—being more temporary than otherwise—are likely to entirely disappear over time or even morph, perhaps with your help, into something more like perfections.

Try to lower the expectations you have of yourself as you try lowering the expectations you have of your son. Too many parents of gay sons paradoxically hold these sons to a higher standard than they hold their straight sons. So they expect more from their gay sons than they expect from his straight siblings (as if he has to make up for being gay by being better). Then having actually become less tolerant and more hypercritical of him than if he were straight, they come to feel very negatively about his not actually being on the level of or superior to his straight brothers and sisters. Disappointed that he hasn't matched up to parental expectations, they see just about everything he is doing as "wrong" and everything "wrong" that he says and does not as a sign of his humanity, but as proof of his defectiveness. Expecting that their gay son be more flawless than if he were straight, and unable to accept anything less than his compensating them for his being gay by being very special, they fail to adjust their expectations to what their son is personally capable of being based on his innate emotional/physical attributes/problems. Now constantly seriously disappointed in what their son has to offer, they go through life angrily feeling that "Having him means fate has abandoned me, for in the lottery of producing children all I could draw was this gay loser."

Don't rage first at yourself for not loving your son unconditionally then at him for causing you to hate yourself. Most parents have mixed negative and positive feelings about most children. It's enough if you make a start toward being more positive by identifying your negativity as not entirely called for and vowing to think more positively in the future. Instead of feeling guilty and angrily blaming not only yourself, but also your son for making you feel negatively, accept your negativity and integrate your negative feelings into a self-view that leaves room for them while remaining overall favorably inclined to yourself.

Don't rely on the overuse of such anger-inducing defenses as:

- *Identification with the aggressor*, where Mom and Dad perceive their son's being gay as an attack upon them and attack him back in retaliation, "kicking him out" of their house because he has "kicked us out of his life."
- *Projective identification*, where Mom and Dad experience the negativity *they* feel toward their son as coming at them *from* their son, leading them to seek vengeance toward him as if under the circumstances that's the only conceivable proper reply.
- *Denial*, where Mom and Dad disguise their anger through reaction formation. Instead of thinking, "I don't like it, but you are still my son, and let's come together over this," they instead proclaim, "We aren't interested in what you do. It's your life, live it as you choose (for all we care)." Thereby, sullen and withdrawn, they miss a great opportunity to fully participate in their son's life not only as his parents, but also as his friends and colleagues.
- *Isolative removal*, where to avoid crises Mom and Dad try to stay out of relational areas they feel they can't handle, walk away from situations where they believe that they are not welcome, and avoid interactions where they think their son will not adequately reward their involvement with him. For they think, "The effort required/the stress involved is not commensurate with the results achieved and can only underscore our angry disappointment in having a gay son."

Avoid vicious cycling where negativity starts and escalates due to focusing on "who is doing what to whom" along two lines: "You did it first," and "Tu quoque," that is, "You are one too." When vicious cycling seems to be getting out of hand, try taking time-outs where you deliberately hold off being angry at least for the time being and instead of expressing your anger, keep calm by reserving getting mad for later.

Since parenting a gay son is a cooperative venture, try asking your son to help you become more positive toward him. Ask your son to join in your attempts to change yourself, that is, to assist you to become a better, less negative parent to him. Ask him to be forthright in telling you how he is reacting to you and why. Ask him to accept you as a difficult parent doing his or her best. Ask him to consider positive things about you, including that your *basic* feelings are loving, even though superficially, and for now, to him it may not seem that way at all.

Try keeping a journal. It may be a good way to help you recognize that your son is not your adversary or out to ruin someone's life, yours or his.

It can also help you stop collecting injustices, thus creating resentments for which there is a price to pay.

Create a journal with two columns on the page: on the left how you feel about your son, and on the right reality, the comparative truth as you do (or should) know it. On the left (entitled "fantasy") write down "how I do feel." On the right (entitled "reality") write down "how I should feel." On the left write down "here is how I do think," and on the right write down "here is how I should think." On the left write down "here is what I see happening," and on the right write down "here is what is actually occurring." Put down every negative fantasy you might have about your son on the left side of the page and on the right side document alternative, more positive, less fantastical responses/fanatical interpretations of reality. This journal can help you expose irrationality that interferes with your calm as you study it coolly and dispassionately, and at regular intervals. This way you obtain a reality check on how you do, but shouldn't, filter perceptions of your son through your special personal scenario consisting of heavy feelthink that by warping reality creates perceptual biases. This way you teach yourself that going through life with a gay son is not the entirely negative, highly dangerous experience you fear it might be. For as you now begin to see, danger is less present in his and your life than you at first had feared; he is not as flawed as you at first came to believe; and he is full of inherent goodness, as you are now just beginning to learn.

Use your journal to tell you what you need to assimilate to help you pull back from stressful and possibly dangerous responses that occur because you react with alarm merely to signs that your son is growing up, and as if what you disapprove of are not transitional but rather fixed permanent actions on his part—that is, impulsive actions of the moment, not positional statements of a lifetime.

Finally do not buy into divisive social myths. For many parents of gay sons, anger with their gay son is often less a personal issue than a socially induced problem. Thus there is the particularly dangerous social myth that homosexuality is on the slippery slope to incest, bigamy, polygamy, and bestiality. This myth is based on old-time beliefs that have not been updated for ages and so still contain ancient wisdom that, like the ancient wisdom that a flat earth is the center of the universe, is out of date in light of more recent, mare valid scientific discoveries and moral advances.

And always remember not to blame society's negativity to gays in order to avoid taking responsibility for negative feelings that are in fact not society's problem, but a problem of your own making.

Chapter 16

Other Therapeutic Approaches

Family Therapy

The term "family therapy" describes a number of different therapies that have in common simultaneously focusing on more than one family member—as they actually bring each subject into the consultation room for joint evaluation and treatment.

The therapeutic *goal* is to resolve both individual and collective family emotional difficulties such as individual-collective fear of intimacy. The therapeutic *method* involves taking problematical relationships among family members as the point of departure, hoping to reduce tension by resolving relational conflicts as a way to ameliorate family stress, reduce family anxiety, diminish family dissonance, and improve family well-being. The theoretical *framework* varies, but it is often eclectic, that is, it combines insight-oriented approaches with cognitive-behavioral, interpersonal, and supportive therapies.

The therapist who uses *insight-oriented* approaches hopes by providing full awareness into personal and interpersonal difficulties to reduce family displeasure through seeking its reasons, importantly exploring the past and how it negatively influences the present. The therapist who uses *cognitive* approaches explores logical distortions about what it means to have a gay son, and what being gay is all about, in a quest to help the family thoroughly air, understand, and rethink the flawed logic/faulty reasoning that is causing some of its presenting problems. Many cognitive therapists simultaneously utilize a behavioral approach. They might encourage the parents to teach their son by example, that is, to *model* the good life for him using illustrations from their own successful relationship and rewarding life. For instance, parents can show their son how the working heterosexual relationship they are in has lessons for how he as a gay man can have a homosexual relationship that also works by in significant ways paralleling the heterosexual relationship his parents have. One set of parents said that their goal was to "heterosexualize" their son's homosexuality. They told their son what they believed worked in their relationship to illustrate what might work for him and his partner—demonstrating by words and deeds how two people (his parents, older, and in some respects wiser, than he) had learned things over the years that they wanted to pass on to their son now as constituting methods he could profitably use to resolve problems he was having in his own life and in his relationship with his partner. These parents concluded that modeling was the best approach for them to employ as a way to influence their son positively because that method lacked intimidation, which would likely lead their son to respond, not as they might have hoped, by thinking, "Dad and Mom know something I can learn," but to respond by thinking, "You are victimizing me by being so controlling." As it turned out, in this they were especially successful not only both because they used this particular method, but also because as part of their approach they took care to listen to who their son was and what he wanted for himself and his partner before trying to make him over entirely in their own image. That is, they modeled the good life as they saw it but left room for the considerable generational gap and personal differences that existed between them and their son, who also had an approach to life that, though not identical to their own, certainly represented a reasonable way for him to live.

Education Therapy

Most parents of gay sons feel at least somewhat overwhelmed by their situation. Education can guide them away from feeling traumatized, anxious, and fearful about what they perceive to be their current predicament and future travails to help them see things as they are and will be, and so to avoid grieving and overcome getting depressed over their so-called loss by correcting painful negative imaginings and replacing them with truths about the far less than harsh reality involved in their having, and having to raise, a gay son.

Educated parents learn that there is every reason to avoid pessimism about their "predicament" and feel more hopeful about their, and also about their son's, future prospects. Education therapy helps increase the joys and reduce the challenges of having a gay son by clarifying what being gay means, and so how to understand and respect that exactly. It challenges and dispels myths about having a gay son that contribute to misunderstandings that can lead to anger and resentment, thus eroding parental support for their child.

Sometimes parents actually need to learn the simplest of things, such as how being gay differs from pedophilia—a sexual attraction to the young that overlaps, if at all, only in some highly peripheral aspects with homosexuality. They can learn that a father doesn't need to feel guilty about causing his son to be gay because he (the father) was passive and that a mother doesn't need to feel guilty about causing her son to be gay because she was enveloping (or the reverse, the father by being castrative and the mother by being distant). And they can develop their parenting skills overall through learning the difference that exists between being loving and being overpermissive, as well as between healthful manipulation and exploitation. They can discover reasons to discard their irrational remoteness, hurtful disrespect, shattering rejection, and destructive hatefulness. They can also learn to hear their son out and gain knowledge from him as he tries to tell them things about himself and his life—things they simply need to know to combat such of their negative emotions as anxiety and relieve such of their symptomatic disorders as depression.

Educational therapy directs parents to supplemental reading that can answer some of their questions—thus raising intellectual awareness to combat the negative effects of cumulative self-reinforcing distortive, often emotionally based, confusion and self-doubt.

Group Therapy

Here I offer some guidelines on how you as parents of a gay son can decide if group therapy is right for you, if so where to find the most appropriate group to join, and how to evaluate whether the group you are in is the right one for you.

There are two main categories of group therapy: (1) self-run, self-directed, often leaderless groups; and (2) groups run by a trained professional. The former may or may not be activist-oriented groups. The latter are of various theoretical persuasions ranging from traditional (often psychoanalytically oriented) to eclectic to fringe.

Self-run, self-directed, often leaderless groups like those run by PFLAG offer you as parents help in the following ways. The group:

- Helps keep you from feeling alone by offering you a sense of belonging and ties to a community that shares joys and sorrows around a common cause
- Helps you distinguish what your son happens to be from what you as his parents think he is, ought to be, and should become—because that is what you want from him, often because that is what you expect from yourself

- Gives you a chance to reveal your innermost secrets and talk about your most trying experiences in a noncritical, supportive, nonpunitive setting
- Provides you with an opportunity to abreact in order to express your passions, thus reducing harmful emotional buildup
- Gives you an outlet whereby you can get difficult feelings out of your system and out into the open, which is helpful in itself and additionally therapeutic by providing you with an opportunity to share how you feel with peers in anticipation of getting valuable feedback from them; you get feedback from other supportive parents eager to share their own experiences, both positive and negative, as well as consensual validation of too rarely acknowledged/accepted feelings, including those which are strongly negative (this helps you counteract the social negativism that exists all around you related to having a gay son and the way you parent him)
- Gives you specific advice on what to think and how to behave with your son not only overall, but specifically at tense moments ranging from disclosure time to any first signs that he might be getting into trouble in his activities of everyday living (ADLs)
- Offers you valuable ideas and suggestions for solving specific problems such as whether to intervene when your son is living dangerously and being self-destructive, and how to do so without being too invasive/controlling, or fixating on the gay issue to the exclusion of other, just as important (related and unrelated), matters that should also be of concern to you and your son
- Teaches you what you need to know about being gay by explaining what being gay actually involves, specifically that (except in some cases of bisexuality) because being gay is not a choice, it is almost always not variable but immutable and exists in gay men down to their bones
- Shows you that though a son being gay isn't selected by but for him, his being gay *in a certain way* does involve his making a number of choices and that here is where just as you might help a child of any sexual persuasion, you might step in and assist him with specific life problems he might be having of a personal or social nature
- Teaches you to differentiate what is normative in your own (straight) society from what is normative in his (gay) society, thus helping you appreciate and manage the fundamental disparities/cultural differences between the two
- Helps cushion interpersonal blows by being there for you as a shield, helping protect you; and by being there for you as a sword, inspiring you to act forcefully with others to actively bring about inner family and social harmony—for example, by holding off/suppressing outside bullying both directed to you and to your son
- Teaches you how to work toward creating social reform favorable for your gay son, as well as for all gay men and lesbians, bisexuals, transgendered, and questioning people

In two situations group therapy may not only be unhelpful, but may actually be harmful. First, it may disappoint by promising to offer you, then not actually providing you with, definitive solutions to difficulties that in fact require more technical input than any group can give. Leaderless groups and groups not run by a trained professional can prove especially inadequate for seriously emotionally ill parents, particularly those who perceive their situation to be, when it is not, highly traumatic and those undergoing a severe grief reaction/depression because their son has (they believe) figuratively or literally abandoned them. (In such cases, it is likely that you may need a professionally run group and possibly even individual therapy to supplement/replace the professional group experience.)

Second, badly run groups exist. Attending them can be less desirable than not being in group therapy (or in any therapy) at all. Though badly run groups may still provide some of the comforts of belonging, the benefits of reduced isolation, shared knowledge, and inspiration from others on how to do better and bring about social change, the distinct downsides of such groups can negate even these considerable benefits. An especially counterproductive downside involves overly encouraging parents to paper over specific parent-son problems by the use of advocacy that is more like denial, thus bypassing or ignoring the need for actual problem solving. In my experience an excessively extreme focus on gay issues can encourage parents to overlook the larger specific problematical issues that surround having a gay son, even when these are actually the issues causing the most havoc. Life is distorted when the gay issue is the only one explored and, not, as it should be, part of a discussion of the broader concerns involved in being a good parent to your, as to any, son.

Another downside, one parents have frequently complained to me about, is that a group merely by focusing on problems can thereby intensify them, making them seem bigger and more intrusive than they actually are. This then *fosters* trauma instead of *mitigating* its effects, and even inculcates traumatophilia—a tendency to resort to, and even like living in, a (traumatic) present where over and over again parents revive terrifying experiences because they have actually come to enjoy scaring themselves in order to test, and retest, their strength and endurance. They also trend toward traumatophilia to come out ahead by having met and overcome a traumatic happening with aplomb and bravery. Some parents quit certain groups because they felt group attendance required them to continually experience problems they had actually solved—to in effect act as if the problems were still acute when they had become chronic or inactive, or had entirely disappeared. That, one parent said, "only intensified my problems by encouraging me to dwell on them." As a result of reliving problems, parents ultimately experience damage, including to their self-esteem. Others have specifically complained to me that getting overly involved in advocacy, as the group encouraged them to do, led them to withdraw from outside relationships with parents who weren't activists or who didn't even have a gay son, to the point that they became somewhat isolated and ultimately depressed because they associated with no one besides those (relative few individuals) with whom they could share this (but only this) specific life experience.

Activism Therapy

On the positive side, activist parents, especially those who join relevant action groups, can achieve personal resilience through the group experience via attaining strength from numbers and receiving validation from others similarly inclined in their quest to change things for the better in the world through attaining political influence, obtaining funding, fighting defamation, combating stereotyping, counteracting media portrayals of gays in an unfortunately defamatory way, and helping pass laws against discrimination and hate. By raising your own and others' awareness, sensitizing yourself, and educating yourself and others to become attentive to false generalizations that reduce gay men in the eyes of all concerned, you as parents can do something, and perhaps a great deal, to help influence the world's view of gays in a favorable direction. Too, joining your son in such events as gay pride parades can help your son improve his self-esteem via enhancing the pride that comes not only from feeling good because he is gay, but also from feeling good because "I know my parents support and love me, and, among other things, that gives me an ally and a defense against those who would devalue me."

But activism can be excessive when it stereotypes gay men not as all bad, but as all good, creating a situation where parents don't do their job because having bought into "good" myths about homosexuality, they ignore neutral and negative facts about their son just because these do not fit. Having encapsulated/buried beliefs contradictory to the fully affirmative view—first having walled them off and second having overcompensated through denial, instead of irrationally devaluing, they defensively overvalue their son, creating a picture of him that however admirably positive is incomplete and inauthentic, and as such forms an inadequate foundation for any ongoing helpful intervention that he might need. Activism is especially harmful when it stops parents from basing their relationship with their son on who he actually is and what he should be, thus keeping parents from intervening when he is actually acting uncreatively or behaving self-destructively. You feel, but he does not get, better because in being insufficiently against him, you leave him without the supportive *tough* love he might need and the structure that can best come from considered, firm guidance from you in the form of helpfully strict limit-setting and the establishment of rules for valid, useful, necessary standards of behavior.

Another danger from activism involves overlooking how being too confrontational can be unsafe with many homonegative people—those who do not take kindly to being opposed in this, or in any other, sphere. There are many situations where activist parents must protect themselves physically. To do so they may have to act with strength that is *silent* (though without cloying passivity), on the one hand finding a way to discourage abuse yet avoiding passive submission, but on the other hand avoiding dangerous confrontation by first saying "please" and "thank you" but then additionally emphasizing, "I mean what I just said."

Chapter 17

Advice for Gay Sons

A happy, successful parent-child relationship requires bilateral accommodation where parents get along with their sons, *and* sons get along with their parents—as both generations act in a responsible fashion toward each other, meeting each other halfway—as the son adjusts to his parents much as he expects his parents to adjust to him. That requires that the son understand his parents' perspective much as he might expect his parents to understand his. It follows that gay sons instead of being strictly focused on what their parents are doing wrong and asking their parents to behave and telling them in no uncertain terms what they have to do to behave well, should instead ask themselves if their parents are always and entirely their (the son's) problem, in the wrong, and need to do all the changing. Perhaps some of the responsibility to change/reform could be the son's, not his parents—because he, the son, seriously misunderstands and even victimizes his parents. So instead of complaining about them, he should become more sensitive to their feelings. Instead of oppressing them, he should more eagerly help to ease their burdens.

Gay sons should try to empathize with their parents to understand how they feel about having a son who is gay. Empathy involves identification so that the son can see himself from his parents' perspective—not only from the vantage point of "What are my own joys and burdens?" but also from the vantage point of "How do my parents likely feel, faced with my being gay and confronted with something that is hard for them to fully understand, and that they just want to go away?"

A son should recognize when his parents have responded to his disclosure transferentially, that is, to their gay son as if he has become a blank screen upon whom they have projected their own emotions and beliefs to create their personal new reality so that his parents see him not as he actually is, but according to their own psychology. It follows that gay sons should not take everything that their parents say about them personally, and seriously, but should instead see how many of their parents' views and attitudes are internally (self-)determined. This is particularly true for parental homonegativity, which so often likely consists less of parental bigotry than parental feelthink, that is, it originates to a great extent in the so-called wisdom of emotionality. So as a son you should think, "Just because they criticize me doesn't mean that I necessarily pro-voked/deserved the criticism. Therefore, I don't need to respond so fear-fully or contentiously." It also follows that gay sons can best respond to their parents empathetically if they take into consideration their parents' background, personality structure, any personality disorder from which they might be suffering, and their philosophy. In terms of their philosophy, if yours is an old-school *conservative* (rather than a progressive liberal) family, you should as much as possible avoid being confrontational to avoid/minimize abrading your parents' special sensibilities having to do with both homosexual and all sexual matters. You should seriously con-sider how your being gay negatively impacts family tradition. You might even consider agreeing to form a pact with certain parents to spare them as much pain as you possibly can about your coming out. For example, if your parents request that you keep being gay from certain identified rela-tives and friends, you might agree to come out *selectively*, admitting you are gay to your parents but not being as open with all of the rest of the family.

If your family has *avoidant* tendencies, respect their fear of intensity/closeness and come out gently and gradually, recognizing that intensity/close-ness threatens them as much as or more than does remoteness. If as you disclose they seem to feel overwhelmed by something they can't handle, pull back a little by not disclosing too forcefully, not pushing them to get involved, not attempting too hard to cut through their denial, and not too actively trying to all at once convert what you believe to be their "homonegative mis-anthropy" into a greater respect and love for you, and for what you are, and no matter what.

If your family has *depressive* tendencies, they will likely need as much reassurance from you as you need from them. They will likely respond most favorably to this reassurance: that although they may have had some input into selected problems, if any, of your gay life, or in other aspects of your life, they are in no way responsible for having made you gay. You might also reassure them that in the future all will be well, for having a gay son, and you in particular, doesn't mean that their life is over. So instead of grieving they can recognize that because they haven't lost any-thing in the first place, they have nothing to grieve about at all.

If your family has *histrionic* tendencies that make them prone to histrionics, do what you can to avoid provoking them to having a catastrophic response to your coming, and being, out. Hopefully if you come out dispassionately, they will resonate with your calmness and so will experience less anxiety than they otherwise might have felt.

If yours is a family with *PTSD* tendencies, that is, a family constantly letting old traumas (which the new "trauma of your disclosure" reactivates) seriously affect them, consider disclosing gradually rather than suddenly overwhelming them with your confessional. Then should they overreact, and especially if they overreact angrily, do not condemn them for that, but instead tell them that you appreciate that they feel stressed, and that you plan to give them patient support throughout the process to help them avoid a terror-filled showdown—one that you admit you may have had a hand in actively provoking.

If yours is a family with *passive-aggressive* tendencies, help them get beyond their simmering negativity by asking/challenging them to be more honest and forthright. Challenge such of their homilies as "Anything you do is okay with us" when these are actually a way to express their anger along the lines of "Who cares what you do?" Similarly challenge subtle retaliative withdrawal; insincere saccharine positivity that poorly and incompletely covers basic, and perhaps truly biting, negativity; and flimsy deceits they actually expect you to see through so that you can discover "by accident" what exactly they truly had in mind. Thus a father, unwilling to come clean about his negative response to his son coming out, instead simmered then expressed his negativity in a roundabout way by giving his son's sister a new house "because she needs a nice safe place to raise a family." But he never told his son he gave her the house. Instead he told him that he had merely rented it out to her. He knew perfectly well that his son would ultimately see through the falsehood. When he checked with the town, he would find out that the house was a gift then predictably respond by feeling hurt after recognizing that what his father was doing was subtly angrily demolishing him by telling him "Because you are gay, you don't need/deserve as many favors from me as does your sister. And because you don't have children, you don't need a whole house, for what a house is, is a place to have a real family."

If yours is a family with *hypomanic* tendencies, that is, one on an "all is wonderful advocacy high" installed so that they can avoid feeling and expressing how depressed they actually are, tell them in a level-headed dispassionate manner that your reality is not so bad as they fear it to be, and that they *can* face what it actually is without necessarily becoming euphoric as if their going into denial is the only way they can spare themselves the pain of recognition.

If your parents continue to reject you even after you made it clear to them that their doing so lowers your self-esteem and diminishes your sense of well-being, try to somehow bypass or work through their negativity to rescue at least a little of what is good in your relationship with them. For example, join support/therapeutic groups with them to together explore their negativity to you as well as your negativity to them (and your negativity to yourself).

But if they continue to reject you, at least for now shift from dealing with them and their problems directly to rising above both—in order to take care of numero uno: yourself. Try passive acceptance where you decide to live with a bad situation as best you can—just going about your life accepting family disharmony by pushing it to the background without your becoming dysfunctional as a result, and getting depressed due to feeling marginalized. In this, a state of healthy denial, you ignore family problems without leaving the family. You set up internal firewalls where having become inured to your difficult parents, you develop personal pride independent of a desperate need for their affectionate supportive feedback, retaining your perspective/sense of humor as you let their bad attitude/ actions pass through you in spite of it all—while you remain if not fully intact, then relatively untarnished. Letting things pass over and through you this way avoids wasting time and effort protesting a situation where complaining won't help. It also spares you further punishment from taking that beating that can, and likely will, arise out of your aggressively speaking up and fighting back. This way you are still their target, but you are no longer their victim, and so at least you won't have to go through life overly involved in being actively and constantly disappointed in and struggling against your parents' homonegativity—to the point that that begins to so affect your self-esteem that you can no longer rise above yourself. It also for the time being avoids a showdown, leaving open the possibility of going back at some later date.

There are, however, risks associated with passive acceptance. You can find yourself prostrating yourself in the hope of gaining affection/some realistic advantage. It can ultimately further lower your self-esteem thus keeping you from affirming and strengthening those personal values which give clarity and weight to your positive self-image. And deciding that "some things just aren't worth getting distressed over" is a good solution only when it doesn't go to the extent of allowing yourself to be beaten down to the point of becoming too weak to care anymore, leaving you even more vulnerable than you were before and open to being hurt by sadistic family members who take your compliance as an opportunity to escalate being hurtful to you because they feel that their emasculation of you, as they perceive it, having been somewhat successful, has put you in a one-down position that in turn offers them further opportunity to abuse you—as they aspire to ever higher transports of devaluation because they can get away with it. And, of course, never become so passive that you develop Stockholm syndrome—where you grow to love parental negativity to the point that you long for, actually come back for, and even provoke more of it. Also try to find strength in carefully chosen intimates. Of course, avoid those who repeat your parents' negative interaction with you either in minor ways, such as by carping ("Why didn't you call me up immediately when you got back from your trip?") or in major ways, such as rejection as in dumping you then saying, "It's because of who you are and what you did" (while denying it was because of their own problems ranging from inconstancy to cruelty). And consider joining activist groups that counter the shame coming at you from your parents with input coming from a group whose intention is to help you instill pride in yourself.

Try not to stop seeing your parents entirely. While that level of distancing may initially feel right, it is still wrong if only because it requires constant watchfulness to maintain, which can't help but divert you from devoting yourself in spite of it all to becoming a whole, satisfied, authentic person.

Be especially careful not to avoid your parents based on a partial view of them derived in paranoid fashion not from the reality of who they are, but from your fantasies about what they may be. I saw my mother as predatory because I had heard from experts and peers alike that I ought to see her that way, and I continued to believe this (though if anything, she was less predatory than uninvolved). A good deal of the problem was mine. For being somewhat paranoid, I evaluated her not realistically, but through the lens of my suspicious distortions about her so that I came so see her, and my father, not as the allies they at least to some extent were, but as the adversaries I fully imagined them to be. I broke my own rule of not attributing full negativity to people whose negativity was at worst partial. Breaking this rule caused me to suffer a lot first, because of my imaginings and second, because my own prophetic, self-fulfilling negativity toward my parents could but lead them to treat me badly in the very way that I at first only imagined/feared. Thus my being irrational created an unnecessary adversarial relationship with them because at first it existed only in my own mind, but seemed rational, then later came to pass through a self-fulfilling process. I was making my issues into their issues, and doing so by projecting my own low self-esteem and extreme self-doubt onto them to the point of thinking that they were treating me in much the same shabby and even bigoted way that I was treating myself. Getting past this imagined negativity (originating in projected low self-esteem and self-doubt) required not that I change my relationship with my parents, but that I alter my relationship with myself— through personal growth involving thorough self-exploration with the goal of developing insight into myself, accompanied by cognitive restructuring geared to correcting my own illogical formulations about my parents, and in particular how my alarmist response to any criticism/devaluation that seemed to be coming from them was, at least partially, coming not from without, from them, but from within, from me.

Gay sons should always remember that not all parental negativity toward them arises directly and specifically out of their being gay. True, there are specific difficulties for parents associated with having and raising a gay son, and these lead to parental misperception and hence parental misbehavior that ultimately has the effect of making parents actually quite difficult. But there are also real difficulties associated with having and raising any son/child at all. Therefore, much parental negativity directed toward you is likely to be a response to something other than your being gay. In particular, their negative response to you is likely to be to any personality/personality problems you might have that have provoked not *antigay* prejudice and discrimination, but an apparently homonegative (but in fact homosexually neutral), reflexive counterresponse on your parents' parts. This is not based on your being gay, but on how you behave toward them and in general toward other people as well.

Try to pick a lifetime partner who will add to your parents' life as much as he adds to yours, one who can even actively participate in helping your parents navigate the difficult transitional period they will likely go through when you, by embarking on a loving relationship with a partner, lend an air of permanency to your being gay, raising for them the good possibility that since you aren't going to change they will be losing you forever. Also keep in mind that a breakup with your partner can affect your parents almost as much as it affects you. Most parents don't like to see you, their beloved son, sad; and while some view a breakup as your comeuppance for being gay, most share your grief. If you would only let them, they can even help you soften the impact of the breakup on your emotions and on your life.

Anticipate that after you come out you will likely need to establish a new more comfortable equilibrium with your grandparents, especially those who might be narrow-minded about homosexuality, as grandparents commonly are due to the generation-specific cultural norms that existed in their time (but are no longer so relevant). In a common scenario, while grandmother is a kindly woman who loves her children and grandchildren unconditionally, grandfather is a depressed man who needs to finger-point/affix blame; a lonely man who fears that his children will go off and abandon him as part of their involvement with his grandson's problems; a conservative, controlling man who needs to condemn his children, your parents, as being defiantly liberal; and an obsessive-compulsive prudish man who feels negatively about anything sexual, perhaps because he is a scrupulously religious man with more a sexually than a homosexually negative credo. I know of grandparents of a gay son who stopped talking to their own children because they were too nice (not disapproving enough of) to their gay son. You can help your parents here by working with grandma/granddad the same way you work with your parents. In particular, try to view any undesirable response on your grandparents' parts not strictly as the product of their ill will, but as a sign of their imperfect humanity. Patiently help grandpa and grandma resolve the tensions that exist between them and your parents, as well as between them and you.

If you feel that you need, or actually happen to be going for, individual therapy, consider inviting your parents to attend at least some of your sessions. If you are in group therapy consider asking if you can bring your parents along at least occasionally. Their joining in can help them avoid feeling that the therapist/group by competing with them for your love and/or being unsupportive of them marginalizes them, targets them as adversaries, or leaves them no longer in control in the family to the point that they feel like, and are now close to becoming, complete outsiders.

Your parents have all the responsibility for you going out; they should get at least some love from you coming in.

Notes

Chapter 1

1. J. Kort, *Gay Affirmative Therapy for the Straight Clinician: The Essential Guide* (New York: W.W. Norton, 2008), 157–158.

2. American Psychiatric Association, *Diagnostic and Statistical Manual of Mental Disorders*, 4th ed. (Washington, DC: American Psychiatric Association, 1987).

3. Tracy Morgan, http://www.care2.com/causes/civil-rights/blog/tracy -morgan-i-would-stab-my-gay-son/ (accessed November 20, 2012).

Chapter 2

1. J. Kort, *Gay Affirmative Therapy for the Straight Clinician: The Essential Guide* (New York: W.W. Norton, 2008), 155.

2. N. Schwind, "Letter," in *My Child Is Gay: How Parents React when They Hear the News*, ed. B. McDougall (Crows Nest, New South Wales, Australia: Allen and Unwin, 2006), 27.

3. K. Jennings and P. Shapiro, *Always My Child: A Parent's Guide to Understanding Your Gay, Lesbian, Bisexual, Transgendered or Questioning Son or Daughter* (New York: Simon and Schuster, 2003), 199.

4. Ibid., 261.

5. Ibid., 240.

6. Ibid., 194.

7. Alexandre Dumas, http://www.goodreads.com/quotes/75172-as-a-general -rule-people-ask-for-advice-only-in-order (accessed November 16, 2012).

8. R. A. Bernstein, *Straight Parents, Gay Children: Keeping Families Together* (New York: Thunder's Mouth Press, 2003), 4.

9. Jennings and Shapiro, *Always My Child*, 15.

10. J. Kort, *Gay Affirmative Therapy for the Straight Clinician: The Essential Guide* (New York: W.W. Norton, 2008), 164.

11. Bernstein, *Straight Parents, Gay Children*, 61.

Chapter 4

1. C. Christian Beels, "Family Therapy," in *The American Psychiatric Press Textbook of Psychiatry*, ed. J. A. Talbott, R. E. Hales, and S. C. Yudofsky (Washington, DC: American Psychiatric Press, 1988), 930.

2. Ibid., 930.

3. Ibid., 943.

4. Ibid., 942.

5. Ibid., 929.

6. Ibid., 943.

7. Ibid., 944.

Chapter 10

1. PDM Task Force, *Psychodynamic Diagnostic Manual (PDM)* (Silver Spring, MD: Alliance of Psychoanalytic Organizations, 2006), 240.

2. Ibid., 248.

3. Ibid., 247.

4. Ibid., 247.

5. Ibid., 251.

6. Ibid., 250.

Chapter 11

1. Jennings and Shapiro, *Always My Child*, 10.

2. Ibid., 34.

3. American Psychiatric Association, *Diagnostic and Statistical Manual of Mental Disorders (DSM-IV)*, 4th ed. (Washington, DC: American Psychiatric Association, 1987), 396.

4. Ibid., 685.

Chapter 12

1. J. M. Oldham and L. B. Morris, *New Personality Self-Portrait: Why You Think, Work, Love, and Act the Way You Do* (New York: Bantam Books, 1995), 403.

2. Jennings and Shapiro, *Always My Child*, 224.

3. Schwind, "Letter," 27.

4. Oldham and Morris, *New Personality Self-Portrait*, 409.

Chapter 14

1. A Mother from Perth, "Letter," in *My Child Is Gay: How Parents React when They Hear the News*, ed. McDougall, B. (Crows Nest, New South Wales, Australia: Allen and Unwin, 2006), 37.

2. R. J. Ursano and E. K. Silberman, "Individual Psychotherapies: Other Individual Psychotherapies: Cognitive Therapy," in *The American Psychiatric Press Textbook of Psychiatry*, ed. J. A. Talbot, R. E. Hales, and S. C. Yudofsky (Washington, DC: American Psychiatric Press, 1988), 870.

3. Merriam-Webster, *Webster's Third New International Dictionary of the English Language Unabridged* (Springfield, MA: Merriam-Webster, Inc., 1986), 2174.

4. J. R. Bemporad and H. Pinsker, "Schizophrenia: The Manifest Symptomatology," in *American Handbook of Psychiatry*, 2nd ed., ed. Silvano Arieti and Eugene B. Brody (New York: Basic Books, 1974), 532.

5. A. T. Beck, "Cognitive Therapy," in *Comprehensive Textbook of Psychiatry/ IV*, ed. Harold I. Kaplan and Benjamin J. Sadock (Baltimore: Williams and Wilkins, 1985), 1437.

Index

About the Author

MARTIN KANTOR, MD, is a Harvard-trained psychiatrist who has been in full private practice in Boston and New York City, and active in residency training programs at hospitals including Massachusetts General in Boston, Massachusetts, and Beth Israel in New York City. He also served as assistant clinical professor of psychiatry at Mount Sinai Medical School and clinical assistant professor of psychiatry at the University of Medicine and Dentistry of New Jersey-New Jersey Medical School. Kantor is a full-time author whose published works include more than 20 other books, including Praeger's *Now That You're Out: The Challenges and Joys of Living as a Gay Man,* Praeger's *Homophobia: The State of Sexual Bigotry Today,* and Praeger's *Essential Guide to Overcoming Avoidant Personality Disorder.*